Missing the Bus, Making the Connection

*The Patricia Marsden-Dole International Series*
Patricia Marsden-Dole, *general editor*

T.A. KEENLEYSIDE

**MISSING THE BUS, MAKING THE CONNECTION**
Tales and Tastes of Travel

Penumbra Press · Manotick, ON · 2008

PENUMBRA PRESS, *publishers*
Box 940 · Manotick, ON · Canada
K4M 1A8 · penumbrapress.ca

Printed & bound in Canada

Penumbra Press gratefully acknowledges the financial support of the Government of Ontario through the Ontario Media Development Corporation's Ontario Book Initiative.

*Library and Archives Canada*
*Cataloguing-in-Publication Data*

Keenleyside, T.A. (Terence A.),
    1940–
Missing the bus, making the
    connection: tales and tastes of
    travel / T.A. Keenleyside
(Patricia Marsden-Dole
    International Series)
ISBN 978-1-897323-97-7

1. Keenleyside, T.A. (1940–)
    — Travel
2. Food habits
3. Voyages and travels
4. Cookery, International
1. Title
11. Series: Patricia Marsden-Dole
    International Series

GT2850.K43 2008    394.1
    C2008-904983-7

# CONTENTS

## ACKNOWLEDGEMENTS

» IN ADDITION TO FAMILY, a number of people have read and commented helpfully on drafts of this work: Rick Archbold, Pary Bell, Sara Cummins, Ramsay Derry, Arnold Gosewich, Carol McFarlane, and Pamela Roberts. Their assistance and encouragement helped bring this project to fruition.

Special thanks are also due to John Flood for his interest in publishing this book and to Dennis Choquette for his expert editing.

Two stories in this volume, "Trudeaumania" and "The Art of the Possible," were published earlier in *bout de papier* magazine and reappear in this book in slightly different versions with the permission of the journal. The quotation from C.P. Cavafy's "Ithaka" is from the translation in Edmund Keeley and Philip Sherrard, *Six Poets of Modern Greece* (London: Thames and Hudson, 1960) and is included here with the permission of Edmund Keeley. A more recent translation is in C.P. Cavafy, *Collected Poems*, translated by Edmund Keeley and Philip Sherrard, edited by George Savidis, (Princeton, NJ: Princeton University Press, 1992).

*For Danielle, Laura, Max, Sam, Shine, and those who follow*

When you set out for Ithaka
Ask that your way be long,
Full of adventure, full of instruction.

*Ithaka,*
C.P. CAVAFY

## Making the Connection

» RETURNING HOME a while ago from several weeks in Spain, I was reflecting on what had been the most memorable moments of our trip. What would stay with me long after I had forgotten whether it was at the alcazar in Segovia or Seville that Queen Isabella first met Ferdinand — or whether what I was really thinking about was where she welcomed Columbus home from America. And was it at the Museo del Prado or the Thyssen-Bornemisza in Madrid that we saw the best works by the marvelous Diego Velazquez? Or could it be I am confusing him with El Greco and the Prado with Picasso's interpretations of Velazquez at his museum in Barcelona? What sensations, I wondered, would linger when I could no longer conjure up the pain inflicted by the bedsprings of our flea bag in the Ciutat Vella district of Barcelona or the texture and subtle flavour of the tortilla espanola that had, until my unexpected order, sat forlornly in the smoky window of a tapas bar in Cadiz, the top disc in a sagging, under-appreciated stack? What sad, frightening, or amusing tale would we still be telling about that trip when most of the details had slid from ready recollection to the distant, gossamer reaches of consciousness?

It had not been a particularly outstanding trip, but there were, nevertheless, five moments that I decided would elude the veil of time — that were burned forever into our memories — and each pertained to one of the great rewards of travel. The first occurred standing in a classic Spanish deli in central Madrid, the Museo de Jamon. It was crowded and I was clutching a ticket, listening intently for the number *ochenta siete* while I rehearsed the phrases

I needed to make our purchases: "*un pollo cocido, dos panecillos, y una botella de vino tinto de la casa, abierto por favor.*"

The clerk smiled indulgently and responded without hesitation. But when he handed me the bottle of wine, I thought, from the shrink-wrapped top, that it was corked. "*Abierto por favor,*" I repeated, afraid my phrase book had let me down.

"*Si, si,*" he answered cheerfully, and I suddenly realized there was no problem; the bottle had a screw cap.

It was for me an important moment of accomplishment, one of modest pride and an incipient sense of catching on to the culture. In a noisy deli packed with Spaniards making their evening purchases on the way home from work, we had, like them, conducted our business smoothly and efficiently, albeit in imperfect Spanish. In a small but meaningful way we felt part of the community.

While that moment had to do with connecting to the culture, the second pertained to linking with people. We had had a busy day in Barcelona, crisscrossing the Eixample district, with its majestic boulevards and flamboyant, nineteenth-century architecture — features that give the city a grandeur matched perhaps only by Paris. We had climbed high in the filigreed towers of Antoni Gaudi's bizarre, unfinished cathedral, La Sagrada Familia, trekked through the newly fashionable Barri de la Ribera and taken a peek at the church of Santa Maria del Mar, with its richly hued stained-glass windows and model Spanish galleon perched on the altar. Access to our nearby hotel was blocked by a street demonstration, so in the drooping sun of a late-October afternoon, we took an outdoor table at a restaurant in the Passeig Born with a view of the church façade. There we lingered over a plate of fried calamari, a mixed salad, and thick slices of bread brushed with tomato sauce and dusted in cheese. Two boys and a girl, shabbily dressed and covered in dirt from sprawling on the grubby pavement around the tables, were now seated next to us talking in English, one of them with a Spanish accent. The man and woman with them, however, were ordering their lunch in what appeared to us to be fluent Spanish. As we, in our inimitable way, speculated about their circumstances, they were joined by several other couples. More dishes were ordered and a lively conversation that freely mixed Spanish and English ensued. Expatriates, we concluded, although one or two had perhaps married locals or people from other Spanish-speaking countries.

Recognizing this as a good opportunity to learn about the demonstration and how long it was likely to last, I leaned across to their table and fell into conversation with one of the later-arriving women.

"It's a student demonstration. Related to the cost of tuition. It will only last a few hours." She was English — an artist, in fact — but had lived in Barcelona for many years. Her husband was Spanish-speaking and the boy who spoke English with an accent their locally born son. The first couple at the table, we learned, were former longtime residents who had moved home to Ireland with their two kids; but they were now back in Barcelona on holidays, looking up old friends. The Passeig Born, it seemed, was a regular gathering place for British expats.

"So, you're an artist?"

"Yes."

"You wouldn't happen to know Louise Boissevain, would you? From Surrey. Her parents are old friends."

"Of course!"

"Fantastic." Louise had recently opened a restaurant just off the famous Ramblas, the wide promenade running north from the harbour lined with plane trees, shops, and restaurants that draws all Barcelona to the bustling bosom of the city. Her father had e-mailed me the name and address before we left for Spain, but at the last moment I had forgotten to bring the information with me.

But she knew about the restaurant. "It's the Lupino."

"Do you happen to know the address?"

"Calle Carmen 33," her husband answered, and on the back of a napkin he drew a map. "We haven't eaten there yet. Let's all go. How about tomorrow night? We've nothing planned."

It was a special hour, talking to those longtime residents as the light crept across the Passeig Born and the temperature dropped from North American summer to early autumn. We felt we were getting a glimpse of what our own lives might have been like if, years before on our first trip to Spain, on the then-largely undiscovered, innocent island of Minorca, we had decided to stay and eke out a living running a bar or restaurant on an isolated beach. For rarely do foreign nationals become completely integrated into the local population—certainly not in a society as closed as Spain's. However proficient their language skills, however many local nationals they count among their friends, expatriates tend to find each other and develop their own social circles. Into a British one in Barcelona we had happily stumbled, offered a privileged view of their seemingly simple, carefree lives in the sun—on the edge of Spanish culture.

The third moment was, in fact, the first scene in an act of seven parts. We were walking near the royal palace in Madrid, talking about the throne room's Tiepolo ceiling, Bonicelli lions, and shimmering Venetian rock-crystal chandeliers, when a man suddenly stopped us. He was young with glasses and Asian rather than Spanish: a visa student at the university, we surmised. Pointing to our backs, he shook his head and clucked his tongue as he guided us down a flight of steps and into a park away from passing pedestrians. Our coats and pant legs were, we discovered, splattered with what appeared to be pigeon droppings, and the man pulled a bottle of water and tissues from his pocket to clean us up. He spent unnecessarily long patting our only-slightly soiled trousers, but at the time we didn't take any particular notice, so grateful were we for his assistance. When he finished, I thanked him profusely. He smiled and nodded; we parted. It was not until several hours later, walking through the Puerta del Sol in the heart of old Madrid, that I suddenly realized what had happened. The square was in the midst of those bustling hours between work and dinner when all Spain spills outside to shop, talk, and gawk. My attention was drawn to the edges of the crowd — to seedy, moustached men squatting on the pavement or leaning against grey walls, sinisterly surveying the passing shoppers and clutches of youths chatting by the fountain. It was then that I suddenly blurted to Dot, "You know, I think that nice young man tried to rob us!"

"No!"

"Those weren't pigeon droppings on our coats. He sprayed us with some concoction."

The next day, at El Rastro, the seething, jostling flea market of the capital, forewarned and ready, we were, nevertheless, successfully pick-pocketed: seventy-five euros and a credit card from a Velcro pocket in Dot's hiking pants. We tightened our security several notches, wearing our day packs on our chests rather than our backs, carrying with us only photocopies of our passports and just enough cash for the day. Yet five more times across Spain we faced attempted thefts, each with a different, creative twist. Once near a railway station we were approached by a man asking for directions and then by an alleged undercover agent (with fake ID), seemingly suspicious that I and the first man were passing counterfeit bills. He demanded to see our passports and money. Hardened by our initial experiences, we resisted, and we suffered no further losses during these assaults. Nevertheless, the attempted thefts were unsettling and the precautions they necessitated each day a nuisance. They detracted somewhat from the pleasure of our trip and our positive image of Spain.

Still, misadventure is an inherent part of travel and, ironically, one of the rewards, not only because of the stories provided, but because of the insights gained. What struck us most about those assaults was the fact that not once did we feel physically threatened.

Those who accosted us usually approached or left with smiles, and they broke off their attacks without laying a finger on anything but our pockets and packs. That is not to say that violent crime does not occur in Spain; obviously it does. But in seven attempted thefts on the streets of almost any North American city could one ever expect such benign treatment throughout? It is this that will stay with us from those little misadventures long after we have forgotten the aggravation of the moment.

On the train, in the arid, mountainous region of Guadalajara, we had a fourth amusing and ironic moment, one of those curious juxtapositions of place and time that sears a landscape in one's memory forever. I was gazing out the window as the train climbed slowly beneath a ridge where spears of white, jagged rock towered above us. Intermittently, there were welcome gaps in this fortress-like foreground as the range opened to a flat horizon of parched, naked shrubs, scattered trees, and drifting brown sand. No one. No cars, no roads, no houses. A barren land where only the occasional aqueduct snaking across the cruel, remorseless earth hinted at any human presence. Still, I almost expected that at any moment a dappled pony would appear at the top of the ridge, its rider covered in a patterned blanket and wearing a sombrero. Then I turned to the television on the ceiling of our coach — to a familiar, flickering black-and-white image on the screen: a young Gary Cooper in a Stetson trotting across a set that was unmistakably the American West! But where was I? Spain? Mexico? The United States? South Asia? The Middle East? I was everywhere there are deserts and high outcrops of rock, for everywhere there is American popular culture.

Finally, at a *tascas* (tapas bar) in the old quarter of Barcelona, we shared one of those fleeting, euphoric moments that, alone and without any other rewards, are reason enough to travel. It was at the end of another long day on our feet and after two or three nights of indifferent meals in bars and restaurants that, in truth, could not have been expected to yield much culinary worth. After warily working our way from the harbour up a dark alley that reeked of midnight trouble, we walked along a street of dingy, uninviting shops, now mostly barred or shuttered, until unexpectedly the voiceless, stale air freshened with shouting and laughter outside Bodega la Plata at Mercé 28. It is a simple bar, established in the 1920s, on one corner of a narrow, medieval street that promises nothing and delivers unmitigated delight. It was 7:30 and the *tascas*, maybe twelve feet square, was packed, its two open sides enabling customers to sprawl across the street like a swelling crowd at the wicket of a football stadium. We took to the place immediately. It was boisterous, earthy, unpretentious—authentic. Grabbing the one remaining small wooden table next to the marble-topped bar, we ordered a half litre of red wine, two *raciones* (small plates) of the house specialty, deep-fried sardines (served with the heads intact), tomato-and-cheese salad, and bread dipped in the customary tomato sauce and topped this time with anchovies. Everyone else was having the same. That was all Bodega la Plata served. But they were sardines unlike in any other *tascas*: fresh, crisp, succulent. Like the Spaniards pressed around us, we dangled them above our mouths between thumb and index finger and crunched them noisily from head to tail.

Our eyes circled the bar, taking in the aged, leathery faces of labourers in black caps; the natty, dark suits of businessmen who had rushed straight from their offices; the tailored elegance of young women almost exclusively in black; the habitués on stools by the bar, talking as fast as they ate; the lovers in a corner, cuddling over glasses of sherry; the insufferable bore earnestly retelling a joke to a waiter; the old man on crutches stepping gingerly into the street and vanishing. We were the only foreigners there, and for an hour and a half we revelled in a discovery that took us back decades—to a bar in Minorca where we had shared laughter, stories, and a flask of sherry with the locals. It was an evening we never thought could be relived, not forty years on, not on a continent so inundated with tourists, not in a city the size of Barcelona. And yet it was happening. The same simplicity and genuineness, the same happiness and communal sharing. For us, the same joy of discovery — discovering what had, in fact, been there all along. At nine, the Bodega la Plata quickly emptied and the entire street fell silent. We paid our bill (twelve euros!) and walked back to our hotel, our appetites sated, our spirits uplifted. We were on a traveller's high.

Home in Toronto, reflecting on those moments from our trip to Spain, it occurred to me that most of our memorable experiences travelling abroad have pertained to one or another of these five types of connection — sometimes to several of them simultaneously. The book that follows is the product of this rumination. It explores each of these tastes of travel, based on my family's experiences living and travelling abroad. Many of the stories are recent, but others are from decades ago. And that, I think, is how it should be, for not always is the traveller fully aware at the time of a vital connection made. Yet when one is, it lives on in memory forever, now and then tripping lightly to the forefront, enticing the housebound adventurer to light out again.

The first section, Cultural Immersion, recounts times spent struggling with the shock of difference and local complexity, trying to adapt and to become one with the surroundings. Especially, they are stories concerned with those happy, euphoric moments when it works and a special connection to the culture is forged. The stories in part 2, Connecting with People, address the human linkages that result from travel: ties to locals, expatriates, fellow North Americans, and even new bonds with one's own family. Misadventures are the subject of the third section, missed connections the fourth. Like the moment on the Spanish train, the tales here pertain to those times when things don't seem quite as they should be — where there is a disconnect of some kind, perhaps a situation full of promise that doesn't evolve as expected. Finally, part 5, Natural Highs, relates to those special, often-unexpected moments when everything seems right with the world. The sensation may result from making special cultural and human connections, or from sharing a meal in an unexpected setting or circumstance. Traveller's high can happen at almost any time and any place. When it does, the moment should be cherished; for, ultimately, these are the experiences that lead us once again to pack our bags and go tripping.

## Missing The Bus

THIS IS NOT A BOOK that focuses on extreme adventures in exotic places, but rather on the sorts of experiences that await the average, observant traveller with an open mind and an independent approach to exploring the world. To achieve those special feelings of connectedness, it is, however, important to get off the bus and strike out on your own. Memorable moments don't often occur when you are being guided through a country, half-quarantined from its inhabitants — when you are jostling for position in front of the *Mona Lisa* or for a table overlooking St. Mark's Square. They are not likely to happen when your principal preoccupation is to avoid a bout of dysentery from local food and water, or to stay in sight of a man in a fedora waving his umbrella above a throng by the Sphinx. Special moments are far more likely to happen when you are on your own, making your own transport, eating, sleeping, and sightseeing arrangements, coping with the language, drifting down streets away from the crowds, lingering where things seem about to happen, searching for the soul of a place.

In the introduction to the anthology *Bad Trips*, Keath Fraser makes the point that "without fear, travel has no meaning." Anxiety and stress are integral to cross-cultural experiences, to putting oneself in situations where those sudden connections occur that are the ambrosia of travel. Of course, the classic tourist sights are important to see: the Louvre, the Tower of London, Ankor Wat, the Galapagos, the Serengeti. But they are the backdrop — the setting for the play, not the performance; they are the destinations of tourists, not travellers.

In his insightful book *Abroad*, Paul Fussell writes, "We are all tourists now, and there is no escape." Today, when the remotest reaches of the earth have been snapped and videoed by visitors from virtually every country, that may well be true. Yet to move from tourist to traveller — if there is a modest distinction — it is necessary to miss the bus waiting outside the hotel and head out alone, armed only with a phrase book and map. Obviously, better still is to travel independently, or if possible live in, not just visit, another country. Then, on a daily basis, one follows the habits of the locals, shopping beside them for food and other necessities, relying on public transport, walking along uncrowded, lens-free streets, eating at neighbourhood restaurants tourists never discover, seeing sights that are not in any guidebook — making connections.

Many of the stories in this book are a product of living abroad: three years in Thailand and Indonesia in the Canadian diplomatic service, six years in England as a student and sabbatical, and a year in France on sabbatical. For that reason these countries receive the greatest attention. Altogether, however, some twenty nations are covered, and in most cases we have visited them several times — lived in them, in fact, at least for several weeks at a time, renting city apartments, country cottages, mountain huts, exchanging properties, or house-sitting. While we have been fortunate to visit almost sixty countries, no attempt has been made to cover all of the globe. Rather, the focus is on those places we know best, that have yielded great moments and entertaining stories with, hopefully, universal appeal.

It will immediately become apparent to the reader that many of the pieces in this book are not just my stories but my family's; for one of our great fortunes has been to live and travel abroad as a nuclear unit. We enjoy doing things together, and with any luck the book helps to illustrate the pleasure of sojourning *en famille* — with kids of any age — despite the mistakes you sometimes make. My wife, Dot, and son, Tim, have, where indicated, contributed to the collection. All the stories are, needless to say, true and as accurate as memory serves. Even the names are real, except on the rare occasion when a change has been made to avoid embarrassment.

## The Tastes of Travel

WE TRAVEL NOT ONLY to taste the five forms of connection discussed above but to experience different cuisines: to have meals in new, authentic, unusual, and exotic settings. To ingest the food of another land is to taste its people and culture. Not surprisingly, therefore, the subject of eating consumes many pages in this book; it is a condiment flavouring almost every piece. For that reason, many of the stories conclude with recipes prepared by Dot. She has chosen ones that are pertinent to the stories or the countries where the tales take place. In a number of cases, the recipes are her adaptations of local favourites. The emphasis is on family dishes that are relatively simple to prepare, usually healthy, and always tasty.

Food is one of the simplest and most effective ways to relive your travel experiences or to stimulate the urge to be off again in search of understanding and lasting memories. May these tales and the accompanying recipes whet the appetite to miss the bus and make those special connections.

*Bon voyage et bon appetit,*
T.A. KEENLEYSIDE, Toronto

## CULTURAL IMMERSION

I

I am a part of all that I have met;
Yet all experience is an arch wherethro'
Gleams that untravell'd world, whose margin fades
For ever and for ever when I move.

*Ulysses,*
ALFRED LORD TENNYSON

» OUR DAUGHTER, DEB, is appalled every time we remind her. "I can't believe I actually was part of it. It's *so* embarrassing. We had gone for lunch, right? Or at least that's what you thought."

"Right."

"How did you say we ended up in Atami?"

After Deb and her husband, Tad, had lived in Japan for two years, she had renewed interest in the details of that initial moment of culture shock and was doubly appalled by our uncouth behaviour.

"An airline hostess on the flight over told us about it."

We were stopping over in Tokyo on our way to Thailand on my first posting since joining the Canadian diplomatic service eighteen months earlier. To my surprise, I had found it a rather depressing feeling, starting out on a "permanent" job, a sense of freedom lost. And it wasn't helped by being fingerprinted the first day at work. I felt I could see my whole life unrolling before me one in-basket after another, the black, inky smudges of my thumbs inside a yellow folder in a steel filing cabinet, indiscretion anticipated. Now, however, we were off on an overseas assignment, what every officer joins the service to do, and I felt elated. Anxious to see something of Japan other than the capital, I asked the hostess where we should go and she suggested Atami, since we could reach it easily on a bullet train. She knew of a lovely traditional inn there, and in my notebook she wrote the name in Japanese characters.

JAPAN WAS YIN AND YANG before Taoism entered pop culture: chaos contrasted with serenity. In Tokyo, people packed like grains of steamed rice in china bowls—in airless buses and trains, in cavernous restaurants, hotel lobbies, and offices throbbing like all-night discos. Traffic screaming "surrender." Unheeding pedestrians scurrying along the sidewalks in fast-forward as thick as armies of ants dislodged from vast, intricate nests—tall cement labyrinths thrown up hurriedly and exuding impermanence. A grey, stifling smog over vast regions of the city, a choking mix of exhaust and factory fumes. Everything hustled. On that first trip, it was epitomized by our waiter at breakfast in the expansive hotel dining room. As we seated ourselves, he stood waiting to take our orders, and within two minutes of giving them, he trotted back to our table with a tray loaded with orange juice, eggs "easy over," bacon, toast, tea, and coffee. "Sorry to keep you waiting," he said apologetically, with no hint of irony.

But even in Tokyo, then as now, there are scattered islands of calm and order. Buddhist temples up wide flights of steep stone steps where, in almost-empty courtyards, people sit quietly, reflectively, contemplating. Contemplating who knows what? A more spiritual past, the accomplishments of ancestors and national heroes, the mysteries of life and death, what to cook for dinner? Parks where women, hair tied tightly in buns, sit on stools painting little wooden bridges that cross ponds to islands fringed in yellow shoots of bamboo. Children, respectful of their elders' engagement, crouch nearby, using sticks to nudge their sailboats onto the rippling water. Neatly uniformed attendants pass slowly behind them. With wide, straw brooms and in majestic arcs that leave fanciful swirls of sand behind them, they gracefully sweep the crushed-stone pathways. Peace and harmony. Inner balance restored.

The Japanese themselves reflect the yin and yang of their capital. But the physical and human images are reversed. While on its surface Tokyo is all nervous energy, in hidden corners it is ordered and peaceful. The people, on the other hand, exude an outer air of civility and calm. Emotions are checked, thoughts inscrutable. But inside they are often in turmoil; exhausted by long hours of work; edgy from a fish-bowl existence at home, work, and in transit; frustrated—especially the women—by customs they dare not breach; dulled by routine and a lack of recreational space and time. The men vent their feelings where tourists rarely see them, getting drunk in karaoke bars on beer and whisky, rubbing pathetically against female strangers in subways and commuter trains. The women bear their lot stoically. If that is not possible, they seek relief from a restrictive home life through education, or dream of becoming Anne of the Red Hair.

WEARY OF THE CAPITAL, on our last day in Tokyo we followed the air hostess's advice and took the train to Atami. I remember little of the ride, except that every scrap of land not covered in steel and concrete was under cultivation. Green shoots of rice pushed out of patches of earth at the sides of drab grey buildings and in the ruts running beside the tracks. So crowded was the countryside on the southern coast of the island of Honshu that we were barely outside one uninspiring town before we entered another.

In Atami we were the only foreigners on the streets. A smiling, chirping crowd followed us everywhere, enchanted by Karen and Deb and their blond hair. By early afternoon we had had enough of towing Karen and carrying Deb, so Dot and I debated what to do: take the train back to Tokyo and the linguistic security of our hotel or go to the *ryokan* we had been told about for lunch. I had my doubts the inn was the sort of roadside place where you could just stop in for a meal. But Dot is a steadfast optimist.

So I hailed a taxi, handed the driver the scrap of paper from the plane, and off he went without hesitation.

Arriving at the *ryokan* was like stepping from the splashes and squiggles that is the oil-stained palette of Japan directly onto the refined, ethereal canvas of a Romantic artist. The inn was set in a magnificent garden of flowering, manicured shrubs, bonsai trees, and yellow-gravel pathways. The warm spring air was fragrant with the scent of frangipani, and orange and almond blossoms.

Birds chattered in the trees and a brook bubbled obediently under a red-and-black wooden bridge decorated at each end with stone lanterns. Through drooping, feathery branches, far in the distance and below us we glimpsed the blue Pacific Ocean — not beckoning, however, for we knew that in reality it was outside the frame, its beaches too crowded to find a place to sit, its water like the giant over-stuffed, over-heated aquarium that had fascinated Karen on a downtown Tokyo street. Still, the ocean provided the necessary perspective for the landscaper's secular view of nirvana.

As we drove up the long lane to the reception office, several members of the staff bustled out the door and stood in a straight line to welcome us, their royal Canadian guests. The men were in dark trousers and white shirts and the women in traditional kimonos. They all bowed deeply as our taxi halted, and my grip on Karen's hand tightened involuntarily. This was clearly not a Howard Johnson.

When it became apparent we spoke no Japanese, someone was summoned from inside, to whom we explained — we thought — that we had come, if that were possible, just for lunch before returning to Tokyo. There was much nodding and smiling, enough to reassure us — mistakenly — that we had been understood.

A plump, middle-aged lady approached us, bowed, and escorted us through the garden to a cottage nestled beside a pond spotted with water lilies. At the door, she motioned to us to remove our shoes and at the same time handed us plastic slippers. Then we stepped gingerly onto the *tatami* floor of the cottage living room. It was austerely decorated: a hand-painted antique scroll graced one wall; a vase of precisely arranged flowers stood in a corner; and in the centre of the room there was a low, circular table with floor cushions, covered in silk. Nothing more. Our hostess slid open the rice-paper panels of the living room, filling the cottage with the rich perfumes of the garden. We were offered a welcoming cup of green tea, the mix of aromas drugging us as if we were slipping into an altered state of being. *Yukatas*, light cotton dressing gowns with elegant patterns in blue and white, were presented to Dot and me, and the woman motioned for us to undress.

Red faced, I stripped to my underpants while she wrapped the *yukata* around my shoulders. "Uh, Dot," I was beginning to panic, "she doesn't think we're here just for lunch."

"Oh, it's okay, I'm sure," Dot replied blithely. "I mean, how could she think we're staying? We don't have any luggage."

I looked at the mound of belongings on the living-room floor: Deb's carry cot and diaper bag, a rucksack with Karen's books and crayons, and Dot's big canvas bag with sweaters and changes of clothing for the girls. "Oh yeah?"

Our hostess signalled me to follow her to a chamber off the living room. She slid open another panel and there in front of me was a large, blue-tiled tub, steam rising from its surface like mist off a lake at daybreak. When she started to remove my *yukata*, I protested and she drew back in surprise. Using hand signs and speaking words I knew she didn't understand, I tried to explain again that we had come only for lunch. She looked flustered and confused as I retreated to the living room. But then when Dot and Karen raised their fingers to their mouths, she nodded as if she understood and hurried from our cottage. She returned with the man we had spoken to on our arrival and again we explained our intent. At least now it was understood that we wanted to eat and, presently, the woman and two other servants graciously laid out china plates, bowls, and chopsticks at the table in the living room.

Dot and I sat on a deck off the living room while Karen looked at a picture book and Deb napped. "This is awful," I moaned, the heaven surrounding us not relieving the hell I felt inside. "I still don't think they understand we're not staying for the night."

"Sure they know," Dot answered. "Just enjoy the view. The air is so soft and sweet!"

The woman returned. She had changed into a formal, silk kimono elegantly embroidered with cranes, poised as if fishing in a pond. As she knelt on the floor beside us, its full-length sleeves swept the ground like the spreading wings of a giant blue heron, and when she bent forward, the big bow on the back of her kimono fluttered erect — not a bird, but the wrapping on a very expensive gift, hand delivered to a sedate little party. An assistant followed her into the room, towing a cart laden with covered dishes. One by one the lids were removed and a lunch fit for emperors and samurai warriors lay before us. Plate after plate of raw fish. Some thick chunks. Some thin wedges. Some white. Some pink. Some dark red. Some yellow. But everything raw! We studied the plates in horror while Karen poked at the cold, fleshy fillets and screwed up her nose.

"I can't believe what you did," Deb exclaims yet again. "How could you have been so stupid, so gauche?"

"We'd read the post guide. Don't eat anything that isn't well cooked."

"That was for Thailand!"

"We were in Asia. We didn't have anything else to go by."

"This was Japan!"

"It was the sixties," I try lamely. "I don't know if we'd had smoked salmon even!"

"Still, I can't believe what you did."

Whenever we were alone in the room, Dot folded chunks of the fish into paper napkins and hid them in Deb's diaper bag. She did it bit by bit so as not to arouse suspicion, though every time she opened the bag the smell of warming fish challenged the frangipanis for dominance.

Anxious furrows vanished from the brows of the staff. We appeared to be enjoying the meal. The empty dishes were cleared away, and in came dessert: a mountainous bowl of the plumpest, juiciest strawberries we had ever seen. Karen and I looked hopefully at Dot. But she shook her head. "Can't risk it. They may not have been washed in disinfectant."

"Ha!" Deb snorts. "What dummies!"

We watched sadly as Dot stuffed the berries in with Deb's diapers and then, when that container was full, the remainder into her canvas bag. Poor Karen. She was as hungry as we were and she loved strawberries, but she never complained. Always as stoic as our Japanese hosts.

It was late afternoon by the time all the empty dishes were cleared away. No bill came and I was anxious about getting back to Tokyo. "They still think we're here for the night," I said to Dot.

"Noooo, they're just too polite to rush us."

When the woman returned with tea, however, I used hand signals again to indicate we had to go. She looked confused, shook her head, and, pursing her lips, made a sucking sound like the disappointed gurgle of a straw at the bottom of a chocolate soda. Then she left to fetch the man with fifty words of English. It took some time for him to grasp that we had to leave and wanted the bill.

I'm sure he thought we were unhappy with the *ryokan* and its service. To him and all his staff we were occidental oxen charging about an oriental tea shop, breaking every conceivable custom. But to the end they exhibited nothing but politeness and restraint. Our belongings were bustled into a taxi, and as we moved slowly down the drive, the staff stood once again in a straight line, smiling and bowing respectfully.

Karen waved earnestly until we were out of sight. I sighed first with relief and then frustration as I examined more closely the size of the bill for the lunch we didn't eat. And I sighed a third time with anxiety. Would I ever possess the deft, cosmopolitan touch the profession I had so recently entered expected of me?

DOT AND I WERE in Vancouver on our way to Deb and Tad's home on Vancouver Island when memories of the culture shock we experienced that day burst upon us like the cherry blossoms jollying the February sidewalks of Kitsilano. We had chosen a bed and breakfast run by a Japanese-Canadian woman. When we asked the hour for breakfast, we were told 8:35 AM! It seemed prudent to arrive on time. So did our breakfast of French toast. Light, fluffy, and liberally dusted in cinnamon and powdered sugar. At 8:37 AM. Just as in Tokyo so many years before. And when we left later that morning, the staff lined up on the sidewalk beside our car, bowing in unison as we drove away: Atami revisited. In North America, you are never far from the rest of the world.

One of the guests at the B&B was a retired Japanese business-man, an avid golfer delighting in the uncrowded courses of North America. We chatted with him about the stress associated with the sport in Japan: membership fees as high as $600,000 US at the peak of the economic boom, tee-off times arranged a year ahead, whirlwind rounds with hurried drinks and dinners between the front and back nines, hole-in-one insurance should one drive to such misfortune. A survivor, now he could laugh about it all. He told us about a Japanese restaurant he had found just a couple of blocks away. He had already been there twice for sashimi and would be going again that night before 6:00 for the early-bird discount. We tried to interest him in trying somewhere else — one of the stalls at the vibrant market on Granville Island or a restaurant serving interesting fusion cooking; there were several nearby. But his mind was set on sashimi and the early-bird special.

"I STILL CAN'T BELIEVE IT," Deb says yet again as I finish recounting our adventure in Atami. She and Tad are in *yukatas* they purchased when they were living in Hyogo-Ken. And she's passing us the sashimi she's prepared on dishes they brought back with them. "You were terrible. The Japanese must have been astounded."

"Mmmmmm," we say distractedly. We've suddenly lost the focus. "Wow! This is sensational!"

"Of course it is!" Deb exclaims. "What did you expect?"

» EXCEPT FOR CHINESE restaurants in North America, my first real experience with Asian culture and cooking came as a graduate student in London in the 1960s. I was invited to the home of an Indian friend for a day of the board game Diplomacy. Midway through this tortuous activity, performed on a pre-First World War map of Europe, we were served an Indian meal that tore my throat to shreds. Fortunately, I, the least experienced player, was Russia, one of the most difficult countries to be assigned, imperilled by potentially hostile forces on all fronts. The ill-equipped troops of Nicholas Alexander II were overwhelmed by a combined Anglo-French land-and-sea invasion that could not be prevented through the hurried dispatch of duplicitous notes to England, France, and Germany. Thus shortly after what seemed likely in any event to be my last supper, I exited the game and rushed home to be administered to by my young wife. When she caught the first whiff of my breath, however, every nursing instinct abandoned her, and I spent the evening alone and miserable in the bathroom.

Gradually, however, Dot and I acquired a taste for Indian food. The more often you eat it, of course, the greater your tolerance for hot spices; so before long we were eating meals that I am sure were as hot or hotter than that fed to the doomed czar of Russia. As my dissertation on Indian foreign policy took shape, I acquired a wide circle of South Asian friends and became immersed in the culture of the sub-continent, arguing excitedly about partition, Kashmir, and Satyatji Rai's latest film with the nimble dexterity of a Bengali doctoral candidate. Often my fellow students would suggest that we "go out for *chapatis*" — rather like young people at home might at that time have suggested going out for burgers and a shake. The *chapatis*, of course, were only a complement to the main dishes — chicken dansak, shrimp vindaloo, saag lamb, dal. Most of my pals were of northern Indian decent — wheat rather than rice eaters — so we almost always went "out for *chapatis*," hardly ever for rice. "The lamb is good," one of them would say, "but it needs a little more salt." That always amazed Dot and me. How anyone could detect the absence of sufficient salt in the complex, fiery mix in our mouths astounded us.

Our tastebuds were tested further during the three years we lived in Thailand and Indonesia. Whether it's swallows' breasts or fish heads, when you're representing your country abroad you crunch the bones before you, lest you give offence. The result is the delight of expanding one's epicurean horizons combined with the discomfort of amoebic dysentery.

Our kids, however, with their youthful exposure to Southeast Asia, became submerged in Asian culture in ways we never could, and it triggered an interest in, and love for, hot and spicy food that never left. Thanks to them, Asian cuisine is a regular part of our diet.

Karen was almost four when we moved to Bangkok, and very quickly she was "singing" tonal Thai with her friends and arching her hands backward like a lakhon dancer as she crouched in a rainbow sarong in our courtyard. We lived just off the Sathorn Road — around the corner from the residence of the apostolic nuncio. When the real-estate agent showed us the house, she told us proudly, "Very lucky. Next to, how you say it? Number One monk!"

Lucky? Yes. There were four houses in the compound, two occupied by Thais and another by a Swiss businessman and his family. He was fond of fiddling with guns and not long after we moved in, from his balcony across his garden and ours, he shot a balloon out of Karen's hands with a rifle. It was not the sort of thing we were accustomed to in Ottawa (nor that you'd encounter in Geneva), but fortunately he was a good aim. The bottom of our garden flooded during the monsoon season, and when it dried we would discover snakes slithering near the roots of our pink bougainvillea bushes. Behind the house, a banana grove separated us from a small *klong* (canal) and this jungle-like patch provided cover for all sorts of reptiles, mammals, and *quemoys* — bands of robbers who preyed on prosperous *farangs* (foreigners). Perhaps it was due to our proximity to the Number One monk that we survived the threats that lurked around us. In two robberies we lost only a few bottles of booze, and our complement of snakes was no match for the thirty-six-foot reticulated python that inhabited a colleague's garden until it was sacrificed for a succulent soup.

Our house was modern with white stucco walls, teak trim, and light, airy rooms. In one corner of the garden, however, there was a spirit house of classical design: a wooden structure the size of a birdhouse on top of a long pole and shaped like a Thai temple with a steeply pitched roof. The main house had previously been occupied by a French family, and when we first inspected it we noted how well the house boy, Udom, got along with the children of the household. Like that of so many Thais, his age was impossible to guess — somewhere from twenty to forty. He had a smooth, round face, a slender frame, and a relaxed demeanour. His most dominant feature, however, was his wide, welcoming smile. It never vanished, never even varied, unlike his eyes that often did the talking, signalling caution one moment, disapproval another, contentment, disappointment, but never anger. He was neatly dressed that day, the way we were always to see him, in a laundry-fresh white shirt and trousers. But his sleek black hair was slightly tousled. Conscious of it, he kept whisking the strands back from his forehead with his smooth right hand as if a movie star at an autograph session. We hired him on the spot even before signing a lease.

Later, before moving in, I ran into him at the ambassador's residence. One of several additions to the staff for a large party, he was serving drinks. Udom, we were to discover, had a penchant for moonlighting. "Master," he greeted me. I cringed. But, in fact, he was far from obsequious. He knew the diplomatic milieu well and what was ordinarily expected of him. He was also flexible, however, and quickly adapted to our own informal ways, playing croquet with us in the garden and accompanying us to a beach house near Pattaya on weekends. Udom doted on Karen and, hand in hand, they would walk through the compound and around neighbouring streets to meet and play with Thai children. He was also infatuated with our first cook, a ravishing Vietnamese with long, manicured, and painted nails, unblemished by kitchen drudgery. After three weeks of soufflés and chickens with a sauce that never varied, Dot discovered that Udom was covering for her and faced her first experience of firing someone. She was just one of several cooks who failed to meet Dot's and Udom's distinctly different expectations.

Deb was just five months old when we arrived in Thailand, and rather than pablum, her initial staple was a bowl of rice, spiced, we suspected, by our *ayah*, Wan, with a dash of the red chili peppers she herself used by the bushel, carrying them always on her breath as she did Deb on a sprawling hip that pressed hard against her red-and-gold sarong. The mixture Wan spooned into our daughter didn't particularly please her at the time. She had arms and legs like stalks of bamboo and she howled incessantly when the monsoon rains rattled the tin roof over the servants quarters where she spent most of her time. Now, watching her tuck enthusiastically into a dish of hot noodles and admiring her full, happy face, it's hard to believe she's the same kid as the freckled, scrawny one in our photos: the stick doll standing in a red plastic tub in baggy diapers, trying to stay cool under an uninspiring trickle from a garden hose.

Ah! The heat. I still remember climbing down the steps onto the tarmac of the Bangkok airport for the first time. A hot blast rose from the surface as if we were hovering over a stove with elements locked on high. Rays wiggled and danced above the asphalt like fumes released from an open barrel of crude oil. They melted the figures at work on the ground into wobbly Gumbies, or the fuzzy images on rabbit-eared portable television sets that, positioned on wooden counters in corrugated-tin shacks, entertain whole villages. On the parched grass enclosed by the runways, there was a golf course. Through the shimmering haze, we could just make out some players, strolling languidly down a fairway under the protective cover of large, brilliantly painted umbrellas. *Okay, I can handle this*, I remember thinking to myself. *It's not all that bad.* But it was. Not one day or week or month. But month after month, virtually unchanging, unrelenting. Heat that sucked at the pores, made the skin itch and burn, drained one's tank to empty. We came to long for the sputtering mango showers that heralded the beginning of the monsoon and, after them, the late-afternoon thunderous torrents you could almost use to set your clock. They provided a brief respite—a cool balm to the skin, the chance for a mad dash through puddles splattered with crushed pink petals and remnants of coconut shells—until the clouds dispersed and the sun once again mopped up all earthly fluids.

Sometimes in mid-winter, when the thermometer dipped to the low eighties, we would feel a chill while taking an early-morning shower in our large, tiled bathroom. Then we knew we were beginning to adapt. A year after we arrived, my father died suddenly. Udom was not surprised. A cloud of flies had been swarming around one of our cupboards for hours: a bad omen. I rushed home to Toronto in late June. While others were going about the city in shorts and T-shirts complaining of the heat, I wore longs and a woollen sweater. We had acclimatized as best we ever would.

Tim was born in Bangkok ten months after we arrived, a chubby, contented baby who, when he was burped, could shoot a stream of milk right to the ceiling. It seemed to startle even the *tuk-kae*, a large gecko, who clung there every evening throatily calling his name. If Karen was Udom's and Deb was Wan's, then

Tim was Jaraway's. She had joined our household shortly before he was born — the last of our cooks. But she was a trained nurse and soon took charge of the household in areas beyond the kitchen. This did not sit well with Udom, who was used to being "Number One." So before long he told us sheepishly that he had to pay a visit to a sick relative in the north; he would, however, be back for sure very shortly. He packed a suitcase and left the next morning. We never saw him again. True to Thailand, the only country in Southeast Asia with no imperial past, he valued independence more than he did security. Periodically we would hear rumours that he was back in Bangkok, but he never came to see us, not even Karen. We wished he would, just to say hello. We missed him and his classic smile, as well as our games of croquet. He had become a real friend.

Jaraway was plump and motherly — to us as well as the children — efficient and sometimes officious. When she wasn't in the kitchen, she was usually with Tim: bathing him, changing him, feeding and forever burping him. He was an easy, healthy baby, but every once in a while, particularly after a spectacular spray of milk, Jaraway would study him anxiously and then report to Dot, "Not quite right, madam. Not quite right." Ever since, whenever one of us is sick, that is our lament, "Not quite right, madam. Not quite right."

We were cross-posted to Jakarta when Tim was less than a year old and the first words he strung together were in Bahasa. Public utilities were pretty unreliable in those days. I remember him standing at the top of the stairs in a green-and-yellow batik shirt and matching shorts. He had beach-blond hair and bangs that appeared to have been cut with a bowl on his head. He was shouting at the houseboy in a serious, husky voice, "Rachman, *tidak ada air*!" (there's no water). Rachman came running from the back of the house with a full jug, drawn from the great earthenware jar outside the kitchen. He was a quiet, rather timid young man who, perhaps not surprisingly, didn't take to Tim the way Udom had to Karen. Nor did he to me for that matter. A single lump of ice always floated forlornly in my scotch and soda, vanishing like an iceberg in late August. But I couldn't bring myself to bark at Rachman in Bahasa the way my young son could. Instead, frustrated, I would help myself to ice from the refrigerator in the pantry. That was just one of the many ways in which, unlike the kids, Dot and I failed to adjust, confusing our servants and potentially undermining their efforts to advance. Despite our shortcomings, however, our Indonesian cook, unlike the ones in Bangkok, stayed with us throughout and went on to a distinguished career at the ambassador's residence. Syono, just a shy teenager when he worked for us, is the first member of the staff acknowledged for his contribution to Margaret Dickenson's *From the Ambassador's Table*, a glossy compendium about formal dining. I don't know; maybe his ultimate success was due to Tim and the high expectations he had of the kitchen even then. "Syono! *Saya mau makan!*" (I want to eat.)

Once we were on a motor trip from Jakarta to Bali when Tim pulled his head and arms over the back of the driver's seat, baby bottle in hand. "*Hati hati*, Bangbung" (drive carefully), he ordered the young university student who worked for us part time as we sped through the dappled shade of a rubber plantation. Bangbung laughed, but he slowed down, too. Tim showed a knack for languages and imitating voices and dialects early on. In fact, he adapted to life in Asia so well that we came to doubt that the privileged world of diplomacy was what we wanted for our children.

So, growing up they missed a few years of candy floss and Popsicles, but only a few. Instead, they ate sticky rice stuffed into tubes of sugar cane. And they stored away early memories and sensations from Southeast Asia that led ultimately to a passion for oriental food and the creation of their own recipes that blend the flavours of different Asian cuisines. Try one, and *selamat makan!*

## LEMON-GRASS CHICKEN
### SERVES 4

4 skinned and boned chicken
    breasts, sliced in strips
2 tbsp canola oil
1 medium onion, sliced
½ cup lightly chopped fresh
    coriander leaves for garnish
½ cup lightly chopped fresh
    mint leaves for garnish

*Marinade*
6 cloves garlic, minced
3 tbsp fish sauce
    (anchovy extract)
1 hot chili pepper, chopped
1½ tbsp sugar
5 stalks lemon grass, minced*
⅛ tsp black pepper
1 tsp low-sodium soy sauce
juice of 1 lime

*Peel off tough outer leaves
(will end up half original size).
Use only the tender, small,
white bulb and about 1 inch of
inner white stalk. Mince by
hand.*

» Mix together marinade ingredients in a medium-sized bowl. Add chicken and marinate 30 minutes at room temperature, or 3 hours refrigerated.

» In a wok or large frying pan, heat canola oil over medium heat. Add onion and sauté until tender. Add chicken and marinade and stir-fry over medium-high heat 15–20 minutes, or until chicken is cooked through.

» Alternatively, the chicken can be barbecued. Add the sliced onion and the canola oil to the marinade. Thread marinated chicken on wooden skewers and cook on barbecue, basting frequently with the marinade.

» Garnish chicken with mint and coriander. Serve with rice, fresh asparagus, and salad, or stir-fried vegetables.

» I AM LOOKING AT A BELL on the corner of my desk. In size and sound, it's not unlike the ones vice-principals once rang in school-yards at the commencement of the day or the end of recess. The bulbous bottom is five inches high, the handle seven. Its ring is high-pitched, clear, and insistent like the voice of an elementary teacher. But there the similarities with the old school bell end. Mine is much heavier, and it is made of bronze, pock-marked and grey-green in colour, as if covered in petrified dust and dirt. Around its base, in relief, there is a ring of inch-high busts — figures from some ancient legend. And above this circle, as the bell tapers toward the handle, there is a second one of equally impassive faces. The handle is at first horizontally fluted until it reaches a small capital as on a classical column, and then, rising from the middle of the capital, there is a two-inch obelisk. Attached to it, at the top and bottom, are four quarter-moon fragments of bronze that form an oversized knob through which light and air can pass and in which cobwebs gather. To my eyes, the bell is handsome, delicate even, enigmatic, and very old.

Shortly after we were cross-posted from Thailand to Indonesia, I bought this bell from a *tukon*, a sort of peripatetic antique dealer who carts his cloth-wrapped wares through the countryside. We were at a bungalow we rented in the Puntjak, a mountainous area of tea plantations and terraced rice paddies seventy-five kilometres from Jakarta. This is the cool, regenerative region to which the diplomatic community and wealthy escape on weekends, leaving behind the capital's heat, grime, and depressing poverty. And one regular activity in the Puntjak is to sit in a wicker chair in the garden with a clutch of office files while a *tukon* unwraps his bundle and lays out whatever he has for sale. For the experienced collector, buying from a *tukon* is a lengthy enterprise, entailing several hours of cheerful negotiation. Only after all of the goods have again been wrapped up — ever so slowly — and the vendor is reluctantly, but with no hint of rancour, exiting the garden gate without a sale is the last and most realistic price proposed.

My purchase was of a temple bell from the Hindu era in Java, probably twelfth century, the *tukon* told me. Certainly no later than the fourteenth. The two rings of busts, he said, represented characters in the classic Hindu story of the Ramayana. This information delighted me. Clearly the bell was an extraordinary find — an object to be cherished forever. But during the remainder of our posting, I gradually came to a different view. As we prowled the antique shops of Indonesia, I discovered that my bell was far from unique. Especially in Central Java, we stumbled across several facsimiles. Only slowly did I become aware of my naïveté — of the real victor in those protracted negotiations that I, the trained negotiator, had conducted with the *tukon*. I had been duped. The bell was clearly one of many forged by a smithy in the twentieth century and roughed up to look old.

The bell encapsulates for me all the complexities and contradictions of Indonesia and the fascinating ways in which we were to find the country so different from its neighbour, Thailand. The bell, for instance, is Hindu, yet Indonesia is predominantly Muslim. While Thai culture clearly reflects the country's overwhelming Buddhist majority, that is not evidently the case with Islam in Indonesia. The country has the largest Muslim population in the world, and throughout the archipelago piercing voices over crackling loudspeakers summon the faithful to prayer; but the other great religions of the globe flourish here as well. Indeed, in many regions they have even influenced local Muslim practices.

This cultural debt to other faiths is both acknowledged and celebrated. Indonesia's most cherished architectural site, for instance, is Borobudur, a Buddhist sanctuary completed in 850 AD and set among the lush hills and forests of Central Java. It consists of nine stone terraces leading to one massive stupa at the pinnacle. On the walls of each, when we visited, damp green moss half hid the elegant carvings depicting the life of Buddha. *What is this?* we wondered. *Are we back in Thailand?*

Borobudur holds for me another contradiction. It is a UNESCO site and was, during our time in Indonesia, badly in need of assistance for its restoration. Because then-prime minister Pierre Trudeau—who had a deep interest in Asian culture—had expressed a desire to tour the monument on an upcoming visit, I tried to persuade Ottawa to have him announce a contribution to UNESCO's refurbishment fund while he was at the temple. Alas, the Canadian International Development Agency was too preoccupied with finding aid projects that would facilitate Canadian sales of logging, mining, and aviation equipment to consider assistance for a cultural project, albeit one central to Indonesia's generation of income from tourism.

Our bell also reminds me of the quiet, leisurely pace of life in Indonesia compared to Thailand. Bargaining is, of course, a way of life there, too, but the Thais are too busy—too far along the development path—for it to be as pervasive and protracted an exercise as in Indonesia. Driving along the Java coast, we would pull over on a desolate stretch of road and get out to admire the view. In no time, a barefoot man in a white shirt and shorts would trot up and insist we buy a parking ticket, price negotiable. Whenever we entertained, the evening always finished with a sort of sit-in outside the gate to our driveway. There our kindly, aging gardener would be engaged in a long, animated discussion with a cluster of young men, contending they had to be paid for *jaga-ing* (guarding) the cars of our guests. Whatever the circumstances, we always paid up, for the alternative was clear. If we didn't, the parking attendant, the car *jaga-er* or whoever it might be would become the thief!

Perhaps it is this zest for bargaining and negotiation that gave rise to the peculiarly Indonesian political concept of *musjawarah*, a system of protracted deliberation to reach agreement by consensus on conflicting points of view without resorting to a vote so that no one loses face. It requires patience and restraint—noble traits more characteristic of the least developed countries than the rest of the world. And so, too, the bell always reminds me of how impoverished Indonesia was, especially when we lived there, and how unseemly it was of us to bargain at all.

We moved to Jakarta only a few years after the bloody and confused uprising of 1965 that had led to the downfall of President Sukarno, the erratic, anti-Western first president of the country. His nationalization of foreign-owned firms, mounting debts from the purchase of military equipment, and unproductive prestige projects had ruined the economy. It was starting to recover under the more stable, pro-Western, but corrupt leadership of President Suharto. Everywhere, however, there were blemishes reflecting the failings of the past as well as the present: a giant sports complex, built by the USSR for the Asian Games in 1962, already decaying and badly underused; rusting steel frames of buildings halted when Soviet aid was abruptly terminated; department stores with empty shelves; unreliable electricity and water supplies; flooded streets more crowded with *becaks* (bicycle taxis) than cars and littered with putrid refuse; a downtown deserted at night because there was nowhere worth going, not even a decent hotel; and, in daytime, miserable people everywhere with pathetic signs of medical neglect—patches over ulcerating eyes, stumps for legs and arms. Every so often, young demonstrators would march past the iron gates of our embassy bungalow—mostly students wearing brightly coloured headbands, protesting the endemic corruption of the government. Always following them at the end of the parade were truckloads of army infantry, rifles slung over their shoulders.

We lived in a Dutch colonial house near the city centre — a small mansion, really, with a dining-room table large enough for eighteen. A high wooden fence and thick shrubs protected us from the not-so-hidden real world outside. Our second-storey bedroom windows looked out on the garden with its friendly, sprawling mango tree, innocent wading pool, and swing set. But beyond it we could see huge cement culverts lying in a flat field of weeds, remnants of a long-neglected construction project now serving as accommodation for several dozen people. For some reason, our house was called Krakatau, after the infamous volcanic island in the Sunda Strait between Java and Sumatra that erupted so violently in 1883, spilling ashes and debris across the Indian Ocean as far as Madagascar and causing widespread destruction and loss of life. Every night, listening to the hollow clicking sound of wood against wood as a street vendor passed down our street, I would think to myself, *How long? How long before this island, too, erupts?*

Travelling outside the capital was little different, and a reminder of the urgency of family planning. When you drive through the North American countryside, how many people do you pass who are outside, along the road? Two, maybe three or four in an hour. In Java? Thousands. To pass the time, we would estimate the number in a minute — estimate because often the side of the road was so crowded it was impossible to make an accurate calculation. Then we would multiply by sixty and discover we were travelling at, say, 10,000 people per hour! Passing frail, wizened men with grey goatees squatting on the ground, staring at our car with vacant eyes. Sad women in garish batik sarongs with clashing *selendangs* (shawls) over their shoulders sitting in doorways, sewing or peeling vegetables. Half-naked children with swayed backs and distended bellies doing nothing — no energy to spare, no notion of play having ever reached them. Stronger boys, alert to any hope of financial reward, shinnying up palm trees, machetes tucked into their shorts, to hack down coconuts for thirsty motorists. Bare-chested men trotting at the side of the road, balancing large wicker or metal containers at the ends of long wooden poles. People in horse-drawn carriages and *bemos* (little open vans), on bicycles, *becaks*, and ox carts. People on the move but going where?

I remember visiting a Canadian medical team at a CARE project in Surakarta, Central Java. An eye specialist was using a converted barber's chair as his operating table, and a single bare bulb hung from the ceiling to provide illumination. That evening I went to a performance of the Ramayana at the magnificent, ninth-century Hindu temple of Prambanan. In those days it was performed on full-moon nights in front of the 155-foot-high central tower that rose from the trampled earth like a sand castle, delicate and shimmering in reflected light. As I watched the troupe of five hundred dancers and listened to the mystical, percussive blend of the accompanying gamelan orchestra, I was struck once again, as I always am when I look at my bronze bell, by Indonesia's contradictions: the often-tolerant mix of cultural traditions in a society nevertheless prone to periodic, bloody ethnic clashes, the sophisticated art in the midst of such abject poverty. In my subsequent letter to the Department of External Affairs in Ottawa, reporting on my tour of Central Java, I drew attention to these paradoxes. I also made a plea that we structure our aid program so as to address the basic needs of Indonesia's most disadvantaged — that we focus on agriculture; health care; education; and small, integrated community-development projects. For how many moons, I concluded, would Indonesia have to wait for selfless, humanely focused assistance from the West?

Almost forty years have passed since I wrote that report. My bronze bell still tolls with an urgent peal. And the people still wait.

SERVES 4

4 chicken breasts,
   skinned and boned

*Peanut Sauce*
2 heaping tbsp peanut butter
1 tbsp canola oil
1 ½ tbsp soy sauce
1 tbsp lemon juice
½ tsp hot red-pepper flakes
1 tbsp brown sugar
3 cloves garlic, minced
½ cup water

*Salad*
1 large bunch Romaine lettuce,
   ripped into salad-sized
   pieces
1 red bell pepper, seeded and
   sliced
20 Greek olives (Kalamata),
   pitted and quartered
1 medium red onion, sliced
1 medium cucumber, sliced
¾–1 cup loosely packed fresh
   coriander leaves, snipped
2–3 tbsp peanut sauce
2 mangoes, peeled and sliced

» Combine peanut-sauce ingredients in a small saucepan and simmer until smooth. Add more water as necessary to bring to a medium consistency. Set aside.

» Place chicken in a small baking dish and coat with 2–3 tablespoons peanut sauce. Bake at 350 degrees until just tender (about 30 minutes).

» In a large bowl toss first 6 salad ingredients together with the peanut sauce until just moist (adjust amount of sauce to taste). Divide salad among four plates. Top each with hot baked chicken in its juices. Arrange mango slices decoratively around chicken. Pass extra peanut sauce.

» AFTER SEVERAL YEARS in the diplomatic service, I resigned to take up a teaching position in international relations at the University of Windsor. That meant some time spent in southwest Ontario, with our travel largely confined to North America, before going on sabbatical to England.

For Dot and me, going there was like renewing an old friendship with someone who'd moved on during the intervening years — who'd turned out to be upwardly mobile. There was much about the country that was familiar and it was as enchanting as ever, but there was just as much that was new and very different.

In the 1960s we had lived the typical life of expatriate students, managing on limited means: savings, scholarships, income from occasional lecturing, and Christmas cheques from anxious parents at home. There were a number of us in the Victorian and Edwardian row houses on the edge of central London — those two- and three-storey buildings with wrought-iron gates and small-tiled fronts scrubbed regularly not by us, but the English residents. They were mixed neighbourhoods of white- and blue-collar workers, South Asian and West Indian immigrants, young couples just starting out, old-age pensioners, and students from all over the world, especially the Commonwealth and the United States. Few among our neighbours were exceptionally poor. We were not really poor, either. But we thought we were, and certainly by North American standards our circumstances were modest, and that had a radicalizing impact on us.

The flat we rented was on Leathwaite Road, midway between Clapham and Wandsworth commons. Our cheery landlady ran the tobacco shop around the corner where school kids in their grey-flannel shorts or skirts, mauve jackets, and ties gathered after school to buy iced lollies and gob-smackers and mints that were stored in large glass jars. Initially she set our rent at five pounds six shillings a week, but then she took pity on us and lowered the rate to five. There it stayed for all four of our years in London. Ruefully, I noted on a recent visit you can't buy a pub lunch in London today for the amount of our weekly rent.

We chose a flat in Clapham because I had a cousin living on the north side of the common who was doing his Ph.D. at the London School of Economics. My cousin, too, had chosen that area because friends had preceded him there. On the steamship over, he told us, an elderly, upper-class English woman had engaged him in conversation over tea and asked where he intended to reside. "I don't know. Clapham Common, maybe," my cousin had answered, not knowing of any other district in London.

"Clapham Common!" The fashionable lady put down her tea-cup and drew back haughtily. "I was in Clapham Common. Once. It was during the war. I was caught in an air raid at the Clapham Common underground station, and I thought to myself, 'My God! I'm going to die at Clapham Common. What would mother say!' "

In England your preoccupations reflect the side of the social divide you occupy. Thus, in the sixties, we were locked in a constant struggle to keep our bodies at a comfortable temperature. I remember in Hindi classes in Woburn Square at the School of Oriental and African Studies, the North American students huddled in winter coats by the single coil of an electric heater at the rear of the classroom. But there were too many of us for its feeble rays to reach us all. *Oh, to be on a beach in Goa*, we thought as we recited phrases such as *"Bagh Himalaya per milte he"* (there are tigers in the Himalayas).

Once or twice a week, we strolled Clapham or Wandsworth to gather faggots in Karen's pram, using them as kindling to help light our fires and sometimes to conserve coal. Always, it seemed, a grey mist hung over the soccer pitches as young men and boys in striped jerseys, faces scratched and splattered with mud, tore down the wings dreaming of Jimmy Greaves and Bobby Charlton. The residue of the latest shower dripped from the umbrella boughs of the beech and chestnut trees onto the cloth caps and trench coats of old men playing chess at open-air tables. And around the ponds, there was invariably a ring of boys like bass on a stringer standing quietly in their wellies, jars and tins of bait beside them, their lines hanging listlessly in the shallow, brown puddles.

When kindling was scarce on the commons, we resorted to single sheets of newspaper twisted tightly into straw-shaped tubes to start the stubborn coals. Or if nothing worked, we relied on our paraffin heater alone. It had a large, shiny reflector that threw off a lot of heat. But behind it a full glass bottle of a bright-red liquid perched precariously, awaiting a stumble or falling object to set the flat ablaze. Some mornings I placed the heater directly beside my desk, lit it, closed the door, and then had breakfast in the kitchen. Expecting to return to a room warm enough for working at least in a heavy woollen sweater, I would find the parlour enveloped in an oily smoke that smelled like burning candle wax, only worse. I had not set the wick at the proper height, Dot would explain to me afterward. We would rush to turn off the heater, open the windows to a January gale, and then start the whole heating process all over again.

Every few weeks, the local ironmonger came by in his lorry with a big blue-metal tank of paraffin on the back. I trotted down with my red five-gallon jerry tin to have it refilled. "Bet you don't get service like this in North America, do you?" he would say cheerfully.

"No, we certainly don't," I would answer cryptically and leave it at that.

At night I banked the coal fire in our bedroom — it worked much better than the one in the parlour — to take the chill off the room before retiring. But then, through most of the night, we would be too hot to sleep. By morning, however, the temperature would be near freezing again, and patches on the grey, floral-patterned wallpaper that had dried and bubbled in the night would again be dark and damp from the moisture seeping through the crumbling plaster.

Having a bath to take the chill out of the bones was a daring sport that required an efficient, full-time handler. The hot-water tap, fired by a gas heater above the tub, reliably supplied only a frugal trickle. So this source had to be supplemented throughout the bath by relays of water from the kettle on the gas stove in the kitchen. Invariably, in the middle of Operation "Weakly" Warm Bath, the water heater and the burners on the stove would sputter and die. The non-bather had to dash for the box of shillings in the kitchen and reload the gas meter. Sometimes, on the way back to the tub, the lights went out, too, leaving the bather in frightening darkness surrounded by a shallow, soapy pool of tepid water as the assistant felt his or her way down two flights of stairs to the basement to feed the equally hungry, but neglected, electric meter.

For some reason, we always forgot to put our milk bottles out in time for the early-morning delivery, and it was always when the lights went out that a dozen or more of them were clustered at the top of our stairs. A wayward foot, searching in the dark, would strike a bottle and send them all tumbling and tinkling down the stairs. Power restored, first the gas water heater had to be relit, then the pilot on the stove. More water had to be boiled for the desperate bather, and then the broken bottles swept up.

If one was particularly unlucky, a fuse would blow as the power returned. Changing a fuse in England in those days was a task better left to qualified electricians. The discoloured rectangular objects looked like hardware from the Victorian era — the sort of thing you might find in a grab box of souvenirs at an antique stall in the Portobello Road. They had to be taken apart with a screwdriver, a wire removed, and another one set between two terminals. Fortunately, my tutor, the illustrious South Asian historian Hugh Tinker, taught me this intricate art at a welcoming dinner party at his home in north London. Dressed as always in a Harris tweed jacket with a white handkerchief stuffed up his sleeve, he took me to his basement and together we disassembled and reassembled fuses until I could do the job to his satisfaction. Of all the things I learned from the faculty at the School of Oriental and African Studies—the names and roles of classical Indian musical instruments, the impact of the Moguls on the subcontinent, the tortuous path of the independence movement, how to say "there are tigers in the Himalayas" in Hindi—that was the one thing that was truly practical.

Keeping the electricity humming, the appliances functioning, the bathtub water flowing, the fires burning, those were our constant preoccupations. Above all, staying warm. Whenever I sniff a coal fire burning, I think of those student years in London. I love that sharp, sooty smell. I can picture myself in an old stuffed chair beside the fire, iron poker in hand, gently stirring the coals, admiring their steady red glow, listening to their quiet hiss. There is nothing quite so comforting as coming inside on a cold, wet, or foggy night and sitting beside an open coal fire, especially if somebody else had to get the bloody thing going.

"I love London," the journalist John Gray said one afternoon over tea and a fire at our flat. "But it's time to go. We've been camping out long enough!"

WHEN WE RETURNED to England with the kids, it was to the other side of the great divide. We spent most of the sabbatical on a farm in Surrey, in the greenbelt outside London. Stockbroker country. Our home was on Blackmoor Farm, off the road between the quaint village of Ockham and the prosperous town of Cobham. A dirt track descended a steep hill—of which Deb and Tim took instant, delighted note—and then wound through cow pastures and cornfields for a half-kilometre until it reached our place. Despite the prosperous surroundings, however, we were housed in a relatively modest red-brick cottage, originally the residence of the farm's woodcutters. It had been built in 1867 and was obviously intended for Canadians with pretensions of being working class. More than a century later, the cottage still lacked central heating, leaving us to rely, once again, on open fires for warmth. This time, however, our wood supply was so plentiful that we rarely used coal. And situated as we were in genteel surroundings, where in every direction the countryside was like a Constable painting, our time was spent very differently.

On two sides of the farm there were deep, green forests where, in the autumn, I cut and split enough wood to see us through the winter. A network of foot and bridle paths meandered through them and, often, as we sat by our living-room fire, we would hear the hollow click clack of horses' hooves as a group of riders in black caps and britches passed in front of our cottage en route to the forest paths. Deb, in particular, watched them intently, fancying herself in the role. Always the least political, she had no trouble bolting to the other side.

The woods were strewn with ivy, holly, and rhododendron; but more impressive than the flora were the pheasants that littered the forest floor — literally hundreds of them being fattened for the annual autumn shoot. When the big day finally arrived, Roly, our landlord, not yet a close friend, invited me to join the shooting party — as a beater. I politely declined. Was it a political statement? I wondered; or was it really that I was miffed at the humble position I was offered in the shooting party? For hours that day, gunshot rang out around our cottage, springer spaniels tore through the woods barking, and frightened flocks of birds — as thick as the pigeons in Trafalgar Square — scuttered by our windows like low, black clouds in a fast-moving storm. Every few minutes we'd hear a soft thud as a pheasant crashed onto a roof or into our back garden, landing near one of the sticky, brown patches left by Roly's stray cows.

No one on the shoot that day can possibly have failed to bag all the birds he wanted. Indeed, Roly had enough to present us with an undressed brace, a plucking and cooking problem for Dot. And for Tim. I think it was the challenge of wild game—well, sort of wild—that first tweaked his fascination with the art of cooking, as well as his suspicion that his parents didn't know all of the answers, political and culinary alike. If pheasant was what the landed gentry ate, he wanted a taste of their life. From an ordinary roast pheasant, however, Tim has moved on. As I write he is in the midst of preparing dinner for a party of twenty-five. They will dine on "turducken," a chicken cooked inside a duck, cooked inside a turkey with three different dressings: smoked andouille sausage, oysters, and cornbread. A dinner fit for barons and earls.*

For Karen, that year in Surrey exposed her to the yachting set. Roly had his own sloop at Bosham on the West Sussex coast, the quaint little village dominated by the spire of a Saxon church that appears in the Bayeux Tapestry and from which Harold set out for Normandy in 1064. It was also purportedly at Bosham that King Canute commanded the tide to recede, a feat that, daily, those who imprudently park their cars too near the shore would dearly like to see repeated. Eventually, Roly invited us all to sail with him and his wife, Trish, through the busy, mast-studded roads of Chichester Harbour. Not long afterward, a chum of Karen's at Sir George Abbott school in Guildford enticed her into sailing lessons. Together these experiences kindled in her what has remained a life-long interest, albeit without a yacht of her own or membership in a club titled "royal."

For Dot and me, our principal diversion that year was roaming the English countryside in a way our circumstances in London had rarely allowed. Not just our local footpaths, but all through the steep valleys, ancient forests, and open commons of the North Downs. In the autumn, we picked blackberries on paths that followed the banks of meandering, hidden streams and drove to Petworth House, not just for the Turner paintings but for sheep-dog trials as well. In the spring, we lazed on the freshly mown grass of village greens watching the local cricket clubs in glorious inaction like orderlies relaxing on the lawns of private, under-utilized sanitariums. We visited beautiful Wisley Gardens and the local manor homes — Clandon Park, Loseley House, and Polesden Lacey, where George VI and Queen Elizabeth spent their honeymoon. And as others have done since the reign of Charles II, we picnicked on Box Hill on a blanket of bluebells, admiring the gold-and-purple hue of the rolling downs spread out below us.

Dot also became keen on doing brass rubbings in local Norman churches. Her favourite was St. James' in the village of Shere, a good choice, I thought, because I liked the pub. It was at St. James' in the fourteenth century that Christine, daughter of William the carpenter, arranged to have herself enclosed for the remainder of her life in a narrow passage in the outer wall of the church, so that "laid aside from public and worldly sights," she might be "enabled to serve God more freely in every way, and having resisted all opportunity for wantonness" might "keep her heart undefiled by this world." No pint of warm bitter for her, I mused, as I sat in a casement window of the White Horse, waiting for Dot to finish her rubbings.

Horseback riding, shoots, dining on pheasant, yachting, wandering the gentle countryside of Southeast England, ours were certainly the diversions of the privileged. But nothing reflected our altered status from the sixties so much as our exposure to British blood sports. In fact, Dot and I had had some limited experience with this curious feature of British culture back then. One Christmas we had watched the start of a hunt in a village square in north Wales, and blood sports was a subject that arose frequently when I gave lectures for the Commonwealth Institute to sixth-formers at schools all over England. My assigned topics were "Canada and the Commonwealth" and "Canada and the Issue of National Unity." Perhaps it is no wonder that, in the question periods that followed, these subjects were quickly abandoned and I was pressed to disclose my opinion of blood sports.

I knew that this was a topic that divided people along class and party lines, and that a good Labourite would express opposition. But, in truth, I had no strong opinion. I fished for smallmouth bass in the Great Lakes. Who was I to criticize the British aristocracy? Besides, from what I had seen, the risks to the riders in a hunt seemed to exceed those of the fox. So I didn't take a position, much to the students' chagrin. *Wimp*, I'm sure they thought. They were thirsty for debate — bloodthirsty.

Several times during our year in Surrey, Dot and I came upon fox hunts. We would stop beside a farm and watch the men in bright-red tunics and the women in black gather in a cobbled, Tudor courtyard. Glasses of sherry served on silver trays would be handed up to the mounted riders, and after a shrill blast of a hunting horn, at close quarters the party would trot out through the gate and gallop madly across the farm, over a fence, and into the neighbouring field. Invariably, even at the first fence, some old gent with a shock of pure white hair would come unseated, fly over the head of his horse and land, if he were lucky, in a soggy patch of grass and mud, still clinging tenaciously to the reins of his horse. Once, walking along a footpath in the North Downs, a ragged-looking fox, moving slower than I would have expected, crossed gingerly in front of us and disappeared into the woods. Sometime later, we heard the bleat of a hunting horn and, several minutes after that, a pack of hounds and a dwindling, straggling line of riders passed in front of us. The fox seemed safe, we thought, and would probably sleep more soundly that night than most of his saddle-sore pursuers.

While fox hunting was not entirely new to us, that year in Surrey we were introduced to another curious blood sport of which we had no prior experience: beagling. The not-so-rich-man's hunt, in which (until the ban in 2004 on both activities) a hare is pursued by a pack of beagles pursued by a party of walkers. Sport for the lower reaches of the upper class. The one we attended started from a neighbouring farm, and we were invited by our landlady, Trish, to come along and participate in this rather odd form of communal walk.

The attire of beaglers was not as flashy as that of fox hunters (Deb would have nothing to do with them). Yet, nevertheless, the sport seemed to have its own strict dress code. The official members of our beagling party — the regulars — were dressed in black riding caps, green velvet jackets, white silk shirts with ruffled collars, riding britches, and brown leather walking shoes — so sensible for trudging across sodden fields! The others — the tag-alongs on a casual outing — came in green overcoats, trousers of a subdued shade (largely forest green), and — most importantly — green Wellingtons. In a way that has always struck me as peculiarly English, we were not apprised beforehand of the appropriate uniform. While my own clothes were suitably drab for the occasion, Dot unfortunately arrived in a red winter jacket and yellow wellies. "I should have thought," said Trish, using that favourite English expression of reproof, "I should have thought that you would have known!"

*Known what*, I wondered, *that red and yellow warn the hare that it is being chased, or distract the beagles from their work?* Feeling bewildered and a little humiliated, at the rousing command of a bugler standing in the middle of a yapping pack of underfed dogs, we set off across a wet spring field, pursuing the leaders of the chase who pursued the beagles, who were sniffing for the track of a hare. At first, with the dogs not yet having picked up a scent, the party moved in a tight, orderly knot — at a brisk but comfortable gait, appropriate for a country walk, except that this one was not along footpaths. That being the case, at the end of the first field, my attention was drawn to another feature of beagling attire I had not heretofore noticed. All of the gentlemen apart from me were carrying four-foot-long sticks, forked at one end. These, I discovered, were to pry apart strands of barbed-wire fence so that the ladies might pass more decorously from one field to the next. How uncouth of me not to have come suitably equipped!

It wasn't long before the beagles caught a scent. Or at least we presumed that is what happened, for as suddenly as another blast of the bugle reached us stragglers, a field behind the leaders, the pace quickened and the yelping of the beagles intensified. From that point on, there was not much order or cohesion to the outing. The regulars, and one or two particularly earnest neophytes, started jogging to stay up with the pack. The rest of the party, however, (being English after all) continued at the same stately speed, falling farther and farther behind the beagles.

"Doesn't much matter," chirped a pink-cheeked woman in a green woolen cap walking beside me. "The hare will eventually circle back. You can stop for a rest any time you like."

Indeed, I noticed that several in the party were no longer walking. They were hanging over fences, talking to friends, kneeling on the ground debating the name of a rare wildflower, or flipping through their bird guides for the picture of the warbler twittering high in the bare branches of an apple tree.

"Besides, it's not very often that the beagles actually run a hare to ground anyway," my companion added with a laugh. "And that's not the point in any event, is it really?"

We walked on doggedly. Our numbers, however, continued to dwindle, just as always happened at fox hunts. But this time it wasn't because of broken legs, concussions, and horses that refused at particularly high fences. Rather, several groups slowed, looking for patches of dry ground and tree trunks or fence posts to serve as backrests. Then they sat down and opened their picnic hampers, exposing teapots, china cups, and all. Others drifted off to the local pub for a pint and a bit of grub, confident they wouldn't miss anything and that they could find the beagling party later.

Among the small band that continued the chase, conversation was intense and excited. One topic dominated all others. The "antis." Were they lurking on a nearby lane? When and where would they likely strike? Or had the diligent efforts to conceal the locale of this week's hunt succeeded? Wasn't it shocking what the antis did last week? Spraying the tracks of the hare with an aerosol can. What would they think of next?

It was only then that I finally understood the allure of beagling, the essential core of the sport. It was not about running a hare to ground. It was about the antis. How to outwit them and preserve the sanctity of the chase. But beagling was more than that, I realized in a sudden moment of enlightenment. It was English society in microcosm. It was about animals, walking, wildflowers, birds, picnics, and pubs. It was about animated conversation, politics, and theatre. It was a playing out of the eternal struggle between the classes.

Lukewarm baths and blood sports. Doesn't much matter which. I love England. On both sides of the fence.

* *Tim used the turducken recipe from Chef Paul Prudhomme of New Orleans. You can get it at http://www.chefpaul.com/turducken.html. But be prepared for a cooking marathon. The recipe is nine pages long, single-spaced, and the birds need twelve hours in the oven.*

TIM » MOM HAD THIS GREAT TRICK to get me to eat my vegetables — got me every time. She'd stab the offender with her fork and pretend it was an airplane that was doomed to crash unless it landed in my mouth. How could I resist when the lives of helpless passengers could be saved by one, simple, altruistic act?

Debbie had thicker skin. She would sit rigidly, mouth clamped shut as innocent pea people crashed dramatically onto her plate — ruthless. She hated everything edible. She was skinny.

She was the ace up my sleeve when the whole airplane thing began to wear on me. I could always deflect attention away from myself by comparing my ingestive efforts to hers. "Why do I have to eat my cauliflower? Debbie hasn't even touched hers" — that sort of thing.

Neither of us was at all prepared for English school lunches. I was too old for edible airplanes, and Deb's strategy of passive resistance wasn't going to work on the English — look what Gandhi had to endure. We were entering no man's land and we didn't have a soul to turn to for support. We'd have to look out for each other in the cafeteria, work as a team.

For the most part, the English are gastronomically neanderthal. Most of our English peers gobbled down such odious concoctions as fried bologna, liver and onions, and rice pudding (it came with some syrupy red sauce that, rumour had it, was made from human blood). They saw it as the treat of the week. Deb and I weren't entirely alone, however. Otherwise there would have been no need for Mrs. Cowan. Mrs. Cowan lay at the root of a general feeling of scholastic dyspepsia that nagged at me for the entire year we spent in England.

Pink Floyd's famous song *Another Brick in the Wall Part II* ends with a voice saying, "If you don't eat your meat, you can't have any pudding. How can you have any pudding if you don't eat your meat?" It is the voice of Mrs. Cowan. It still haunts me. Mrs. Cowan was a massive, steak-and-kidney pie of a woman with blotchy skin and bad breath. We used to make a game of counting her nose hairs. Twenty-six left, thirty-three right.

Mrs. Cowan's job was to stand beside the slop bucket and decide if you'd eaten enough to move on to dessert.

"But I don't even want pudding. I hate semolina."

"I don't care what you hate; you'll eat it. And you'll start by finishing your greens."

You couldn't leave the cafeteria until you'd made it through enough of your dessert to satisfy Mrs. Cowan, and if you were in Mr. Jeffrey's class, as I was, being late for class wasn't an option. He had his own special closet filled with different instruments of torture — a different one for each conceivable offence. I was trapped. So was Debbie. Her teacher was in cahoots with Mr. Jeffries. Alcatraz.

It was said that Mrs. Cowan lived off the contents of the slop bucket.

"She doesn't have a home. They let her sleep in the gym."

"She ate her own children and now she has to work here as punishment."

"Next year, they're going to let her cook."

We called her "The Cow," never to her face, though. We were terrified of her. She could make your life a living hell. A bunch of us made Ollie Winters cry once by daring him to sneak up behind her and say "moo."

She was evil.

We hated her.

Mashed potatoes were our salvation. My sister can be credited for realizing their potential.

All the really horrible meals came with mashed potatoes. It was the administration's one oversight. Deb discovered that, by scooping out a hole in the centre of your potatoes, you could make room for things like liver if you chopped it up into tiny pieces first. Then you could pack the potatoes into a tight little ball so that it looked like almost nothing. If you reserved a little gravy to reduce the contrast between white potato and the odd protruding piece of meat, kept a straight face, and controlled your shaking legs, you could breeze right into dessert. Desserts were generally no big deal, but if you did get stuck with a liver-semolina combo you could then beg for lenience based on your performance with the liver.

My sister is a genius. In that one year, a special bond developed between us. She has since survived raw horse and pond scum at a Japanese dinner in her honour. I, too, can now eat just about anything. But I always leave a little something on my plate — a piece of gristle maybe, or half a Brussels sprout — for Mrs. Cowan.

She has to eat it. They make her.

*Here's a combination that never requires deception:*

## PISTOU MASH WITH CHOPS

*Mash*

4 large potatoes
¼ cup milk
1 tbsp butter
1 tbsp pistou (see p. 72–73)
6–8 fresh basil leaves, snipped
2 heaping tbsp grated
   Romano cheese
1 tbsp pine nuts
1 tbsp chopped walnuts

*Chops*

2 or more fresh lamb loin chops
   per person
juice of one lemon
1 tsp cracked black pepper
1 tsp mint
2 cloves garlic, chopped
salt to taste

» Boil potatoes until tender, drain and mash together with milk and butter until creamy. Stir in remaining ingredients over low heat until warmed through. Serve.

» Sprinkle ingredients over both sides of chops. Allow chops to warm to room temperature (about 1 hour). Grill 5–10 minutes per side. Chops should be rare at the centre and juicy. Let stand 5 minutes for medium-rare.

» PUBS AND PUB LUNCHES constitute one of England's finest institutions. They rank alongside parliament, afternoon tea, and the BBC evening news, a notch above Stratford, strawberries and cream at Wimbledon, Lords, and the FA Cup. You can plan a day around a pub. A twelve-kilometre circular walk from pub parking lot to public bar, timed to make it before last call. Better still is to reach the perfect inn midway along, before the specials are gone and there's nothing but a packet of crisps to wash down with a pint of bitter. There's Ye Olde Masons Arms on a hike from Beer to Salcombe Regis, the yellow gorse your sun on an overcast day; the Square and Compass in Worth Matravers, coming from Swanage by the upper coastal path and returning along the Priests Way; the Wool Pack in Slad, trekking from Painswick through Laurie Lee country, fire-thorn berries spilling over loose-stone walls. I like them best coming in late on a cold, wet afternoon when there's a table free by the inglenook fireplace and you can doze there like a contented cat, paws outstretched to the glowing embers, reviewing the route completed, planning conquests to come.

Scotch eggs are good, too, although they are no longer the pub staple they once were. Like bangers and mash and bubble and squeak, marmite and spotted dick, they remind me that, however much I may feel at home in Britain, I am in another country. Not foreign, but different. At the end of the bar, the scotch eggs used to sit under a glass cover—along with some Cornish pasties maybe—like a neglected museum exhibit: cold, dark, and drying. Unexploded grenades from the Great War. Nowadays, when you do find them, they're often resuscitated before they're served—heated in a microwave and dressed up with a crunchy salad. Dot even makes them with ground chicken instead of pork to reduce the fat and cholesterol. These are, I guess, necessary changes. They've resurrected the scotch egg from the verge of extinction—even internationalized it—to meet the needs of a health-conscious age.

British pubs, like scotch eggs, are an acquired taste; it takes time to adapt to their idiosyncracies. There are regional flavours, too. I remember the first time I went into an off-licence near Paddington Station in the sixties, I asked for a quart bottle of Courage. I liked their simple ads: "Take Courage."

"A wot?"

"A quart."

A quizzical stare.

"One of those large brown bottles behind you."

"Oh! You mean a flagon!"

Two weeks later we had moved into our flat off Clapham Common, and I made my first trip to the local off-license. "I'll have a flagon of Double Diamond please."

"A wot?"

"You know, a flagon."

Another confused look.

"One of those large brown bottles behind you."

"Oh! You mean a quart!"

Dot's father, who was born and raised near Bath, looked forward eagerly to his first visit with us in London and a trip to our local pub. "Half and half. That's the thing to drink," he said authoritatively as we walked to Clapham Junction. "Just the right mix."

We sauntered confidently up to the bar. "Two pints of half and half, please."

"Alf 'o wot, mate?"

We were so flustered we couldn't remember the right combination. Bitter? Mild? Pale? Lager? Stout?

"I think we'll change that." I struggled to sound at ease with local custom. "We'll have two pints of best bitter?" That had worked before; I'd heard others say it.

"Which one?" The publican was growing impatient.

I gave up and pointed to the fanciest of the china handles, decorated with — I don't know — a bishop's mitre or a cherubic friar. "That one," I said diffidently, as if it were the only English I knew.

It was some time, too, before we learned that to feel comfortable, it was best not to hang up our coats and sit at a table. Better to stand by the bar in our macs, dripping water onto the hardwood floor as we sipped from our mugs and surveyed the room, staring down the stares of the regulars. Now, of course, it's not just tourists but even the locals who sit, and not just at stools by the bar. Now, too, you're never sure where to order, especially food — at the bar or at your table. Customs change. You have to keep going to the pubs to stay abreast.

I always go to the bar first. I check the taps. See what's on draft. Look for the scotch eggs under the glass cover. Even if eventually I sit, I always take the first sips of my pint of warm bitter standing by the bar or peering into the fire, picking up snippets of local gossip. And I ask for my scotch egg alone and unheated with maybe a little mustard. I really don't care any longer how you're supposed to do it. I'm an old-timer now.

## INTERNATIONAL SCOTCH EGGS

SERVES 4

1 pound lean ground chicken
1 tsp thyme
1 tsp oregano
1 tsp basil
1 tsp garlic powder
½ cup or more bread crumbs
   (fine)
vegetable oil
4 hard-boiled eggs
1 raw egg (beaten)
salt and pepper to taste

» Mix chicken and spices until well blended. Divide mixture into four and press into patties. Wrap one patty around each egg, patting and forming to completely coat egg in mixture. Dip in beaten egg and roll in bread crumbs (on waxed paper for easy clean-up).

» Deep fry in vegetable oil over medium heat (bubbling but not scorching) until golden brown, about five minutes. Drain on paper towels. Serve hot or cold with mustard or sauces of choice, and salad!

» I LOVE FRANCE. I feel relatively at home there — the way you do in a country where you can at least get by in the language and thus experience the culture more deeply, get a feel for how the place ticks. But there is more to it than that. I am always conscious there of the historical connection to Canada and of the continuing importance of France to French Canadians, indeed, to all Canadians, in helping sustain the bilingual, bicultural character that contributes so vitally to our special identity.

That transatlantic tie — and my own connection to Quebec — was driven home to me the first time I went to get my hair cut in the Riviera town of Menton, where we were living on another sabbatical. The barber had his radio on, softly playing popular music. I wasn't even aware of it, I was so preoccupied trying to follow his French and keep up my end of the conversation. Then, after a particularly long pause in our awkward exchange, he suddenly said, "*C'est votre compatriote qui chante.*"

"*Ah, oui?*"

"*Oui. Robert Charlebois.*"

"*Ah, vraiment,*" I said. But I wasn't really sure who he was.

His entertainer. Not mine. My compatriot. Not his.

Not much later, on September 8, our wedding anniversary, Dot and I watched the ceremony outside Menton's Hotel de Ville marking the liberation of the town from German occupation. A wreath was laid at a plaque honouring the first Allied solider to enter Menton. He was a Canadian lieutenant — a French Canadian — and he died there hours later.

Our mutual suffering.

Those moments of connection in Menton reminded me how I felt the first time I landed at Dieppe in 1958, Canadian flags flying along the quay and the flower beds shaped like maple leaves. Or the day with the kids in 1980 we bought waffles at an outdoor stand near the crescent beach at La Baule on the Atlantic, the Riviera of the north. They came soaked in maple syrup. Canadian maple syrup. Not from Quebec, but Ontario! Or of the discovery we made the same year at the post office in the lovely town of Beynac-et-Cazenac, with its dramatic chateau virtually carved from the rocky cliff rising 500 feet above the Dordogne River: that there was a special connection when it came to the mail as well. On the notice indicating postage rates, for "*Amerique*" it listed "Canada," and after that simply "*Autre Pays*." What's more, the rate was lower for us than it was for Americans. For English and French Canadians alike.

One of my research projects the year we lived in Menton was to undertake a systematic, quantitative analysis of images of Canada in the international media — in newspapers of France, Britain, and the United States specifically. Given the dearth of interest in things Canadian in all three countries, it was not a particularly arduous task. Thumbing through the pages of *Le Monde*, I was struck, however, at the seriousness of its coverage of Canada whenever we did appear on French radar; it was significantly different in that respect from the British and American papers. And not just in its treatment of Quebec, but all of Canada. One thing that I noticed with particular fascination was the tendency of *Le Monde* from time to time to refer to Canadians as "*les cousins*." No such familial term was ever employed by the newspapers of Britain and the United States. I know *Le Monde* was using the term in the context of French Canada, but it made me feel good to see it, nevertheless. French Canada is my Canada, too. It made me feel connected.

What I like best about France, I think, is its Gallic flare, its dash — the same sensation you get in Quebec. France is all about presentation. Look at Paris: no city so entices you to walk virtually its entire breadth — from Place de la Bastille to the Bois de Boulogne — inviting you onward with its broad avenues, statuesque fountains, triumphal arches, gently curving river, historic, tightly packed islands — miniature antique Manhattans — its symmetrical squares, gardens, and even rows of manicured shade trees beside crushed-stone pathways. If I am not marvelling at Paris's magisterial sweep, it is only because I am admiring its women. They are no more beautiful than North Americans, perhaps less so. But they dress and carry themselves with such style. They know the impact accessories can have even on a sweater and pair of jeans. Hand a French woman a simple silk scarf and she'll show you ten different ways to tie it, each with a different effect.

I feel the same way about eating in France, even though the fare is often ordinary and uncreative — so much so that I'm usually impressed only when the bill is also impressive. "Everywhere it's couscous," a Parisian hotelier sniffed to us in 1986. "And they call it cuisine." Still, eating is one of the things I like best about France — not so much the food as the ambiance. Style again.

In 1999, Dot and I dined in Paris with friends at Chardenoux, an out-of-the-way restaurant in the eleventh *arrondissement*. It's a snug little neighbourhood bistro with etched-glass windows, tile floors, and a long zinc bar. I ordered pigeon — good, but not sensational — and all through the meal kept up some silly banter with the waiter about the origins of my pigeon, its care, and feeding. Toward the end of the meal, however, I suddenly noticed a bullet hole in the smoked glass window beside my seat. "Ah," I said to the waiter, pointing at it, *"vous avez tué le pigeon pour moi."*

*"Mais, non, monsieur,"* he said to me dead seriously and with dramatic flare. *"Ca, c'etait pendant la guerre!"*

Collaborator or resistance fighter, I don't know which. Shot during the occupation while he was eating where I was sitting now. Style!

The year we lived in Menton, we loved to lunch on the balconies of restaurants cut out of the rocky cliffs of fortress towns in the Alpes Maritimes. Ste Agnès, for instance: ten kilometres up the hairpin turns of a narrow road, perched on a peak at 2,000 feet. The calm Mediterranean is spread below you — no more than a few kilometres away as the gull flies — floating like a blue plastic raft in the afternoon haze. Or we'd go to Cap Martin, where Churchill and Le Corbusier vacationed, the waves crashing against the wall of our restaurant, fanning the patrons with gentle plumes of spray. Or to the Safari on the Cours Saleya in Nice. Yes, it most of all, its specialties chalked on a blackboard outside the door, its tables always full. We'd order *une omellette Niçoise, aubergines au four*, or *sardines grillées*. And, of course, a *pichet* of *rosé*. On a sunny January afternoon we'd choose an outside table against the restaurant wall, tilt our chairs back to soak up the reflected heat, and watch the street in front of us transformed from fruit-and-vegetable stands to flea market, from midday white to afternoon gold. Always, toward the end of the meal, we would fall into conversation with the French at a neighbouring table, and everyone would agree there was no better place to while away a few hours than under the cerulean skies and against the ochre walls of the Cours Saleya.

But it doesn't really matter where you are in France. Off the tourist track in a residential part of Paris. On a cobblestone street with half-timbered houses in Alsace. On a sun-soaked deck at the top of a lift in the Alps. In Aixe-en-Provence along the Cours Mirabeau. In Burgundy in a field of lavender with "*un bon cru.*" In Bordeaux at a table beside a fountain. Or on a harbour-front square in Brittany or Normandy — the Vieux Bassin at Honfleur, perhaps, where Monet, Renoir, Sisley, and Pissarro went to experiment with light, giving birth to Impressionism, and from whence Champlain set off to found the city of Quebec. Everywhere, if not great food, there is always history, ambiance, style.

As for the French themselves, I confess to a love-hate relationship. They can, of course, be sour and taciturn, and not just the waiters in Paris. Even on a balmy day in February, grumpy old ladies strolled Menton's seaside promenade, coat collars turned up, gloved hands pressing their black purses close against their bodies, tight lips curling as if they had just bitten into a Menton lemon. The old rhyme about the four main resort towns of the Riviera goes:

Menton's dowdy.
Monte's brass.
Nice is rowdy,
Cannes is class!

Certainly Menton had more than its share of aging dowagers—wealthy Parisians and other northerners escaping the worst of winter in France's Garden of Eden, spirits not raised by the experience. It struck us as appropriate that the skull of Grimaldi Man, the oldest known inhabitant of the Riviera, is exhibited in Menton's municipal museum, close to where his descendants parade today, glumly awaiting their own interments. Could one of them possibly be, we sometimes mused, the stooped lady wrapped in a black shawl who in 1971 disrupted our picnic on the grass near the Eiffel Tower, shooing us away with the pointed tip of her black umbrella? 

The French can be brusque and arrogantly dismissive as well. We joined the Menton Tennis Club where Dot, Tim, and I played two or three times a week on the soft, gritty *terre battue*. Early on, a Frenchman challenged me to a match. On red clay, which I had never played on before, he beat me badly in the first set. The second, however, was even until he complained of a sore back and had to retire. A friend asked how the match had gone. "*Je lui ai écrasé,*" he responded curtly, thinking I would not grasp the verb. "I crushed him."

Once, I asked the same Frenchman what he thought of Prince Ranier of Monaco.

"*Inutile,*" he replied. Nothing more. I suppose it was the same way he felt about me. Still, I have to admit there was flare to the way he put things.

The tennis-club experience was not unlike one we had dining recently at La Regalade, one of Paris's "*bistros de la crise,*" opened by renowned chefs at less costly suburban locations during the economic downturn of the 1990s. When Dot innocently asked for information about an unfamiliar menu item, the waitress, wife of the owner, puffed haughtily, "Oh, *you* wouldn't like that!" and refused to tell her more.

Sour, brusque, and dismissive, the French can also be annoyingly bureaucratic, wearing you down with paperwork and delays, hoping you'll just go away and bother someone else. At no time, perhaps, is this more evident than when securing *cartes de séjours* for an extended stay. On arrival in Menton, we visited at least two *commissariats de police* before we were directed to the correct office, the one that dealt with foreigners. There, in a cramped room stuffed with files — of the inadmissible, those whose cases were still under review? — Dot and I were subjected to a long interview. Photocopies were made of our passports, additional passport-sized photos were requested (which, fortunately, we already had), our lease was copied, as well as a letter of introduction from my university and a letter from our landlady confirming that we were, in fact, residing at her property. Then we were given forms to complete. "Mail the completed papers to my office together with the photographs. No, don't leave the photographs now. I want everything at the same time. Mail them in this-size envelope." The commissary held up a square envelope. "Not one of these." He held up a rectangular one. "Put only one postage stamp on each envelope. This one." Again, he showed us precisely what he wanted. "You may come back in a few days for your *cartes de séjours*. But not all at once. That is too much. You and your wife one day, the children another."

When Dot and I returned several days later, nothing seemed to have been done with the material we had mailed. We had to sit in his office while, on an old typewriter, he filled out on new forms all of the information we had sent him. Each time he finished a document, he lifted his typewriter off his desk and put it on the window sill so that he had the space he needed to spread out the form and affix his signature and various stamps. Five times over two days we went through this laborious process before securing our *cartes de séjours*. Why did we ever bother with them anyway? we wondered a few months later, after we felt at home in France. No one ever asked to see them.

Often, if you wait long enough, the red tape just withers and dies. For Tim in particular, trips to the local *lycée* grew less and less frequent that year, but his French increasingly fluent, including local slang. We'd get notes from the *lycée* asking for written explanations of his absences and requesting various forms he never bothered to fill out. "Just ignore it all," he shrugged. "That's what the French do." So we did that and nothing happened. We were getting the hang of France.

Having learned that lesson, I later advised one of my Windsor students, whose application for doctoral studies at the University of Nice was tangled in bureaucracy for months and then rejected, simply to show up at the university anyway and see what happened. He did that. And he was admitted.

To be fair, even the French make fun of their bureaucratic labyrinth, turning their acerbic tongues on themselves. In Paris, years ago, it took ages for the concierge of a seedy hotel—an old Madame Le Farge of a woman—to copy off our passports all of the information she needed. Noting my growing exasperation, she peered at me over her spectacles and said in halting English, " 'is not for me. For Napoleon!"

An English friend once explained to me how he felt about the patients in his practice. They were like family, he opined; but as with any relatives, they could be bloody annoying at times. That's the way it is adapting to the French and French culture—for this English Canadian anyway. *Les cousins*. Well, first cousins once removed, at least.

---

## YOU CALL IT PESTO, I CALL IT PISTOU

» It was in the south of France that we first discovered the classic pistou—that seductive union of crushed garlic, basil, and olive oil. For me it captures the essence of Mediterranean cuisine, the easy camaraderie with which ingredients combine and yet retain their pungent aromas and warm, sun-ripe, distinctive flavours.

Now whenever I see a shiny green bunch of basil bravely resisting the impersonal misty spray of a Canadian supermarket, I rush it home and, before it has a chance to bruise and blacken, chop it (leaves only, washed and patted dry), along with six or so good-sized cloves of garlic.

Then I blend in some olive oil by hand to form a paste and press it gently into a small plastic container (usually an old margarine tub), pour an eighth of an inch of olive oil over the top to preserve it, snap the cover on, and store it in the fridge. Rescued!

It is wonderful to have pistou on hand to enhance almost everything, but especially an emergency pasta. Just put a tablespoon each of pistou and olive oil per person in a pot and warm to take the rawness out of the garlic. But don't allow it to boil or the basil will be destroyed.

The Italian version of pistou — the ubiquitous pesto — includes freshly grated Parmesan cheese and chopped pine nuts with the basic mix of olive oil, garlic, and basil. Though richer, pesto is equally versatile.

Today, of course, there are all sorts of "pestos" on the market, from sun-dried tomato to black olive. However, I still like best the classic French pistou served over spaghettini or linguine. With a nod to the Italians, I always place bowls of pine nuts and freshly grated Parmesan or Romano cheese on the table, along with extra sprigs of fresh basil, salt, and freshly grated black pepper. I add pieces of leftover chicken if there's some at hand and pass my best olive oil for extra sprinkling or dipping of bread.

Pistou is similarly great, but very rich, added to cream, warmed, and poured over pasta.

In Italy and the south of France, they enjoy this congenial creation any way you make it and whatever you call it!

*Note: The basil and garlic must be chopped either by hand using a cleaver and a bread board or an electric food chopper. It does not work in a blender/processor.*

» SOMETIMES IT IS FEAR of foreign languages that keeps people from travelling abroad except on organized tours. Yet it's remarkable how few words you need to know in another tongue to get by. A phrasebook is useful, but I never have it handy when I need it. So at the outset of a visit, I try to memorize key words and sentences: "excuse me, where is the toilet?"; "could we have a table for five, please?"; the numbers from one to ten. After that, I fly by the seat of my pants. I'm better after a glass or two of wine.

Dot teases me that I have a habit of trotting out pet phrases to sound better in another language than I really am. Years ago, hitchhiking through France, I marvelled to every driver about the beautiful trees lining each side of the road—as they used to in much of rural North America before the devastation of Dutch Elm Disease. To this day, whenever we drive a nicely treed stretch of road in any country, one of us is bound to nudge the other and exclaim in fractured French, "*J'aime beaucoup les arbres le long de la rue!*" In Europe, of course, people are used to a mélange of tongues and are good about finding a way to understand you. That year in Menton, we went to dinner parties where French, Italian, and English were served up in equal portions. Few understood all three, so the conversation alternated among them and everyone felt at ease—at least some of the time.

Of all the languages I wish I understood, Italian is at the top of the list, its fleet cadence and alluring, rolling tone like a spring shower, dripping notes of laughter, love, and excitement. Perhaps I feel that way because, when I first visited Europe at eighteen, I fell in love with an Italian girl in Ascoli Piceno, a town in the Appenines north of Rome. It was a festival day and there was a colourful parade of flag-throwers all the town had come to see. Giuliana, her skin like coffee and cream, her shimmering hair the sleek coat of a young cat, was watching the parade in the company of an elderly aunt. I spoke no Italian and she no English, but shortly before our encounter I had met a Greek sailor with whom I could converse in French. By chance he spoke some Italian and was still hanging about. After the parade I strolled through the town beside Giuliana. Her step was light like a ballerina's, her voice sweet and lilting, and her eyes were glued to mine, beckoning like ripe olives. Her arm was linked tightly, too, alas, not to mine, but to her stooped, bull-legged aunt in black, opaque nylons, a black dress, and shawl! The Greek sailor accompanied us as we happily promenaded, acting as our interpreter. She would pose a question to him in Italian and after he'd grasped its meaning in Greek, he would put it to me in faltering French; I would do a quick translation in my head into English and then reply as best I could in French to what I thought was the original question in Italian. I don't think we always got it right, but everyone had fun and there was plenty of smiling and laughter. Best of all, when I got home from Italy, there was a letter waiting for me in Italian from Giuliana. Ah, Italian! Just reading it makes me feel the way Jamie Lee Curtis did in *A Fish Called Wanda*. My father handed me Giuliana's letter, a bemused expression on his face.

He was never good at languages; maybe that's why I'm slow at learning them myself. He never finished Grade 12 Latin in high school, yet he went on to complete his degree in medicine, for which Latin was supposed to be a prerequisite. Dad loved administrative bungles and he often boasted about his bogus medical degree until a bunch of his doctor friends arranged for him to receive a certificate awarding him Grade 12 Latin, post facto.

Maybe it was an unconscious embarrassment over this linguistic deficiency that led him often at the dinner table to quote famous passages from high-school Latin texts to prove he really wasn't that bad at it: "*Caesar erat in Britannia*," "*Arma virumque cano, Troiae qui primus ab oris, Italiam fato profugus Lavinaque venit.*" Most of all, however, he liked to repeat: "*Veni, vidi, vici.*"

WE CAME TO VENTIMIGLIA by car on my forty-seventh birthday. It was a Saturday—market day—and while we'd been there often before, it had never been like this. We spent close to an hour in the long tunnel through the coastal cliffs outside the town: New Year's traffic. We should have known then to turn back, but we didn't because Karen was with us only for the holidays, and we didn't want her to miss Ventimiglia on a market day. It's a big event for everyone from Nice to San Remo. Our plan was to tour the avenues of stalls and then have lunch in one of the many outdoor restaurants. But that day, just getting there and finding a place to park took all morning.

We saw the usual sites as we circled the market, kicking before us the broad, dry leaves of plane trees that drifted along the mottled dirt paths: the rows of simple wooden shops, their shutters lifted to display leather belts, shoes, gloves, and dresses; rolls of brilliantly coloured fabrics, framed pictures of coastal villages and fishing boats carved from woods of different hues; optimistically flimsy winter coats, mittens, and scarves; and an unvarying array of kitchen gadgets of dubious utility, the same ones they hawk at county fairs in North America. At the vegetable stalls, we bought the last of the season's green grapes and several fresh pastas. But the restaurants we viewed with increasing alarm. I am fond of studying menus before making a choice, and as always I was doing just that as we wandered the streets of Ventimiglia. At the best of times it's a senseless activity there; all the restaurants are of about the same calibre and they offer essentially the same basic fare, described on menus sheathed in plastic and resting inside large leather folders embossed with ornate crests. That day it was more useless than usual to examine the specials; every place was packed inside and out, spasmodic gusts lifting the skirts of checkered table cloths clamped to wooden tables and sending waiters scurrying after paper napkins sailing into unpaved, dusty streets. At most of the restaurants people were lined up waiting impatiently to get in, sweaters draped over their shoulders, sunglasses at the ready, tucked into their hair. I spread the word that we had better launch a serious hunt for somewhere to eat.

We moved out of the market area to other, less interesting streets on the edge of town where store owners, the collars of their brown and black leather jackets turned up, hopped from foot to foot outside their shops in slivers of weak winter sunlight. But still there was no place to eat. In a panic, we eventually found one empty table at a bar that offered no food. The table was, however, on the street catching the slanting rays of the sun, so Tim and I installed Dot and Karen there over drinks while we rushed off to buy some goodies at one of the food stalls.

Even these, we quickly discovered, had been ransacked by the voracious hordes who had invaded Ventimiglia that day. Most had already closed up shop or else the owners were wiping down their empty shelves, delighted at the prospect of getting to their favourite bars in time for the second half of the Saturday soccer match. But there was one near the end of a long row of shops that, behind a smudged glass window, still offered up a tiny, tired selection of doughy slices of pizza, *pissaladière*, cheese, and olives. We thought for a moment, looked at each other and then at the old lady behind the stand, sprouting black stubble on her chin, brown face wrinkled, dry river beds cutting across her temple and cheeks. She was, we realized, our only hope for any sort of lunch; we needed all she had left. But how to ask in Italian? "*Tout,*" we knew, was "everything" in French, and in Latin it was "*totum.*" Instinctively, I blurted out "*tutto!*"

"*Tutto?*" the lady repeated, raising a rubber-bumper arm to her head and wiping her chunky hand across her mouth in a gesture of surprise.

"*Si, tutto,*" I said confidently.

Momentarily, we wondered what would happen as the proprietor of the little stand stared at us incredulously. But then she proceeded to wrap up all her remaining wares in brown paper and present them to us in one bundle like soiled linen she happily wouldn't have to wash on Monday.

Triumphantly, we marched back to the bar with our precious cargo. We had conquered the language barrier!

*There are different ways of making pissaladière. Here's our favourite, but it's not recommended if you have a heavy date with Giuliana!*

## PISSALADIÈRE

SERVES 4

Any thick, prepared pizza crust (about 1 pound)
1 tbsp olive oil
2 large Spanish onions, thinly sliced (discard tough, outer layers)
2 cloves garlic, minced
1 tsp fines herbes
1 tsp thyme
8 flat anchovy fillets, drained and sliced into thin strips
12 pitted Greek olives (Kalamata), halved
1 tsp cured green peppercorns, drained
2 sprigs fresh rosemary, snipped
½ cup freshly grated Parmesan cheese

» Heat the oil over medium heat in a large non-stick frying pan. Add the onions, garlic, fines herbes, and thyme; toss to blend. Cover and cook over medium to medium-low heat for 20–30 minutes, stirring occasionally until onions are very tender but not brown. Uncover and continue to cook and stir until liquid evaporates (about 5–10 minutes).

» Spread the onion mixture in a thin layer over the pizza crust (the crust should be about twice as thick as the topping). Cover attractively with anchovy strips and olives. Sprinkle with Parmesan, snipped rosemary leaves, and peppercorns.

» Bake on a cookie sheet at 400 for about 20 minutes, until golden brown.

» I'M INTRIGUED BY THE markedly different preoccupations of travellers around the world. For some the principal goal is to see all the major sites listed in their guidebooks, however briefly, however leg-weary they are at the time. For others it is to shop to the limits of their luggage or customs allowance. Some focus on the hotels they stay in, others on the restaurants where they eat. Some look for uniquely new experiences, others for familiarity. Avid golfers, for instance, approach travel the same way they do life at home, with the number of different links they play (and their scores) determining the degree of their bliss. The classic tourist is, I suppose, most interested in enjoying the cultural attractions of another land; spending the bulk of the time visiting museums, art galleries, and churches; admiring architectural masterpieces; and watching theatrical, dance, and musical productions.

There is yet another travelling type: those whose orientation is essentially sociological, and Dot and I fall into this category. When we arrive in a new country, city, or town, our instinct is to try to experience it as if we were two of its citizens — to become, however briefly and incompletely, part of the community, so that when we leave we can say at least tentatively, "okay, so that's what it would be like to live there," be it Brasília, Berlin, or Batavia. We start by walking the core of a town or city, by tramping the countryside, getting a feel of the layout, the aesthetics, asking ourselves if this is somewhere we would be happy spending the rest of our lives. We visit residential areas, local parks, out-of-the-way restaurants, stores, and recreational facilities. And we try to fall into conversation with as many locals as we can. The cultural attributes of a community are, of course, an important component of its lifestyle, so, of course, we also visit art galleries, museums, and churches and attend artistic productions. But we do tend to focus on the outside first. And often, when we do set out to visit a particular cultural attraction, it takes us ages to get there. This I put down to Dot's particular preoccupation with the little human crises we encounter along the way. If we run into kids fighting over a ball or the rules of a game, we have to stop to see how their altercation plays out, and Dot will probably want to offer some words, or at least a gesture, of consolation to the losers. If we come across a man and a woman on a park bench in earnest conversation, we will sit nearby until we know the outcome. Will their exchange end in tears or a kiss? Are they newly acquainted, engaged, married, or having an affair? If someone is shouting from a balcony to friend or foe in the street in a language we do not understand, we will pause and at least guess at what the conversation is about. So our progress is deliberately slow as we absorb as much as we can of the human dynamic that surrounds us.

Although we still remain first and foremost social observers, over time we have given increasing attention to the cultural focus of the classical tourist. Greece and Italy are, I think, two countries where one is particularly likely to become absorbed in the arts. They are so woven into the fabric of these societies that it is virtually impossible to experience them in a meaningful way without embracing the talents of their painters, sculptors, singers, musicians, writers—their artists working in every medium. Even at eighteen, on my first visit to Italy, I was enthralled by the opera, *Aida* at the Baths of Caracalla, smitten, however, as much by the palpable tension in an audience that was so utterly absorbed in a production it knew so well as I was by the actual music and dramatic staging, especially of the *Grand March*. On the same trip, only months before his death, I saw Pope Pius XII at the summer palace of Castel Gandolfo. Like an apparition, the frail, pale pontiff with long, slender hands rose from his bed to the window to bless the excited crowd that had patiently waited for an hour or more in the courtyard below his chambers. I, too, a resolute agnostic, fell to my knees, awed by the reverential atmosphere and the historic legacy to which I was a witness. This human experience enriched immeasurably my visit the next day to St. Peter's Basilica and the Sistine Chapel. And so for me began the blending of society and the arts that is so inherently characteristic of Italy.

Looking back, however, I realize that it was really in 1986, during a trip to Florence, that Dot's and my tutelage in the artistic wealth of Italy really began. We met up there with my brother who had lived in Italy for several years, in Rome, Padua, and Verona. It was the Ides of March and we were expecting spring blossoms, sun bathing the Tuscan hills and dancing off the white-marble and red-tile roofs of that enchanting city. Instead it was cold and damp, with two inches of snow on the ground as he took us through the Bargello Museum. There, Dot fell in love with the work not of Michelangelo but Donatello— his statues of David, St. George, and St. John the Baptist. "That's okay," my brother reassured her. "Art is a personal thing." And we relaxed enough to pass up some of the rooms at the daunting Uffizi Gallery in order to spend more time in the Piazza Della Signoria, waiting for snatches of sunlight while we admired in their natural setting replicas of statues we had already seen inside, including those of Donatello.

In 1999, along with Karen and her husband, Craig, we rented an apartment in Venice on the Rio di Santa Caterina in the Cannaregio district, away from the swarms of tourists who flood the streets leading to St. Mark's Square as persistently as the autumn and winter storms. It had a little balcony, crowded with pink geraniums, where we could sit with a glass of wine and watch Venice at work. A colourful stream of barges and motorboats passed below us, delivering wine, meat, vegetables, and fruit; collecting garbage, transporting construction equipment, conveying the sick to hospital and the police to investigations. For everything that passed, there were two images: one sharp and real, the other oily, broken, blurred as it quivered along the narrow canal directly facing us, running off the Rio di Santa Caterina. The canal was flanked by a solid wall of grey, shuttered buildings, grills covering the windows of the bottom floors, apparently abandoned due to flooding. Inside our own apartment were two drawing rooms, each with a grand piano. My brother and his girlfriend were in Venice at the same time, staying at a nearby hotel, and they entertained us one evening in our apartment with a piano-and-recorder duet, the medieval music wafting out our casement windows to the cobbled street in true Italian fashion.

"There's a concert at the Scuola Grande di San Giovanni Evangelista," he tells us. "The Orchestra di Venezia and the Balletto Veneziano. They're playing Vivaldi among others. You should go."

So we do that. But first we go to the Gallerie dell'Accademia not far away. "I liked best the series titled *Miracles of the True Cross*," I tell my brother afterward. They offered such a rich, evocative record of the social history of Venice. "Especially Bellini's *Procession of the Holy Relic in Piazza San Marco* and his *Miracle of the Cross at Ponte San Lorenzo*. They were painted for the Scuola Grande di San Giovanni Evangelista, where we heard the concert, you know."

"I know."

"Now I can honestly say I don't like Tintoretto's work. And I'm not nuts about Titian either. But I do appreciate the tones in Veronese's canvases, especially his vibrant blues."

He smiles indulgently, recognizing I've learned a bit since 1986.

He sends us to the island of Torcello, a bucolic oasis on the fringe of the lagoon but the hub of Venice from the sixth to the twelfth century. There we admire the stunningly simple cathedral Santa Maria Assunta, "the noblest memorial of the lagoon," according to one writer, with its marble floors, wooden ceiling, and glowing mosaics of the Madonna and Child, Christ's Apotheosis, and the Last Judgment. He takes us on a barge trip along the Brenta Canal to see the villas that were once the summer residences of Venice's nobility. At Villa Pisani on the outskirts of Padua, eventually owned by Napoleon I, I am enthralled by the great ceiling in the ballroom, painted by Tiepolo and glorifying the Pisani family. Now I am anxious to see more of his work.

"We will, we will," my brother reassures me, for we are going on with him to visit his old haunts of Padua and Verona. In Padua our first destination is the Capella degli Scrovegni, the famous chapel built by Enrico Scrovegni to atone for the sins of his father, Reginaldo. So greedy a lender was he that he was denied a Christian burial and reviled for his miserliness in Dante's *Inferno*. The chapel is covered from top to bottom in frescoes painted by Giotto from 1303 to 1306 and from them emanates a blue glow that envelops the capella and soothes the flagging visitor. Dot is especially taken by the marble panels on the lower sections of the walls, depicting the vices on one side and the virtues on the other. I reserve my highest praise, however, for the brilliant circular frescoe painted by Giusto de Manabuoi, a follower of Giotto, on the ceiling of the baptistry we visit the next day.

For both of us, however, the highlight of Padua is the Basilica di Sant'Antonio, even though, artistically, we're told, it deserves only a quick look. What interests us is the stream of faithful filing past the tomb of St. Anthony, touching and kissing its polished stone. We marvel at the extraordinary offerings that surround it, testament to St. Anthony's powers: photographs of horrendous car crashes that devotees miraculously survived; pictures of missing children, some at last found; the discarded syringes of reformed drug addicts. And at the rear of the apse, in the Chapel of the Reliquaries, we shudder in disbelief as we gawk at what are supposed to be the saintly remains of the gentle, humble friar of Padua, contemporary of Francis of Assisi: parts of his larynx, tongue, lower jaw, and the beard that purportedly grew after his death!

After this encounter with the ghoulish side of Italian culture, we have had enough for the moment of art and history. We need to get a grip on reality. So we go outside where, at one end of the adjacent Piazza del Santo, excited Italians are holding a toy Formula One car race, complete with loud speakers, checkered flags, hairpin curves, screaming engines, and horrific crashes. More work for St. Anthony, inspired by the pastimes of the contemporary society that particularly engages us.

In beautiful Verona we sit in ancient, graceful piazzas — Bra, Erbe, and Signori — each a study in refinement like the medieval paintings we've admired in all the galleries. At Piazza dei Signori, we linger long enough to be moved by the young violinist in formal attire playing Monteverdi outside the Café Dante. Then we visit the Gothic funerary monuments of the Scaligere family, including that of Cangrande I, "The Big Dog" who grins down at us from the mount atop his tomb. To spot the quarters where my brother once lived, we climb the Torre dei Lamberti for a panoramic view of Verona. The fast-flowing Adige wraps snugly round the city centre, tucking it into a tight-fitting corset that shows off its shapely parts to best advantage.

We see Castelvecchio, fortress home of the Scaligeri and now the city museum of art. We cross the river to explore the sixteenth-century Giusti Gardens, visited by Cosimo de Medici, Goethe, and Mozart. An avenue of cypress trees leads you through a formal garden of flowers, hedges, and mythological statuary as you climb to a stalactite grotto and thence to the belvedere for another grand view of Verona — O sweet Juliet! And we walk to San Zeno Maggiore, the best preserved Romanesque church in northern Italy. It honours the fourth-century African bishop San Zeno, who converted all of Verona to Catholicism. Its ivory-coloured facade and bronze reliefs around the main portal are what we've particularly been brought to see, but what absorbs our attention most is the medieval graffiti defacing some of the frescoes inside. The next day, appropriately, we are passing the cathedral when we note that an important service is about to begin. We stop and watch respectfully as a red-and-purple-robed procession of cardinals and bishops enters for the ordination of a new black bishop, recently designated papal nuncio to Burkina Faso.

By now, however, Dot and I are sated with art and antiquities; we crave some social interaction. It's Sunday, so we go to Verona's massive football stadium to see the city play Bari, a first-division match. At the ticket window, I hand over precisely the number of lire necessary to purchase two seats in the upper tier. But the attendant gesticulates that I have not given her enough. She wants 10,000 lire more. I throw up my hands in incomprehension the way the Italians do. "*Per la signora*," she says, pointing at Dot. At last, I grasp the problem. The admission is purportedly higher for women than it is for men! We have the answer to our perpetual question. Despite its physical and cultural beauty, Verona is not somewhere we would choose to live forever.

Thanks to Italy, over time our approach to travel has subtly changed. But social observation is still our dominant preoccupation. Looking back to that trip to Florence in 1986, when my brother first took on our cultural education, I realize that what had the most lasting impression on us was not Florence and its treasure chest of artistic riches, but the train ride there from Genoa. We got into conversation with a young man from Naples and soon the subject turned to food and spaghetti sauces in particular. There was one sauce his mother made that he said surpassed all others — *all'amatriciana*. When we said that we didn't know of it, he started to scratch out the recipe for us on the back of an envelope. But part-way through he got stuck, excused himself, and went to another compartment for advice. Soon a third Italian joined their conversation, and then a fourth. And before long the whole car was a confusion of voices — a cacophony of anger, laughter, lecturing, and lilting poetry as everyone threw in an opinion on how to make spaghetti *all'amatriciana*. That is the Italy we love the most.

Italy is like homemade bread straight out of the oven — garlic bread: warm, aesthetic, robust, yet also refined; the more you have, the more you crave.

And garlic bread goes best with spaghetti, whether its *all'amatriciana* or any other sauce, and whoever the mama who makes it!

## OUR MAMA'S
## SPAGHETTI SAUCE
### SERVES 4 OR MORE

¼ cup vegetable oil
1 onion, chopped
½ pound lean ground chicken
1–2 hot Italian sausages, sliced
½ pound white mushrooms,
    sliced
1 portobello mushroom, sliced

» In a large frying pan, brown onions, chicken, sliced sausages, and mushrooms in the vegetable oil. Drain fat.

*Add*:
1 small can tomato paste
2 medium-sized cans
    peeled tomatoes
¾ cup chopped celery
¼ cup chopped parsley
6 cloves garlic, chopped
1 tbsp oregano
½–1 tsp hot red-pepper flakes
1 tbsp sugar

» Simmer uncovered on low heat until rich and thick (approx. 1 hour).

*Add*:
1 green bell pepper, chopped
15–20 Greek olives (Kalamata),
    pitted and halved
1½ tbsp capers, drained
1 tsp cured green peppercorns,
    drained

» Simmer for an additional 15 minutes. Serve over spaghetti or spaghettini pasta.

*For easy, disguised leftovers, mix extra sauce with cooked rice or leftover cooked pasta and fill topped, seeded, and hollowed green-pepper cases with the mixture. Top with breadcrumbs and grated Parmesan cheese. Bake in a little (1 cup) V8 juice for about 1 hour or until peppers are tender.*

## CONNECTING WITH PEOPLE

II

Thanks to the human heart by which we live,
Thanks to its tenderness, its joys and fears

*Ode on Intimations of Immortality,*
WILLIAM WORDSWORTH

» PHOTOGRAPHY AND TRAVEL go hand in hand, joined by our compulsion to record our passing, the need to jog our memories, and by the kindergarten urge in us all to show and tell. To show how good we are — how eclectic, how artistic, how professional. Who hasn't stood in front of a crumbling column while a phalanx of cameras clicked, recording the same pile of ruins, indistinguishable from hundreds of others stretched across continents of antiquity? Who hasn't been jostled out of the best angle for the perfect shot by another Leica — bumped by some lout with a bag full of lenses? Who hasn't been asked to photograph young honeymooners in a park — shown exactly where to stand so that all of their soldier-stiff bodies are visible? Who hasn't had to resist the urge to tell some neophyte positioned four-square in front of the Grand Canal that actually the picture would be much better if only he would move back a little and use a gondola for foreground? And who hasn't suffered through tortuous evenings of albums, slides, videos, and now jpegs while hosts and hostesses correct each other's faulty recollections and earnestly advise their guests, "Now this is essentially the same view looking the other way"?

Photography is rarely something about which people are sensible and objective. My own conceit is that I take great photographs of images reflected in water. I think I do, and I attribute it to learning from a master, the famous Montreal photographer Klaus Matthes.

As soon as we arrived in Bangkok, I was hurled into myriad activities at the embassy: multilateral talks regarding aid for a dam and irrigation project in Cambodia, designed to woo its egotistical and erratic leader, Prince Norodom Sihanouk, away from neutrality; meetings of the Economic Commission for Asia and the Far East; the negotiation of a loan for the purchase of workshop equipment for Thai secondary schools; interviews of potential Colombo Plan trainees to be sent to Canada for study and work experience; preparation of a new catalogue of films for distribution via the embassy; plans for visits by the National Defence College of Canada, the auditor-general, and the minister of industry, trade and commerce, the jovial Jean-Luc Pépin. On top of all this, uppermost in the ambassador's mind was the impending celebration of Canada Day. The preceding July 1, there had been scant coverage of Canada in the Thai press, and he was determined that this year it would be different. What he was most anxious that I do was to write scintillating copy about Canada that the media would be busting to use — insightful portraits of our regional and cultural diversity, paeans to the virtues of Canadian softwood lumber and Candu nuclear reactors.

I was flipping frantically from one file to another in the in-basket spilling over on the corner of my teak desk when the communicator handed me the latest telex from Ottawa. One more matter requiring urgent attention. It announced the impending visit to Thailand of Klaus Matthes. He was coming in connection with a new project he and his partner, Mia, had just launched. It was to be a photographic collection on the universal theme of love. Klaus was after images from around the world that explored the many facets of this theme, and he wanted our assistance in finding them for the Thai portion of the study. He was also collecting literary fragments from the pens of famous authors, poets, and statesmen. These Mia was going to edit for the text that would accompany the photos. He needed our help getting in touch with Thai writers worthy of inclusion in this illustrious collection.

By the time Klaus arrived I had a rudimentary knowledge of the Thai literary scene. Most of the authors of note were, it seemed, in one way or another related to the royal family. Venturing into this project meant mixing with privilege and aristocracy, something for which Klaus seemed ill-prepared when, one morning, Sutitra, our lovely receptionist, rang to say that he was in the lobby waiting to see me.

It was the late 1960s. Pierre Trudeau had recently become prime minister, and with him a new wave of sartorial informality had reached even as far as the stilted, cautious domain of Canadian civil-servanthood. In Ottawa, white shirts were out, replaced by all sorts of pastel shades, worn with flashy ties. So, too, were grey suits. Now they vied with beige, olive green, and sky blue. Elsewhere in Canada, of course, the revolution in fashion had gone much further. The prime minister had worn sandals into the House of Commons. Slacks and bulky knit sweaters were showing up in the workplace. And on the streets anything was okay. Cheap T-shirts with big, blurry photos of Che Guevara. Faded blue denim, bedecked with black and white "peace" buttons. Flowers in the hair. Bare buttocks and breasts.

Thailand, of course, has a reputation for sensuousness and promiscuity. Once, a senior official at the Ministry of Education presented me as a gift a strip of tickets like the ones you might buy for rides at a fairground. Only these were for a new drive-in brothel on Sukumvit Road, offering a 50-per-cent discount. Despite such overt sexuality, however, none of the new informality in dress in the West had reached polite society in Thailand. It remained highly conservative. Dark suits, white shirts, and sombre ties were de rigeur for men at the office, traditional sarongs or Western skirts and dresses for women. Shorts and halter tops were frowned upon. Public nudity was unthinkable. To the Thais these new fashions reflected the moral decadence of Western society. It was, I suppose, the sort of thing that had led the foreign minister one evening at a formal reception to lash out at Dot for no apparent reason: "We are not like North Americans," he shouted angrily.

"We don't fornicate in the streets." No wonder they took such a dim view of the endless parade of hippies who stumbled through Bangkok in those days on their way north, looking to "get high with a little help from [their] friends."

As I escorted Klaus to my office, I was already apprehensive. It was clear that he had embraced not the drugs but the attire of the new generation. I am not a natty dresser; my wife and kids—anyone who knows me—will attest to that. But even to my undiscerning eyes, Klaus looked, well, scruffy. Like the knife-and-scissors grinder who once a year passes down our street, ringing his melancholy bell. Or the shoe repairman with the shoe-box-sized store around the corner. People fading into memory. Pleasant, mild-mannered, but a little dishevelled. Klaus was unshaven, wore leather sandals, rumpled charcoal slacks, and a blue cotton shirt with several threads loose around the shoulders. His hair complemented his clothing. It wasn't entirely unkempt, just somewhat disorderly, scraggly—not attended to. He was like a dog who had been groomed at breakfast but then had a good romp in tall grass. Klaus had too much on his mind to worry about his appearance. He was dealing with heady issues.

"The world is in chaos. Nuclear annihilation is an ever-present danger." Sad eyes stared at me intently from a kindly, worn face that had clearly seen and experienced much tragedy. "It is critical that we foster closer, personal bonds among people around the world, ties of love and understanding. That is why this project is so important. It can make a difference to global peace and security."

"Peace and Security." That was our business—the ultimate objective of the foreign service, albeit one that in a hard-nosed realist era vied for time and resources with expanding trade and investment opportunities. But Klaus's business? I had to call on all my diplomatic training not to laugh in his face. A collection of photographs and quotations on the theme of love pertinent to our highest goal? What nonsense! What inflated egos people have! How incapable they are of seeing themselves and their preoccupations objectively. That was how I saw it then, an earnest young officer weighed down by heavy matters of state. I had the files in my in-basket prioritized. Admittedly, my first concern was to have Canada plastered all over the Thai press on July 1. Only then, I thought, would I enjoy the ambassador's trust and confidence and have the liberty to order the rest of my agenda as I saw fit. Second came multilateral issues that tended to have pertinence to peace and security: the multilateral aid project in Cambodia, for instance, whose objectives were as much political as developmental. Third were bilateral matters in Canada-Thai relations, essentially questions pertaining to aid, trade, investment, information, and cultural affairs. Fourth on the list was meeting the demands of other departments of the government and of official Canadian visitors to Thailand. Fifth and last was addressing the needs of private Canadian citizens.

"I'll do what I can to help you," I told Klaus. "But I'm terribly busy."

He looked at me startled, his dark eyebrows rising like volcanic mountains from a flat plain. "But what could be more urgent? We must get this work completed as quickly as possible. Humankind is at stake."

"I've arranged some meetings for you with Thai writers," I answered. "On the weekend my wife and I will take you for a drive into the countryside so you can get photographs. We'll go to Ayuthaya."

Now as I look back at my years in the foreign service — at what I actually accomplished in all my late-night hours on that plethora of multilateral and bilateral files — when I think of the ultimate collapse of that multilateral project in Cambodia and of the barbarism that was soon to erupt in the "killing fields," I see it all rather differently. Klaus, I think, was probably right. His photographic project about love was probably the file most deserving of my attention.

"You have a suit with you, I trust?" I asked.

"Why, no! I didn't bring one. In this heat—"

"You have to have a suit. This is a very conservative country, and the writers you will be meeting are cousins of the king."

"But I don't have one. They'll have to accept me as I am. I'm sure they'll understand when I tell them about the project."

"Klaus! You have to have a suit." I looked him over again, focusing on his size and build. Medium height, medium weight like me. "Dot and I would like you to come to dinner tonight if you're free. I'll fix you up with one of my suits."

Klaus agreed, but his mind was elsewhere. "I've brought along a portfolio of our work to show the authors I meet." He undid the large black folder resting against his chair and one by one handed me black-and-white enlargements from their recent publication, *Le Corps Secret*.

I sifted quickly through the prints with growing alarm. They were lovely. Artistic and evocative—provocative even. The use of light and shadow was remarkable, inspirational in tone and placement. This was clearly the work of a creative genius. But there was a problem: nudity. Every photograph was an erotic shot of a nude body.

"Klaus," I said as calmly as I could manage. "These are truly beautiful. There is no doubt about that. You have extraordinary talent. You know, and I know, that this is art: exquisite art, not pornography. But that is not how the Thais you are going to meet will see it."

Once again, volcanoes erupted across his temple, and I explained to him as best I could the nature of Thai culture. "Do you have any other photographs with you? Some that are less avant garde, perhaps?"

Klaus rummaged through his portfolio and at last produced some prints from *Bonjour Québec*. A tall-spired, clapboard village church across a field of virgin white snow. A fast-flowing river in pristine countryside, heralding the rebirth of spring.

"Perfect. These will be just fine."

So off Klaus went the next day to his interviews, clutching his downsized portfolio and neatly dressed in a dark-grey suit. I felt very proud of him, my little charge, as he left our teak-panelled offices on the seventh floor of the Thai Farmers Bank building. And proud of myself, too. Never before had someone ventured off in my clothes. And never has anyone since. Not even my son.

But it was the weekend we spent with Klaus that has had the most lasting impact on me. That is when we had the opportunity to observe him at work — to study his photographic technique and especially his interest in reflections. As we drove north over the flat central plains of Thailand, the rice bowl of the nation with its vast, prairie-like fields of cassava, sugar cane, pineapples, and especially rice, he would call on me to stop while he walked along the road, looking for the best angle for a particular shot: a young boy in the middle of a flooded paddy, his bare, brown back glistening in the sun, lovingly hugging the back of a buffalo like a kid in North America might dream of riding a palomino through a rocky canyon; a boney-legged fisherman dressed only in tattered khaki shorts casting a net in the canal beside the road. Tucked close to him, a young girl in a simple yellow cotton dress, staring in wonderment from beneath a fringe of black, glistening like new fishing line. In Ayuthaya, at Beung Phra Ram, the lake in the centre of the city, he catches two Buddhist monks with shaven heads — novices in saffron robes, small red umbrellas resting on their bare right shoulders — quietly contemplating the placid water. One is smoking a cigarette, subtracting from the merit he is earning from his three months in a local wat, extending perhaps his cycle of rebirths. Among the ruins of the ancient capital, Klaus finds a large stone Buddha in the sitting Bhumisparsa position, left hand resting in his lap, right hand touching the ground, summoning nature to witness his resolve to attain enlightenment. Under the Buddha's right arm the branch of a fig tree protrudes ridiculously, the wide shiny leaves appearing to tickle his stomach in a vain effort to distract him from his meditation. At the junction of the Lopburi and Pa Sak rivers, he shoots a weathered, wooden ferry with open sides and a low-slung roof leaving the Chan Kasem pier. It's moving slowly but assuredly with antiquarian dignity, a workhorse like the small tugs that towed log booms to mills across the Canadian North. A young couple in the stern have tossed a white garland into the ferry's wake the way they might a handmade float at the festival of Loi Krathong, ensuring that they will be lovers — if not in this life, then perhaps the next.

And everywhere Klaus captures reflections and the play of light: the boy and his buffalo on the lime-dappled surface of the rice paddy; the sweep of the fisherman's net over the canal before it strikes the water; the dark shadow of the branch across the gleaming body of the stoic Buddha, tortured by the blazing sun; the umbrellas of the monks, widening circles of blood staining the pond; a black patch on the river that mirrors the curvature of the ferry's transom and a smudge of white that is the reflection of the sinking garland. A master absorbed by his craft.

For the rest of our time in Thailand — indeed, ever since — I have tried to imitate Klaus's art. On the early-morning train to Khon Kaen, I try to catch the kaleidoscope of shapes and colours glancing off the jewelled peaks and corners of temples, or the melt-ing-orange-Popsicle hue cast by a line of monks. They are holding their begging bowls in front of them in both hands as they pad barefoot along a ridge between two watery fields of rice. It is at dawn that I like Thailand the best — those moments of coolness and promise, charged with an optimism that dissipates into lethargy and cynicism by midday under the enervating oppression of the sun. At night, at a *nang*, I want to capture the eerie light on a cloth screen created by shadow puppets carved from dried buf-falo hides. During Loi Krathong in Bangkok, I'm after the candle-light swimming on the surface of the lake in Lumphini Park, as

Karen and hundreds of Thais on a full-moon-lit night push from shore their banana-leaf boats shaped like lotuses. At Songkran, the New Year's celebration of the lunar year, mixing with the crowd near Wat Phra Kaew, what I try to record is the hard glint on a chunk of ice hurled recklessly at a youth expecting to be sprayed only with water.

And later, in Indonesia, what I shoot most of all is the reflection of volcanic mountains in the terraced, swollen paddies of Java where bright-green shoots of rice have just been planted. Every time I take out my camera, I think of Klaus Matthes and his brow wrinkled by the burden of trying to save humankind with a collection of photographs about love. My teacher.

I'm good, I think. Come for dinner. I'll show you my slides and albums. My reflections. And the view of the Chao Phraya from opposite banks of the river.

» IN BANGKOK, a mélange of cultures has led to a cuisine that often blends the traditions of several countries: Thailand, China, and Vietnam in particular. But there are other influences, too, including Western, and together they have made it one of the great gastronomic destinations of the globe. It is, however, not just a city of alluring culinary convergence; it is one stuffed full of things to see and do.

There are the floating markets, for instance, now so world renowned that, at Wat Sai in particular, tourists outnumber the flotilla of women in lampshade straw hats and indigo shirts selling fruits and vegetables from their wooden canoes. What our eldest daughter, Karen, always liked best was the early-morning taxi ride there by long-tail boat. She'd stare astounded at families washing their hair and brushing their teeth in the mud-puddle klongs running beside their thatched, stilted homes, sublimely indifferent to the palm branches, coconut shells, dead pigs, and half-drowned rodents drifting by.

One of Dot's favourite places was the Temple of the Emerald Buddha, with its glittering, gilded stupas, gleaming orange and green roof tiles, pillars studded in mosaics and, finally, its diminutive image of the Buddha, the talisman of the kingdom. It sits in a glass case atop a pedestal, wrapped in one of three royal robes, changed personally by the king at the beginning of the hot and rainy seasons, and also at the cool one that hovers briefly but never lands. Then there is Wat Pho, resting place of the largest reclining Buddha in Thailand. Covered in gold leaf and forty-six metres long, the image is of the Buddha passing into nirvana. The secular equivalent of this experience is also available here, for at the same time, Wat Pho is the home of a national school of massage. Wat Traimit (the Temple of the Golden Buddha) and Wat Arun (the Temple of Dawn) were Dot's and Karen's choices for making offerings of incense, candles, and lotus buds, and of mine for listening from a quiet corner to the soothing, transcendental hum of monks chanting *suttas*, or Buddhist discourses.

Of course, the Chao Phraya River itself is one of Bangkok's top attractions. It wriggles along the edge of the city like a giant python, the main artery connecting the city to the sea and its glorious past — when teak and water, not precast concrete and auto fumes, defined its character. And in Bangkok, it's the world-famous Oriental — not one of those ubiquitous Hilton hotels — that has the commanding location. It struts majestically beside the Chao Phraya with all the pomp and circumstance of the Chakri dynasty. There, in fan-backed wicker chairs in the airy author's lounge, we'd drift back in time and have high tea with Somerset Maugham before a cocktail with Conrad. Or on its decorous patio overlooking the river, we'd watch King Chulalongkorn (or was it actually Yul Brynner?) being borne along the river by royal barge.

Another highlight of Bangkok is the Grand Palace, a compound, in fact, of four extravagant halls. Little of it is actually open to the public, although it is possible to wander around the exterior. I was inside only once — in the Dusit Hall — for that arcane custom of presenting credentials, a fleeting moment in the company of royalty.

In loose-fitting tails I'd borrowed from the racks of the Americans, I sat in an anteroom with the rest of the embassy staff chatting with royal attendants, resplendent in white and gold uniforms with red sashes across their proud, ample chests. While we waited, we were served saccharine orange pop on silver trays and briefed about the royal portraits that covered the red-silk walls. Oh, that pop! I hadn't tasted anything like it since some pre-pubescent birthday party when we were served its likeness with chocolate cake. But I was to drink it graciously for three years in both Thailand and Indonesia—in government offices, at schools, hospitals, businesses, signing ceremonies, and anywhere else I went on official business. How sweet it had become since my childhood. How much more like chocolate cake. How unlike a scotch and soda!

Eventually we were instructed to line up in descending rank in front of high, ornately carved teak doors. Suddenly, at a command we never heard, they opened, revealing to us the long, lushly carpeted throne room. There at the end, sitting under several tiers of golden canopies, sat the diminutive figure of His Majesty King Bhumibol Adulyadej, Rama IX, of Thailand. He looked expressionless as in the over-bright colour photographs on desks and walls all over the country. A bespectacled, homely, and modest man. But someone who was, I knew, loved and revered by his subjects— "the lord of life," "the light of Thailand"—and now honoured everywhere as the longest-serving monarch in the world. No one ever spoke ill of him; all one ever heard was praise. Indeed, with such respect was he treated even by the press that, whenever his photograph appeared, it was always at or near the top of the page, never where, if the paper were folded, it would hide underneath.

As rehearsed, we bowed, moved forward ten paces, bowed again, advanced a further ten paces, and bowed once more. Our diplomatic "suite" was now directly in front of the throne, from which the king descended so that he was standing directly in front of the ambassador. The letter of recall of his predecessor and the letter appointing him as the new ambassador were then presented to His Majesty. In those days, they were still signed by the Queen, and they started, "My dear brother." Later, when I took part in a similar ceremony in Indonesia, I discovered that the letters to the president of the republic began differently, less intimately: "My dear cousin."

The presentation concluded, the ambassador and the king delivered brief speeches in their respective languages, meaning that the Massachusetts-born king understood perfectly the ambassador's hope for the continuation of the cordial relations that had for so long existed between our two countries, and the ambassador grasped nothing of the king's expression of reciprocal sentiments. As their remarks concluded, gloved attendants hurried from the wings with glasses of champagne. I quaffed mine quickly — to wash away the aftertaste of the soda — and that proved astute, for shortly the glasses were reclaimed. We were not to linger long in the presence of royalty. There were other ambassadors waiting.

Before we departed, however, the ambassador summoned us to come forward one by one to be introduced to the king. I remember I wanted to do more than simply bow and shake hands. I wanted to chat — to ask him, for instance, about the tragic death of his older brother in 1946, an event shrouded in mystery that led to his becoming king at the age of eighteen. I was primed on all the topics I knew were dear to him: music, painting, writing, sailing, and photography perhaps most of all. But it was not my place to initiate a conversation, and the king simply smiled wanly between tightly sealed lips.

I remember, too, that as I returned gingerly to my designated place in line, walking backward, lest I give offence, I mused how much more dashing I would have looked to him if, rather than borrowed tails, I had been decked out like the diplomats of some other countries in a braided uniform with a splash of medals, touched off by a ceremonial sword in a silver scabbard. Then perhaps he would have spoken. Alas, that was not and is not Canada's style.

Now, in unison, all of the ambassador's party bowed to King Bhumibol, walked backward ten paces, bowed again, did an abrupt about-face, and marched to the door. There we wheeled for a final salute, spun again, and exited the royal chamber. My cameo, unarmed appearance with the King of Siam was over.

In the past, in one of those arcane customs in which the world of diplomacy abounds, some countries had been required to perform more than three sets of bows on entry and departure. The number depended on states' relative power and status vis-à-vis Thailand, and was negotiable. Apparently, however, so much time was spent in tedious debates — in rows that risked diplomatic rupture, open conflict, who knows what? — that finally three sets of bows was established as the standard for all: for Americans and Canadians, tails-renters and sword-bearers alike!

*Here are two of Karen's recipes that combine national flavours in true Bangkok fashion:*

### CURRIED BEEF TRIANGLES

MAKES 15–20 TRIANGLES

*Filling*

2 tbsp canola oil

½ pound extra-lean
ground beef

½ small onion, minced

4 cloves garlic, minced

1 tsp minced fresh ginger

1½ tbsp curry powder

2 tsp cumin

1 tsp ground coriander
(or 1–2 tsp minced fresh
coriander root)

⅛ tsp freshly ground
black pepper

¼ cup water

1 tsp finely chopped hot red
chili pepper

½ tomato, finely chopped

¼ cup pine nuts, toasted (to
toast, stir-fry nuts in a dry
pan over low heat until
lightly browned)

½ cup chopped fresh coriander
leaves

*Pastry*

1 package frozen phyllo pastry

» Sauté beef in 1 tablespoon of oil, remove from frying pan with a slotted spoon and set aside. Drain fat from pan. Sauté onion in the rest of the canola oil until tender. Add garlic and spices, and stir-fry over medium-high heat for about 1 minute. Return meat to pan. Add the water, chili pepper, and tomato, and stir until well blended. Simmer to infuse uncovered for 5 minutes, stirring occasionally. Remove from heat, stir in pine nuts and coriander. Let cool.

» Follow instructions for working with phyllo pastry dough given inside package. The pastry strips can be cut shorter to make smaller finger-food-sized portions. Bake as directed. Triangles can be made ahead and frozen.

*Dipping Sauce*

1 tbsp olive oil
1 small onion, finely chopped
4 cloves garlic, finely chopped
3 tsp finely chopped ginger
2 tsp finely chopped hot red
 chili pepper.
⅓ cup orange marmalade
¼ cup water
2 tsp dark brown sugar
juice of 1 lime

» Sauté onion in oil until soft and golden. Add garlic, ginger, and chili pepper, and sauté briefly (1 minute). Add marmalade, water, sugar, and lime juice, and simmer gently, stirring frequently for about 2 minutes until mixture thickens slightly. Remove from heat and serve. Dipping sauce is also good with meatballs or spring rolls.

---

## ASIAN CABBAGE ROLLS
### SERVES 4

1 whole cabbage, steamed and
 set aside
¼ cup canola oil
1 small cooking onion,
 finely chopped
1 tsp curry powder
2 tbsp finely chopped garlic
½ hot chili pepper,
 finely chopped
1 tbsp Chinese salted soya
 beans, rinsed (available at
 Asian grocery stores)
5 reconstituted dried shitake
 mushrooms (reserve liquid)
2 tsp low-sodium soy sauce
½ cup pine nuts, toasted
2 large carrots, grated
¼ cup chopped fresh
 coriander leaves
2 cups cooked rice

*Sauce*
1 tbsp low-sodium soy sauce
2 tbsp water
1½ tsp sugar
½ tsp hot sauce
 (e.g. sambal ulek)
1 tsp lemon juice

» In a wok or large frying pan, briefly stir-fry the onions in the canola oil over medium heat (about 2 minutes). Add the curry powder and stir-fry just long enough to release the flavour from the curry powder (about 30 seconds). Push the mixture to the side of the pan. Add the chopped garlic and chili pepper, stir-fry briefly and move aside. Repeat this procedure with the beans and then the mushrooms, lastly stirring in two tablespoons of their reserved liquid and the soy sauce. Remove from heat. Mix in pine nuts, carrots, coriander, and rice.

» Carefully peel leaves from the steamed cabbage (it's easier to separate the cooked leaves than to remove them raw).

» Put about 2 tablespoons of the rice mixture on each leaf near the narrow end and roll toward the wider end, turning in the ends part way along.

» Place cabbage rolls in a shallow oven-proof dish. Mix sauce ingredients together and pour over rolls. Bake covered at 350 for 45 minutes or until tender.

» THERE ARE IN MY VIEW only two ways to experience the essence of Canada: by canoe or on cross-country skis. Those are the best means of traversing its wilderness lakes and forests with the grace of a heron and silence of the wolf — at one with nature. They can be exhausting modes of transport, it is true. Carrying a canoe over a steep, rock-strewn portage will knock the wind out of the fittest tripper and drive searing pins through stooping shoulders. So can a long, herringbone assent up a mountain with a pack on the back and a biting wind in the face. But struggle is a necessary prelude to life's greatest joys — to resting on a paddle dipped in the lily pads of an unnamed lake, or gliding down a powdery track that ends at the shore of a creaseless blanket of white, dozing in the weak, mauve light of a January afternoon.

When I think of canoes and skis, I think of hot, thick, home-made soups. I see us on logs by the dying embers of a fire, over-turned canoes at our backs, spooning the soup from metal cups. Or I see a Thermos being passed around a log cabin on a Gatineau trail, while snow-fringed socks dry by the wood stove.

Those are moments in the middle or at the end of a day worth far more than the effort of getting there. And those are soups that nourish both body and soul. Pea and lentil soups with chunks of spicy sausage; bean and tomato soups as thick as chili con carne; curry soups that restore feeling to the toes and fingertips of skiers and nurse, like Tiger Balm, the shoulder blades of voyageurs. My nostrils stir with excitement at the thought of them now. Their hearty breaths mingle with the wood smoke of our campfire or the acrid odour of a crisp, overdone sock.

When I think of paddling and skiing I also think of the Scandinavian adventurers who played such an important role in early North American homesteading and in bringing the wilderness to the reach of ordinary people. Especially I think of Jackrabbit Johannsen, that incredible Norwegian who laid out so many of the ski trails in the Laurentians early in the twentieth century, continued skiing and paddling almost to the end of his life, and then went home to Norway to die — at the age of 111!

To pay our respects to those Scandinavians so important in the history of our frontier, we knew that, at least once, we had to go skiing in their homeland, the birthplace of cross-country. So we did that one Christmas, choosing Norway. As a boy, I had read a book about its children, during the German occupation, lashing gold bars to their skis and carrying them cross country to railway depots. There, according to this tale, they buried the bars in the base of snowmen until they could be ferreted out of the country. Whenever we skied in the late 1940s, we pretended we were Norwegian kids, gliding past the unsuspecting German guards. Choosing Norway meant I could play that game again.

We rented a cabin near the town of Gol, on the Oslo-Bergen railway line. Cabin 602 near the base of Skogshorn Mountain. On the train to Gol, almost right away, we were befriended by a group of Norwegian university students in the next compartment. They were on their way home from Berlin for the holidays, and had already begun to celebrate over a large bottle of whisky that Dot and I were immediately invited to share. I had heard before that once Norwegians open a bottle, the party continues until they finish it, a not-impossible task in this case since the students were going to the end of the line. But in the typically generous manner of Norwegians, they were determined that we finish the whisky before we reached our destination despite the tight time constraints that imposed on us all. Naturally, conversation was lively — and all about skiing, especially the appropriate waxes for the conditions we were likely to encounter. There was much heated discussion among the students and a lot of contradictory advice was proffered. In fact, the instructions didn't end until they had helped us down with our luggage at the little wooden gingerbread station in Gol and the train was pulling away. One of the students, swinging wildly from a door of the train, shouted into the crackling night, "You know the best advice? Just forget everything we've said."

We laughed and waved until the train was out of sight, rather wishing we could have gone on with the students to Bergen and switched to coffee. I have always felt a special bond with Norwegians. Something to do, I guess, with surviving long, hard winters. But there is more to it than that. A similar pragmatism and skeptical point of view, a cautious attitude toward powerful neighbours, and the same self-deprecating sense of humour. Of course, there is also the shared appreciation of good whisky.

But not everything about Norway is similar. We spent the first night at a modest motel in the town of Gol. An anniversary reception was taking place when we arrived, and we were invited to help ourselves to the remainder of a *koldtbord*, a Norwegian smorgasbord laid out on a long table in the motel's adjacent dining room. Salmon, pickled herring, eel, meatballs, fish balls, roast pork, and dried reindeer. No chicken and penne at this buffet! There was another aspect of the motel that pleased me even more, a large ante-chamber with hooks and pegs when you entered your bedroom — for winter coats and boots, skis, skates, and poles. Now why do we never build our motels and hotels with such a wonderful practical touch, especially in the north?

The next morning, we did an enormous shop along the attractive main street of Gol, for we had to purchase all our supplies for our two-week stay. The alternative suggested to us was to ski down from our cabin the twenty-five kilometres to Gol and then climb back with our groceries, the way rural Norwegians traditionally did it. Getting to town, it was clear to us, would be all, not half the fun.

Laden with our luggage and groceries, we presented ourselves at the office of Arnie, whose cabin we were renting. Arnie was a cheerful, husky man in his late thirties. He'd studied at the University of Illinois on a ski scholarship, so his English was excellent. But there was an antiquarian ring to his slang. Arnie had his dad with him to help load our supplies into a pickup truck, and then we all headed up the hills as far as the road would take us. The climb was steep and mostly through forests that sloped into narrow gorges with half-frozen streams at their base. The evergreens—tall, straight, and snow-laced—were comfortably familiar, just like the trees you see from the train along the north shore of Lake Superior. They cast long, black shadows on the ice-cream scoops of snow, turning to golden butter in the afternoon light. Eventually, however, we rose above the dense woods, spilling into rolling fields of snow that extended upward to a blue horizon that was slowly darkening. Several stars were already visible when, two kilometres below cabin 602, we pulled to the side of the road. Arnie and his dad, maybe sixty, maybe seventy (it's hard to tell with Norwegians), loaded our supplies onto toboggans that they strapped around their waists; and with heavy packs on their backs as well, they sprinted off on their skis. We followed with the scraps that remained.

It was our first ski of the season, and I remember the pack I had been assigned shifting uncomfortably every time I poled, yet it was embarrassingly small compared to the ones Arnie and his father shouldered together with toboggans. I arrived at our *hytte*, built from rough-hewn logs, behind everyone else, out of breath and dripping as if I'd just mowed a lawn in an August heat wave. But Arnie and his dad hadn't even broken into a sweat. They looked as fresh and relaxed as when we'd set off. "Peachy keen, huh?" Arnie said as he handed me a glass of juice. His dad's blue eyes sparkled boyishly as he studied me, sagging in a chair; but I knew behind his cheerful grin he was thinking, *pathetic, just pathetic!* It was like being in the company of Jackrabbit himself, and I felt humiliated —as if I had let my country down.

Arnie led us around the simple, sparsely furnished cabin and explained how to light the gas heater in the living room/dining room. We couldn't use the fireplace because the damper in the chimney flue was broken, so the gas heater would be important in the event of a power failure. We did have electricity, but there was no phone, no radio, no TV, and our toilet was a plastic bucket in an unheated shed adjacent to the cabin. Arnie showed us the two bedrooms, one with flimsy insulation and a single bed for Karen, and another with four bunk beds for the rest of us. He explained that to get water, we had to lift the cover off an outdoor well, crack the surface ice with the metal tip of a ski pole, and then haul the water up by the bucketful. No problem, we said. We were used to living simply at our summer cottage.

We arranged to have a taxi meet us at the road two weeks hence, and then Arnie and his dad headed down the track we had cut from the road, Arnie shouting back, "Hope your holiday is peachy keen!" *Peachy keen.* It was like opening a closet stuffed with Pogo comics, penny loafers, and Madras shorts. But now that phrase is with us always.

We were alone. It was December 23, and though there were other holiday cabins in the vicinity of Skogshorn, none were in use. Everyone seemed to be in Oslo for Christmas. As best we knew, the nearest human beings were in the little town of Golshefellet, six or seven kilometres away. Except, that is, for the driver of the snowplough on the road below us. Every so often that night, we could see the blue light on the roof of his machine flashing dimly as he struggled valiantly to keep the road open, our lifeline to civilization.

It was still dark when we rose the next day, but soon dazzling sunlight was dancing off the pristine snow and we felt encouraged. Snapping our boots to our bindings, we set out to explore our surroundings and carry gold bars to Golshefellet. Wherever we went, there were no tracks so we had to cut our own. That made it slow going even in the open above the tree line where the daytime sun helped pack the snow and form an icy crust. But in the forested areas it was impossible to ski; the snow was so deep and powdery it buried the kids, and we had to retreat to the relative safety of the snow fields.

On the way home that first day, we cut our Christmas tree — the top of a spruce of indeterminate height, dusted in white and pushing triumphantly through the thick pile blanket gathering higher around it every week. It was dark by four so we skied by moonlight. And that became our daily pattern: a big breakfast, an all-day ski that lasted until after dark, and then a long evening recovering over bowls of hot soup in our little *hytte*. For the first three days we saw absolutely no one. Then we started coming across tracks in the snow we hadn't made. They were different from ours — much narrower and they never widened no matter how steep the downhill sections they traversed. It saved us time and energy to use these tracks made by Jackrabbit's descendants; but our skill was not always up to their demands, and we often spoiled their elegance, leaving messy, misshapen patches in the snow where we sped out of control or failed to negotiate a turn. We wondered what passing Norwegians would make of them — crash sites, perhaps, of the German Luftwaffe pursuing the disappearing gold.

It was the 27th, I think, before we encountered any other skiers. We exchanged greetings and chocolate and continued on our respective ways. So it was a lonely holiday in many respects, and the silence and long hours of darkness frightened the kids at first. They weren't used to tightly regimented rationing, either, though in truth they were spared the worst of it. Enviously recalling the generosity and abandon of the students on the train, Dot and I measured out our evening ounces of scotch with laboratory precision. But it was an unforgettably wonderful holiday, too, perched on the top of the world—a world of ermine, green crowns, and tiny log palaces trailing wisps of smoke into a clear blue sky. And there really was no need to be afraid; you could see the Germans approaching for miles. There was time to lash on your skis and glide to the cover of the forests below or make for Gol and the reassuring voice of Arnie.

To comfort the kids, we snuggled in the bunks at night and told stories until they fell asleep. To pass away the long evenings, we played cards, read aloud, wrote poems, and composed our own words for familiar Christmas carols:

O little town of Golshefellet
How far from us you lie!
We're 'bove the trees, snow's to our eaves
And n'er a soul goes by.

While in the black night glimmers
Our solitary light
The butts and jeers of Norway's skiers
Ring through this hytte tonight.

How silently, how violently
The blinding snow is driven
Against the door and through the floor
The powdery gift is given.

O sturdy Norse on frozen hills
We know you're full of smiles
Canadians quake, while Vikings take
A ski of forty miles!

However bad our verse, it was comforting to hear our own voices — loud, cheerful, and off key. It was comforting, too, to tuck into the thick soups that Dot cooked up from the supplies we had transported to the cabin. They were all, needless to say, peachy keen.

---

**CURRIED PEA SOUP**

SERVES 4

4 cups frozen green peas
2 tbsp olive oil
1 medium onion, chopped
1 medium apple, peeled,
    cored, and chopped
1 tbsp curry powder
    (medium-hot)
4 cups 2-per-cent milk
1 tbsp plain yogurt per person
mint sprigs

» Bring peas to a boil in ½ cup water. Cover and cook until very tender (about 10 minutes). Drain and set aside.

» Sauté onion and apple in olive oil in a soup pot until soft, stirring to prevent sticking (about 15 minutes). Add curry powder and stir-fry briefly (5 minutes) to release flavour. Stir in reserved peas. Add milk and stir until milk is hot but not boiling. Purée until smooth. Swirl in yogurt to decorate and top with mint.

*Serve hot in winter or cold in summer.*

## (VERY) HEARTY PEA SOUP

4 quarts of water

3 cups split green peas, rinsed
and picked over

1 pork hock about 1½ pounds

1 pound spareribs, cut into
manageable pieces

1 pound pork belly, whole or
in thick slices

1 pound smoked sausage
(or any precooked
spicy sausage)

½ celeriac (celery root), peeled
and chopped

½ cup coarsely chopped carrots

1 medium yam, peeled and cut
into bite-sized pieces

3 leeks or 1 onion,
coarsely chopped

2 tbsp chopped fresh parsley

½ cup chopped celery greens

2 medium potatoes, peeled and
cut into bite-sized pieces

salt and pepper to taste

2 large pots, one of which is
large enough to hold all
ingredients eventually;
a soup kettle is ideal

### Day One

» In the larger pot, soak the peas overnight in 2 quarts of cold water.

» In another pot, simmer the meat (except the sausage) with 2 quarts of water, covered for 3–4 hours, stirring occasionally to avoid sticking. Remove the meat, cool and store it and the broth it cooked in separately in the refrigerator overnight.

### Day Two

» Add the vegetables to the peas and the water in which the peas have soaked and simmer covered for 2 hours or until peas are tender.

» Skim the fat off the meat broth and discard. Add the broth to the vegetable pot. Cut the meat in small pieces, removing as much fat as possible and add the meat to the soup pot. Discard the fatty pork belly. Simmer the combined ingredients for another hour, adding the sausage, sliced, for the last 20 minutes, and stirring frequently to avoid sticking. The cover can be left off the pot if the soup appears too thin or left on if too thick. Water can also be added to adjust texture.

*This soup tastes even better after being stored for a day or two in the refrigerator and reheated with careful stirring.*

» BOOKING ACCOMMODATION abroad unseen can be a dicey thing. Does the glossy photograph in the brochure of a turquoise pool beside a stone terrace shaded by a plane tree cleverly hide the motorway across the wall that roars like Manhattan and spews fumes like Sudbury? Does "quaint" indicate a listed property of architectural and historic significance or simply an absence of central heating and running water? Does "secluded" mean pastoral and charming or merely that there is nothing in the area of any interest?

Based on a picture in a booklet, we once rented a thatched, Elizabethan cottage in Devon that oozed quaintness, charm, and seclusion. But the only bathroom turned out to be off the kitchen — an unpleasant descent from the bedroom in the middle of the night down a narrow, twisting staircase. Besides, you couldn't get past the stove to the loo if the oven door was open. All through a wet, windy winter, water seeped through the wattle walls and under the casement windows and front door, turning the sickly yellow carpet in our tiny living room into a dish rag that never wrung dry. The coal fireplace smoked relentlessly and the gas heater only warmed you if you sat directly in front of it, inhaling its noxious fumes. We have the friends we made to thank for a wonderful time, not the Tudors.

Menton was different. That year we used an agency in New York to find us an affordable villa in the south of France. It didn't much matter where, for our primary objectives were to immerse the kids in French, be warm, and well fed.

Descriptions and photographs flowed regularly to Windsor and we scrutinized them carefully. Villas in Arles, Orange, and Nîmes with sun-soaked patios and pools. Rough-stone cottages at the edge of silvery olive groves in the isolated hills of Provence. Apartments along the Côte d'Azur with balconies overlooking the Mediterranean, bowls of fruit and bottles of wine resting expectantly at tables under red, white, and blue umbrellas. Everything, however, was outside our price range. The agency was ready to give up on us, but then it got a new listing — a property that was available for the first time for out-of-season rental: La Colla, in the hills behind Menton on the Italian border.

There were, the agent told us, two homes on the property. The one for rent was a three-bedroom villa with a garden. It looked like a plain, rectangular box in the xeroxed photograph the agent hurriedly sent us. And it was beyond the crest of the initial slope out of Menton, looking inland toward Ste. Agnès and the Alpes Maritimes. No sea view. Not very appealing. The second was the landlady's residence, an old house at the end of an adjoining garden. She was eighty-six and rather fussy and cantankerous, we were told by a former summer resident of whom we made inquiries. A daughter who lived in Monte Carlo and visited daily was the person in charge of rental arrangements.

Over the phone with the agent, I was about to reject the property without even putting it up for discussion when she said, "Oh, by the way, the landlady is a princess."

"A princess?"

"Yes. The Princess Imaterinsky."

"No kidding?"

"How can you turn down a princess, a Russian princess?"

She was right. I was immediately intrigued. That night La Colla went before council for discussion. Like me, Dot was excited. What stories we would hear! What family history! What an entrée to the Côte d'Azur as it had been in the Belle Epoque —

in the era of the Empress Elizabeth of Austria and Edward VII who, as the Prince of Wales, was a regular at Cannes.

"Cool," Tim said. "We can walk down to the sea and swim every day. Do some windsurfing, water skiing, maybe a little hang-gliding. I like it."

Karen was at university and would be unable to accompany us, but it sounded to her like a good spot to chill out at vacation time. By then we would have met lots of people. Someone would have a yacht and maybe invite us sailing. "Whatever, the bread and wine will be great!"

Deb was a little more problematic. She has a sweet but somewhat imperious disposition and is, as Harry told Sally, "high maintenance." Every speck of fat must be dislodged from a chop or steak before she'll eat it. Even from hamburgers, flecks of white gristle are surgically removed. Half the raisins are extracted from her bowls of Raisin Bran because there are too many to tolerate. They are stored in the refrigerator and then used on plain bran flakes, which are deemed inedible without them. In bed she wears industrial-strength ear protectors so that her beauty sleep will not be disrupted by the odious noises of the masses. Thus in our household, for a long time, she had the title Lady Deborah and we joked about how she was destined some day to marry Prince Edward. But at sixteen she discovered Tad, and Edward was out of the running. Nevertheless, on her eighteenth birthday — several months before going to France — we elevated Deb to the status of princess anyway. Her Royal Highness the Princess Deborah. "How do you feel about La Colla?" I asked Deb. I knew she wasn't that enthusiastic about the sabbatical in any event, since it meant being away from Tad and doing her last year of high school by correspondence. "Would you mind sharing space with the Princess Imaterinsky?"

"She's Russian," Deb said dismissively. "There are lots of Russian princesses." I took that as her tacit concurrence.

But as it turned out, it wasn't a case of our simply saying we'd take the property. There was the matter of whether or not the princess would have us. A letter arrived from her daughter, Natasha. Mother, she wrote, was concerned that La Colla might be too isolated for the children. And the princess would not want them bringing gangs of young people on motorcycles up from the town — people to whom they had not been properly introduced. One had to be very careful nowadays about whom one invited to the villa what with all the crime and violence along the Côte d'Azur. Maybe the old bag *is* difficult and cranky, we thought, but by now we all wanted to meet her and form our own opinions.

I responded with appropriately conservative sketches of Deb and Tim: assurances that they didn't do drugs, were selective in their friendships, studious and resourceful enough to cope with La Colla's isolation. At last, through her secretary daughter, we had the princess's consent to the rental and off we set for Menton.

La Colla was far better than any of us had imagined from the xeroxed photograph the agency sent us and the description of its isolation from Natasha. Our villa was plain on the exterior, but its ochre walls covered in pink, climbing roses glowed like a campfire in the evening sun. At one end, off the living room, there was a large English-style garden with the snapdragons at their peak when we arrived in late August. Beyond the princess's house, there was a small orchard with a fig tree full of ripe fruit. From there the property sloped downward along the edge of a valley, and in the distance you could see the Mediterranean. Behind the two houses, the land rose steeply on a series of terraces covered in old olive trees. It was there that I set up a table and worked out of doors until mid-November and again from early April. At the top, just before you reached the narrow road that crossed over the hill and then plunged down to Menton, the property was flatter and tree-less and you could lie in the grass gazing inland at the arid, rocky Alpes Maritimes, snow-covered in January when we were still eating outside, backs to the sun-splashed walls of the villa. The inside was spacious and comfortable as well, and the large bedroom windows opened to the majesty of the Alps and the sounds of the valley below La Colla—a chorus of frogs creaking like old rocking chairs and roosters crowing at dawn. The villa was all that brochures advertise but fail to deliver. It was quaint with the feel of a bygone era and pastorally secluded, yet close enough to Menton that we could walk down the steep footpath from the hill above us to the town centre in half an hour—329 steps from the top to the base of the double staircase paved with black and white pebbles that leads to the Parvis St. Michel by the cathedral. A few more steps and we were at Place du Cap at the eastern end of Menton's pedestrian walk. It is the nicest little square in Menton, enclosed by cream-coloured, turquoise-shuttered buildings, a statue of the Virgin Mary cut into the facade of one. An old olive tree, surrounded by Impatiens, occupies the centre and several restaurants spread across the square like beckoning picnic hampers.

WHEN WE PASSED through the gates of La Colla for the first time and motored up the quarter-mile grassy track to the back door of our villa, the Princess Imaterinsky and Natasha were waiting to welcome us. Natasha—her regal head bound in a swirling silk scarf—was sitting at a card table completing the inventory for our premises and the princess—less elegantly yet smartly attired in a sweater, slacks, and faded-blue straw hat—was scolding her for working so long and hard. Both spoke impeccable English, and with British accents, we noted. Sent away to boarding schools, no doubt.

We started to unpack our car, including the groceries we had bought in Menton before the tortuous drive up the hairpin curves to La Colla. First out were the long baguettes from the *boulangerie*. From under her broad-brimmed hat, the frail princess studied them suspiciously with clear, thoughtful eyes that spoke of adventures completed and another journey serenely awaiting. Then she blocked my route to the kitchen. From a deep pocket in her trousers she pulled out a silver chain with a small pendant dangling from it and thrust it in front of the loaves.

"Ah! You see!" she said triumphantly. "The *pendule* isn't moving. You shouldn't eat that bread; it isn't good for you!"

"Oh, really?" I said politely, but thinking, *No way! One minute at La Colla and she's trashing the best thing about France!*

As each bag of groceries came out of the car, it received the same pendular inspection. Most of the vegetables passed muster, the chain and pendant swinging happily from side to side. But not the steak Dot had bought for our first dinner, nor the little tarts of strawberry and custard that were to be a special treat. For them the pendule drooped listlessly from the bony, wrinkled hand of the Princess Imaterinsky. There was no palsied shake to any of her body, I observed. Not if she didn't want it.

All this was done cheerfully and in high spirits, as if the princess didn't really expect — at least not right away — that we would be influenced by her judgment of our victuals. We weren't. Everything went into the kitchen, and she protested no further. Instead, the pendule was turned on us. Holding it directly in front of each head in turn, she focused intensely on the pendant. Each time, for a horrifying second the chain lay motionless, but then for all of us it started to move in a wide, confident arc from side to side. The princess put her pendule back in her pocket and, calling cheerfully to her chickens, all of which had names, scrambled lithely up to the next terrace to feed them. She liked us, it appeared. And we liked her.

So began our year at La Colla. Almost every day, while I worked at my card table on one of the terraces under an olive tree, Dot would drive down to Menton and wander through its maze of twisting alleys and tunnels, under beams that supported ancient, tilting houses, and up and down steep, winding staircases. A kasbah transported from across the Mediterranean. Then she would shop at the covered market and maybe at a nearby store buy salad spoons or a pepper grinder, made from local pink-and-cream-coloured olive wood, its veins and polish like Italian marble. At lunchtime, there would be a new treat for us to try as we lounged in the garden or in the dusty driveway below our house, enjoying the dancing shadows of a plane tree playing on a patched and crumbling wall. Three days a week — or really whenever they felt like it — Deb and Tim would go to the local *lycée* — more for the sake of their French and to make friends than for academic instruction. At other times they worked on their correspondence courses in their bedrooms. It was tough sledding for Deb, but Tim found his work a cinch. He'd lie on his bed with Radio Monaco on full blast doing his math and English and by noon he'd be done and head off to Menton or Nice to join up with his growing circle of friends — mostly students at the University of Nice who always seemed to be on strike and ready to party.

Invariably there was something going on at La Colla. Little vans were constantly coming up the long drive and we eagerly awaited their arrival, intrigued to see what would unfold. One would arrive with parcels of books for the princess. Another with workers to repair a gas heater or a well. Still others would come with feed and sawdust for the chickens. A delightful retired plumber who had worked for the princess for forty-five years stopped in periodically to do odd jobs, repairing stove pipes, ovens, and blocked drains. Little trucks brought wood, oil, propane, bottled *gaz*, and coal. All were required because the heating system and appliances were carefully divided among various energy sources lest there be a strike or shortage affecting one or more areas. Even our stove, we discovered with the aid of the plumber, had gas burners but an electric oven.

A Franco-Russian friend of the princess dropped in periodically to buy eggs. Others came by for nutritional or homeopathic advice. Alba, a plump Swiss woman from down the road, popped in regularly to do the princess's laundry. Joseph, the swarthy, soulful gardener, came several times a week. He was the victim of a swindle in which he had apparently lost property due to some obscure feature of French law, so he was always happy to put down his hoe and talk to us at length about his troubles. It was through him that we learned about Prince Imaterinsky, one of scores of royals, grand dukes, and archdukes who at one time or another made Menton home. The prince had died in the 1950s. What a fine gentleman he had been, Joseph told us. In his day all of the expansive grounds of La Colla had been kept immaculately by full-time staff. Now, however, the olive trees above the houses were no longer properly tended and bore little fruit, while the terraces below the driveway were wild and overgrown, the domain of rats and snakes. Joseph would shake his head and reluctantly pick up his hoe again, "*Trop de travail pour un homme trois jours de chaque semaine.*"

And then there was Maria who cleaned the princess's villa and did other odd jobs. Petite, irrepressibly cheerful in the manner of the French who have spent their lives straddling the Italian border, and patient about our linguistic deficiencies, she spoke slowly with an enchanting Italian accent. In particular, we loved to hear her say "*alors-e.*" She was from the village of Castellar, a short walk above us, and she took Dot there to see her house and meet her family. They became good friends, and Maria taught Dot two of our favourite dinners that year: *porc au moutarde* and rabbit royal, as we call it in memory of La Colla.

Much of our time seemed to pass in idle conversation with the princess, her daughter, and this steady flow of local visitors as we fell into the languid rhythm of southern France. The pace, the heat, the haze, the terraces, and the flowering vines all reminded us of Asia. There were even lizards on the screens and roosters and yapping dogs to wake us at ungodly hours. As in Asia, we found ourselves forgetful and slow to get things accomplished. Dot was always ready to go to Menton around noon just when the shops were closing — until 2:30 or 3:00 PM! So pervasive, indeed, was the afternoon siesta on the Côte d'Azur that we discovered that even the rifle-toting guard on the observation deck of the Nice airport left his post from noon until two. In the France of those days at least, even terrorists, it was presumed, did not work during the sacred midday break.

Once a week, the princess would have her old grey Rolls Royce pushed out of the garage and she, dressed casually as always, would drive alone down to Menton to shop. How she managed to negotiate the endless switchbacks in that oversized car I have no idea. I wished always that I could be in Menton to watch her arrival and see her parade through the market doing a pendular inspection. Everyone must have known her and anticipated her weekly arrival with great pleasure. The rest of the week she would be busy with her chickens, a dozen stray cats, and her orphaned dog, Putchka. Or she would read and pick fruit and vegetables, weighing them on an old balance she kept outside her kitchen and selling them to us at the going price in town.

Frequently the princess would arrive at our back door to inquire how we were getting on: if we had found a tennis club to join, if the children were bored, and if we were making friends. "I must introduce you to Vladimir the next time he's here for his eggs," she would say. Then she would remind us to be careful to lock the villa and car at night and tell us the latest news of Riviera thefts as reported in the *Nice Matin*. She got very worked up about crime, but whenever I read the *Nice Matin* the stories were on a par with those we read later when we lived in Devon under the terror of the "knicker nicker."

For Dot, the princess would have books on various spiritualists and new diets that simply had to be read. One day she told us that one of the cats was missing. But the next week we heard that everything was okay. The cat, she had learned through meditation, had been found and was living with good Buddhists near St. Agnès. There were frequent lectures, too, on the virtues of homeopathic medicine. Natasha shared the princess's obsessions. But both were gentle proselytizers. Everything was offered cheerfully and without pressure. Late one night, I twisted my ankle badly leaving a restaurant and was administered to the next day by Natasha. She gave me some little white pills that put me in an instant sweat but miraculously erased the pain. "Were you awfully drunk?" she asked casually in the soft, non-reproachful way she and the princess always addressed us.

Although the princess left La Colla only for her weekly shopping expedition, she received many visitors at her home in addition to the steady flow of workers and other locals. A daughter periodically drove down from Geneva to see her and another flew in from Hampshire. They, too, spoke flawless English. An artist friend in her nineties came to have lunch with the princess and their deceased husbands. They would climb to the open field at the top of the property with a wicker basket, spread out their picnic, and commune with Prince Imaterinsky and "dear old Toby." We noticed that the artist addressed the princess as "Margaret," and that seemed odd for a Russian. But we decided they were boarding-school chums and that that was the name her English friends had given her. Everyone else always referred to her simply as "the princess."

While many paid social calls at La Colla, they never tarried long, especially over their goodbyes in the driveway below our villa. With the chickens clucking and Putchka yapping for his meagre dinner of rice, nuts, and garlic, the princess would interrupt the conversation with a cheerful, "*Must* you stay? *Can't* you go?"

There was something very special about La Colla. It reminded me of Paul Scott's *Staying On*. It was as if the south of France, like India, had been a British colony. It was independent now and most of the expatriates had long since gone home; but still some of the old families had remained in their decaying villas, now often divided into separate flats available for rent. They were determined to go on as before as if nothing had changed. Indeed, it was more than that. It was as if the Russian Revolution, too, had never happened. Princess Imaterinsky was still a Russian princess.

Or was she?

One evening I heard her calling and banging two pans together at the chicken coup below the garage. She had fallen and couldn't get up. She was cheerful as always, but in great pain. We called for an ambulance and I went with her to the hospital. Before we arrived, she handed me her pendule for safekeeping. I was honoured.

The princess had broken her hip, and ten days later she died of pneumonia in hospital. I remember that night taking a long walk out the laneway to the gate and along the back road that led toward the Italian border, a rough, pot-holed route where sometimes I encountered North African refugees illegally entering France on foot. It was lightly overcast, but the glow of the moon penetrated the clouds, turning them silver, and the dark, bare branches of the scrub oaks were silhouetted like marionettes against the luminescent clouds. I could feel the princess watching me, smiling quietly, maybe even approvingly. I could see her half-reclined on the cement cistern below her house while her chickens pecked at their evening meal and she gazed across the valley to the mountains in quiet communion. The next day I returned the pendule to Natasha.

We never learned her whole story. She never said she was or wasn't Russian. But one day Natasha showed us the old black albums of family photographs, including ones of the princess as a little girl — in Shropshire, England. She'd left England in the 1920s, Natasha told us. A bit of a rebel, apparently. And she'd met Prince Imaterinsky in Menton. His family had fled there before the revolution.

So, in fact, we were misled by the booking agency. La Colla, too, was not quite as advertised. And during our stay, Deb was not the only English princess in residence. But no matter. Margaret will always be a Russian princess to us. Her Imperial Highness The Princess Imaterinsky.

I miss her and I think of her often. Especially when Dot makes rabbit royal or *porc au moutarde*, I visualize a pendule dangling from my wrist. I give a skyward wink, and then I let my aging hand shake. Because I like those recipes Maria passed on to us, those immutable memories of La Colla.

---

## RABBIT ROYAL

### SERVES 4

1 large rabbit, quartered

¼ cup all-purpose flour, seasoned with salt and pepper

3 tbsp olive oil

1 onion, thinly sliced

¾ bottle dry white wine, heated

3 sprigs fresh thyme or 1 tsp dried

2 sprigs fresh rosemary or ½ tsp dried

6 whole cloves garlic

2 bay leaves

15 black peppercorns

1½ tbsp Dijon-style mustard

salt and pepper to taste

» Dredge rabbit in seasoned flour. Sauté it in the oil in a non-strick frying pan over medium heat until evenly browned. Remove rabbit to a stew pot. Add a little more oil if necessary and briefly sauté onion in the same frying pan until just tender but not brown. Add the onion and remaining ingredients to the stew pot; stir well and cover. Cook over low heat until tender, stirring frequently to avoid sticking. Remove cover toward end of cooking to allow sauce to thicken. Rabbit can take from ½ to 2 hours to cook depending on its age.

## PORC AU MOUTARDE

SERVES 4

1 scant tbsp butter
4 cloves garlic, chopped
1 cup 1-per-cent plain yogurt
2 generous tbsp Dijon-style
   mustard
2 pork tenderloins, cut into
   approximately ¾ inch
   rounds
salt and pepper to taste

» In a small pot, bring butter and garlic to a simmer and remove from heat just as the garlic aroma rises. Stir in the yogurt and mustard. Return to very low heat and heat sauce through, stirring occasionally until mustard loses its raw edge (about 10 minutes). Do not boil as this sauce loses its punch if it cooks. You can stir 1 tablespoon of flour into the yogurt before adding it to the pot to prevent curdling. Naturally, the French use cream not yogurt and reduce it by simmering slowly until the cream thickens.

» In a non-stick skillet, over medium-high heat, sauté the pork in a little butter or margarine until just cooked (still pink in the centre). Arrange on plates. Pour warm sauce generously over meat. Any extra goes well with broccoli and/or baked potatoes.

» NOT MANY PEOPLE make bread sauce any longer. Pity. Because to me it's the simple cog in a roast turkey or chicken dinner that makes the whole thing spin. The glue that holds the meal together. The paste, really. That's what it looks like. The stuff they kept in a big jar in kindergarten that you brushed in gobs onto a sheet of red paper before sticking on a yellow cow.

That's what you do with bread sauce — dunk splotches of it on your dinner plate next to the white meat. Then you bunch onto your fork a chunk of turkey, sausage, some stuffing, cranberry or red pepper jelly, and a blob of this innocuous-looking paste. The result is sensational. The zest of the cloves in the bread sauce transforms the entire mouthful into an addictive blend of flavours. Dot always makes a generous supply when we have turkey or chicken because it's a must with leftovers — and in sandwiches. Perfect for keeping things from popping out.

We never had bread sauce when I was growing up. But Dot's family did. Her dad was from Somerset, and it's very much an English condiment. That's why bread sauce became an issue the Christmas we spent in Menton.

Shortly after our arrival at La Colla, we were befriended by an Englishman named William who had inherited a lovely old villa in the Garavan district of Menton. His principal preoccupations were tending to his spacious garden — one of the finest in the town — and entertaining. He was, in fact, the self-appointed receptionist for English-speakers moving to or passing through Menton, and he helped widen the wonderful circle of eccentric friends we made that year. When we first met, I made the mistake of asking William what he did for a living. "You mean work?" he asked horrified. "Oh, good gracious, I don't *work*!"

By December we had become good friends and were invited to his villa for Christmas. "No, no," we protested. "You have entertained us far more often that we have you; you must come to La Colla and have Christmas dinner with us." After several polite refusals, William finally consented.

It wasn't until shortly before Christmas that we realized that having William and his Jack Russell terrier, Polly, didn't really mean just one more at the table plus one on the floor. Inevitably, there were English-speaking people passing through Menton even at Christmas whom William was receiving and introducing to the expatriate society. They could not be abandoned at the holiday season and thus, since we were hosting Christmas dinner, they had to be accommodated at our rather small table: a retired British naval captain and his wife who resided in Menton part of the year, an English businessman and spouse, journalist daughter and husband.

Our numbers thus raised to twelve, including six people we had never met, dinner required some planning. Several days before, William and Polly came on their own for supper, and for what turned out to be protracted negotiations.

William always had roast potatoes with the Christmas turkey; our family mashed. Dot and William presented the respective merits of their choices, but consensus was impossible. So it was agreed we would have both. We always cook sausages in the pan with the turkey; William expected squash. Another stalemate. William insisted on Brussels sprouts, Dot on creamed onions. The discussion was long and tedious, and in the end both were inscribed on the menu. Dot had never cooked a Christmas dinner without green peas, William one that neglected green beans. Each bargained hard, but the result was the same. We would have both.

At the end of this portion of the negotiations, there were to be seven vegetables from which the guests could choose in addition to the turkey, sausages, and gravy. Thank God, I thought, that Tad wouldn't be there; he would have tried to crowd them all onto his plate at once together with double portions of white and dark meat!

Only with respect to bread sauce was there an immediate consensus. Neither Dot nor William had ever had a Christmas dinner without it. There *would* be bread sauce. That matter quickly agreed to, the question was *who* would prepare it?

The principal negotiators eyed each other suspiciously. *Is William really handy in the kitchen?* Dot wondered. *Maybe at Le Clos du Peyronnet the main dishes are catered.*

*Can such a critical component of Christmas be left in the hands of a colonial?* William worried. *It would be a pity to disappoint my visitors from England.*

There was only one solution. Each would prepare bread sauce. Somehow we would find a place for both recipes at the table.

On Christmas Eve, the others went to bed early — to be rested for the peeling, the basting, and the stirring. But Karen and I drove up to Gorbio to meet William at the church for the midnight carol service and *crèche*. It was, he said, a must. All the village turned out and there was always a long procession through the nave of costumed children and animals.

Gorbio is much like other quiet mountain villages, with narrow winding streets and grey shuttered homes — poorer looking than many, in fact. But we were fond of it, and had gone there several times for lunch on the balcony of a restaurant looking over the valley below the town where the countryside is gentler and less enclosed than in the arid reaches above. Indeed, from the sunny slopes below Gorbio come some of the earliest fruits and vegetables in the region and some of its best wines and olive oil. As well, more than a thousand species of wildflowers bloom in the valley, more, purportedly, than in all of Ireland. So it was with happy anticipation that Karen and I met up with William at Gorbio's simple little church for the midnight service.

But this year the *crèche* put William in a funk. There was no goat in the procession.

"There was a goose," I said encouragingly afterward. "I liked the goose."

"There's always a goat!" William said crossly.

"I thought the kids were cute."

"There has to be a goat." William wouldn't be consoled.

*How is Christmas going to be?* I worried. *What if William is still in a mood? What if he's disappointed in the vegetables after all the preparations? What if no one likes his bread sauce?*

The evening started elegantly enough. William's friends brought half a dozen bottles of Moët & Chandon champagne. There were cheery toasts to the Queen, President Mitterand, and absent friends and relations. The conversation flowed.

But in the kitchen there was chaos. With insufficient counter space for all the vegetable pots as they came off the stove, they had to be spread out on the floor while others were rushed onto the range. William had the roasting pan on the floor as well and was dumping flour into it to make the gravy once two burners became free. Dot was dancing around him trying to move from stove to counter and back. Polly was barking and begging for treats.

I carved the turkey onto plates at the sideboard in the dining room from which they were rushed to the kitchen floor for the vegetables and then back to the dining-room table. When I had finished, the carcass was removed to the kitchen and pots and pans piled on the sideboard for convenient seconds. Still, there was insufficient room and others had to be scattered round the dining-room floor where Polly could nose at the lids.

With so many guests wedged tightly around the table, there was little room for anything but cutlery, plates, glasses, and wine. But a small circle was reserved at each end, nevertheless. And there

Dot and William proudly displayed their respective china bowls of bread sauce.

The Keenleysides disdainfully ignored William's bowl and ladled out hearty spoonfuls from Dot's. William did the opposite. The English visitors politely partook of both and declared them of equal merit.

And so a sort of truce prevailed, as in the Franco-Canadian fisheries dispute. And there was a growing calm and quiet as the frantic cooking and serving ended and stomachs filled.

But *we* know. We know the real truth. Dot's was better. Sorry, William, you're a fine gentleman — the toast of the expatriate community — and everyone liked the squash. But when it comes to bread sauce, well, Dot's is the best. That's all there is to it.

---

### BREAD SAUCE

1½ cups milk

1 medium onion, peeled and quartered

10–15 cloves

7–10 slices plain white bread

⅛ tsp hot red-pepper flakes

» Fill a small pot with milk, onion, cloves, and red-pepper flakes. Simmer gently for ½ hour. Remove onions and cloves.

» Tear bread into bite-sized pieces (discarding crusts) and add to milk mixture, stirring constantly over medium heat until thick and creamy (like firm porridge). Use more or less bread as necessary. Serve warm with hot meal or cold with leftovers.

» RETURNING TO WINDSOR from France was tough for Tim. He was now entering his last year of high school and alone at home. Deb had left for Queen's University in Kingston that fall, and it was four years since, from the platform of the railway station, he had trumpeted Karen off to the University of Toronto. He was restless to get on with his life and to him Windsor seemed hopelessly provincial and restrictive after the Côte d'Azur. Over and over again that year, he complained about the poor choice of dry rosés in the liquor store.

We tried to boost his spirits by eating out a lot, playing tennis, and going to the movies. It helped, but still he grumbled. Compared to Nice the food in Windsor restaurants was indifferent; the hard courts were pedestrian after *la terre battue*, and he had preferred going to the films in Monte Carlo, where one night Boris Becker had sat behind us munching on a big box of popcorn. Besides, he complained, it wasn't the same as when all five of us used to pile into the car with a big picnic dinner and go to a drive-in. "You know that film, *Swedish Fly Girls*?" he asked me. "We never actually saw it, did we?"

"No," I laughed. "We couldn't have; it was restricted."

I only ever read the newspaper ads for *Swedish Fly Girls*, but it was clear it was a sleazy film about raunchy airline hostesses. Periodically, however, it came up in our conversation because, whenever Dot and I felt like seeing something trashy, I would joke, "How about *Swedish Fly Girls*?"

"We could see it now," I said encouragingly to Tim. "Maybe we could get it at a video shop."

"Naw," he sighed resignedly. "Wouldn't be the same as at a drive-in."

Tim waxing nostalgic. We knew, indeed, he had grown up.

In fact, I remember precisely the night he came of age. It had been the previous spring at a party at Vladimir's — the man who came to La Colla to get his free-range eggs from the princess. His last name, DesAubrys, didn't seem to fit his first, but that's because he was, in effect, a double emigré. His family was French, but they had fled to Russia at the time of the French Revolution. Then, with the Russian Revolution, they returned to France. Classic Côte D'Azur. It was through Vladimir and his charming and renown Dutch-Indonesian artist wife, Youdi, that we were introduced to *la dolce vita* of the Riviera. They had a villa at the top of the hill above La Colla, overlooking the old centre of Menton with the red-roofed campanile towering above the shuttered houses and the placid Mediterranean beyond. The DesAubryses were fond of throwing parties for an eclectic mix of painters, writers, musicians, dancers, intellectuals, and the idle rich. Sometimes they lasted until dawn. Usually at their dinner parties, card tables were set up in the living room and on the patio looking down on the harbour.

One night I was at a table with an Oxford don who gave us graphic details of his facelift and liposuction operations. "You should try it," he urged. "They'll do wonders for you." At the same dinner, Dot was flattered to be the only woman at a table with three men until, that is, two of them got locked in a quarrel about the third with whom, it turned out, they were both in love. She spent the rest of the evening mediating their dispute.

Occasionally Deb and Tim came to these parties with us. The night Tim came of age, we were all there at a big, boisterous function that spilled from their expansive living room onto the candle-lit patio with the lights of Menton glittering below like diamonds and ovals of amber trailing from the diaphanous gown of a grand duchess. I remember talking to an American painter friend of

Youdi in a black, wide-brimmed hat and cloak with a red silk scarf wrapped around his neck that tumbled to his waist. He had two carefully groomed dachshunds in tow—with dazzling rhinestone collars. We were discussing the overdevelopment of the Riviera, and everywhere else for that matter. "Plastic," he said. "Everything is plastic."

"When will it ever stop?" I asked mechanically, meaning it rhetorically.

"*God*, I don't know. Probably end in flames." He dragged out every word for dramatic effect. "I guess we'll all melt down into one big ball of plastic." He turned and fell into conversation with a young male friend who, it seemed, was taking classes in physiotherapy and needed subjects on whom to practice. "My *dear*," he exclaimed, "take my body and experiment!"

Beside me now was a beautiful young woman in a bright-red tunic and short blue skirt that showed off her shapely legs to well above her knees. She had blond hair that glimmered and curled seductively above her shoulders. It bounced lightly when she tilted her head, her blue eyes sparkling at me alone. *This is better*, I thought, and that feeling grew as conversation proved animated and easy. The upcoming Grand Prix at Monte Carlo, the Cannes film festival, the best restaurants at Antibes and Villefranche.

Until, that is, I asked her about her occupation.

"I'm an airline hostess. For Scandinavian."

"No kidding?" I tried to sound nonchalant, but I couldn't control the grin that quickly spread across my face and just stuck there. *A Swedish fly girl! I'm actually talking to a Swedish fly girl! And she's enjoying our conversation! This is fantastic!*

From that moment on, however, I couldn't concentrate on what she or I said. All I could think was, *A Swedish fly girl! Wait till I tell the others!*

At the Des Aubryses', there was always a large crowd, and before long conversations were interrupted as others joined a group, trays of canapés, olives, and stuffed mushrooms were passed, or people bumped into one another, apologized, and started to gab. So I became separated from my Swedish fly girl. I didn't see her for the rest of the evening, nor did I get a chance to tell the others about my encounter.

Not, at least, until we were driving home. Then, as soon as we were alone in the car, I burst out excitedly, "Guess what? You won't believe whom I was talking to?"

"Who, *who*?" Dot and Deb were eager to hear.

"A Swedish fly girl! Can you believe it?"

"Really?"

"Yeah," Tim interjected, glancing at me. "I met her, too. Got a date for tomorrow. We're playing tennis at the club, and doing lunch."

"But, but, she's too old for you!" I stammered.

"Yeah?" he smiled slyly.

Cut out by my son, living the Riviera high life.

He had come of age.

## GET-STUFFED MUSHROOMS

15 medium mushrooms
4 medium-sized tomatoes
6 tbsp breadcrumbs
1 tbsp pesto (see p. 72–73)
2 tbsp freshly grated Parmesan
    cheese
salt and pepper to taste

*Leftover tomato cases are good
stuffed with:*

• chopped mushroom stems
mixed with equal amounts of
breadcrumbs and grated
Parmesan and a tablespoon of
pesto. Tuck a small cube of feta
or mozzarella cheese into the
centre for variety;

• ratatouille topped with
grated Parmesan;

• various pasta sauce remnants
mixed with cooked pasta
or rice.

» Bake at 350 until tomato
skins are tender.

» Wash mushrooms and remove
stems (save for use in stuffed
tomatoes). Scoop out the soft
insides of the tomatoes into a
small bowl, being careful to
avoid piercing the tomato skins
(save these cases to stuff later).

» With a fork, mash together
the tomato pulp, breadcrumbs,
Parmesan cheese, and pesto
until the mixture is the
consistency of mashed
potatoes. Press stuffing into
mushrooms to fill each cavity.

» Bake in a shallow baking dish
at 350 or until tops are golden
and mushrooms tender
(approximately 30 minutes).
Let cool slightly and pass with
cocktail napkins.

» ON SABBATICAL once again from the University of Windsor, Dot and I chose to return to England for our sixth year living there. This time we rented a cottage near the East Devon coast. It was on a typical country road with high hedgerows that led to the village of Littleham. At a crossroads at the end of the lane was the thirteenth-century church where Lady Nelson, Lord Horatio's spurned wife, is buried. Across from it was our local, ironically named the Clinton Arms. If we walked several hundred yards along the road in the opposite direction, we reached a public footpath that took us over the rolling East Devon golf course to the coast at Beacon Hill, the highest point between Exmouth and Budleigh Salterton. We covered all of East Devon that year and large chunks of the coastal pathway system in Dorset and West Devon as well, crossing through fields of grazing cattle and sheep, over fences with little doors terriers can scamper through, and past mounds of earth where newborn lambs played "king of the castle."

The cottage we rented was thatched and attached — one of five in a row, reached by a dirt track that continued to a dairy farm. We had tried first to rent the one next to us but were told by the booking agency it was not available for the period we wanted. Curiously, however, it was empty most of the year. But every so often a couple would arrive late in the evening and leave at dawn. The first time they came, we were awakened in the middle of the night by piercing screams and anguished moans, as if someone, chained to the stone floor of a castle dungeon, were being flogged to death.

I was about to call the police when I suddenly realized what was happening. One of the owners was using the cottage as a rendezvous for an illicit affair. It was bad enough that he or she was cheating, but on top of that, the liaison was costing them a small fortune in lost rent. We had never heard such frantic lovebirds in France. We certainly didn't expect to spot them in the sylvan West Country. Our English friends were highly amused by our discovery, and dinner parties at our cottage tended to run late, with ears pressed to the porous walls in eager anticipation of nature's call.

For all the explosions in traffic, construction, and suburban sprawl that have scarred England over the decades we have known and loved it, there is a timelessness about the country that runs deeper than any other place and draws us back again and again. Part of the charm, of course, is England's civility. That, as everywhere, is under attack, to be sure; but still nowhere is there quite the same gentility, the same respect for tradition, the same whimsy. China cups for tea in parks. Champagne at Lord's and Henley. Strawberries and cream at Wimbledon. Punting on the Cam. Evensong in parish churches. Even crime—in rural England, at least—often has a gentle, unthreatening character. "Granny Warning" screamed a headline in the *Sunday Observer* that year, reporting on four old ladies who'd nicked 300 pounds' worth of toys from a store in Theydon Bois, Essex. "Police With Riot Shields Tackle Man Armed With Garden Fork" shouted another. According to the *Exmouth Journal*, the police apprehended two youths on the roof of the Magnolia Centre, ordered them down, and "gave them suitable advice about their future conduct." Regularly, the same newspaper asked readers if they could help the police with unsolved crimes, listing the details: "offender(s) entered insecure rear yard of premises" (that is all!); "offender(s) smashed a secluded rear window, climbed in and made an untidy search but took nothing"; "offender stole three rose shrubs from a front garden." Now, in England that *really* is a no, no!

The weather, too, is reported in a cheery, whimsical manner, change suggested when none really seems forecast, as in "Rain, with brighter, showery periods later in the day." During the bleak Devon winter, we were told one morning that "in the midlands and the north it will start off wet; however, there will be showers in the afternoon, clearing by evening, which will lead to mist and fog."

Nowhere, perhaps, is British whimsy more evident than in the personals columns of its newspapers. I like those in the *Guardian* best where, frequently, in true liberal fashion, advertisers unashamedly bare their contradictory natures, seeking affluent partners, but with the "usual *Guardian* values." My favourites from our year in Littleham:

1964 vintage, full bodied, dry, with a slightly nutty flavour, seeks female who can talk and listen — psychologists need not apply.

42, Reformed Scarlett, seeks a Rhett who gives a damn.

Attractive, successful professional woman, 34, seeks similar 30s for fun and friendship. Must like cats, music, films, countryside, good food/wine; no accountants/train spotters.

Like the French, the Brits, too, are fond of put-downs. Early on during my time at the School of Oriental and African Studies, I passed the distinguished British historian A.L. Basham in the hall. "Now, Keenleyside, how are you getting on?" he asked me kindly.

"Very well, sir, thank you," I responded and then added with typical, Canadian modesty. "But the more I learn about India, the more I realize how little I know."

"Yes," Basham retorted. "You Americans come here thinking you know everything. But I'm afraid we have to prick that bubble."

Usually, however, there is a softer, wryer tone to their cutting remarks. Reporting Basham's comment to a New Zealander friend who had previously studied at Oxford, he told me that, once, he and a Canadian friend had a heated academic argument with a don over tea. They were getting the better of him when he sipped noisily from his cup and resorted to the clinching argument, "You know what the trouble is with you, Jim, and, er, you, Philip." Another long pause while he slurped the remainder of his tea. "You're not English, are you?" Then he put his cup down and shuffled out of the room.

Of all the curious traits of the British, however, the ones that fascinate us the most are their reserve and concomitant repression of emotion even in the face of events that so clearly call for a reaction. When I was researching my doctoral dissertation, I remember reading the memoir of a distinguished English statesman of the 1930s whose name now escapes me. Discussing the courtship of his subsequent wife, he recalled how the first time they were out on a date, he lost control of his car going around a curve, careened off a cement island in the middle of the road, veered across the oncoming lane on two wheels, spun completely around and ended up on the right side of the road (i.e. the left), heading in the direction they had been travelling. Neither of them being at all injured and the car unharmed, the biographer wrote, they carried on without comment. Imagine a North American couple ever marrying with such an example to presage the probable openness of future communications. Yet the author never forgot the event, thought it important enough to include in his memoir, to acknowledge, in effect, his and his wife's emotional deficiency. How can it be, I often wonder, that the Brits can have such a rich literary and theatrical tradition— that they can write novels and perform plays that so exquisitely and with such subtle understanding explore the depths of the human psyche—and yet at the same time be in their own daily lives so reserved and in control of their feelings? How is it that words like "dearie" and "luv" can tumble so freely from their lips, yet rarely "I love you."

I don't know the answers, but thank God the Brits are the way they are. It's part of the fascination of going back and back.

THAT ANTIQUARIAN BRITISH reserve was vividly on display during our sabbatical in Devon. It was perhaps best illustrated in the tortuous course by which we came to know the fellow residents of our row of little thatched cottages, especially the gentleman at Number 5. My letters home charted our progress in establishing contact.

### September

I WORK AT A LITTLE yellow-top table that we bought at a used-furniture store in Exmouth because there was no desk in the cottage. I've installed it in a tiny bedroom on the second floor, where, after I run the electric heater for an hour, the temperature reaches fifty degrees, warm enough, the manual says, to turn on my computer and printer. So, huddled in my winter coat and blowing on my fingers to keep them limber, I go to work, contemplating the ironic fact that in England it is possible to publish and also perish. From my table, I have a good view into the back garden of the cottage at Number 3. Several times I have caught the eye of the woman who lives there with two boys, usually as she's hanging clothes on the line. But the moment we make contact, she looks away, pretending she didn't see me....

The boys at Number 3 have taken to filling water balloons and lofting them over the cottage roof so that they splatter by our rear door. Every time we make eye contact, however, they look away, just like their mother....

Our landlady phoned to tell us that Simon, the man in the end cottage, will be coming around to our place with a letter for her, using that as an excuse to introduce himself....

Have at last made contact with one of the boys next door. He was at home ill apparently and was recuperating by, once again, hurling water balloons over the roof. At one point during the day, we were out in our garden when their dog—a deerhound —leapt over the fence to our place, crushing Dot's freshly planted pansies. This forced the young lad, about ten, to come out of his cottage and call the beast back. Communication thus became inevitable. I asked him if he were sick and he said he hadn't felt well when he first got up. "Ah," I said, "that explains your poor aim with the water balloons." And with that he quickly retreated inside. Simon has still not popped by with the letter for our landlady. I guess he just can't find the appropriate moment.

Our brief conversation with the boy, Jason, has led to communication with the mother. I was out in the front garden the next day when she herself actually came out on the pretense of doing some work, but actually, I think, to speak to me. She told us that her son reported that we were "very nice," presumably because we didn't scold him over the balloons. She's actually quite pretty. Thirty-five-ish, blond, but looks scraggly and worn out, as if she's spent too many years tending open fires in a damp, dimly lit cottage and cutting peat moss on a Dartmoor bog.

Our landlady rang to say that Simon has now lost the letter....

### October

SUSAN, NEXT DOOR, has asked if we would be good enough to babysit their dog, Bracken, while she and the boys are away for two days....

The postman mistakenly left a letter for Simon at our cottage. In fact, it occurred to me that it might have been Simon himself who dropped it in our letterbox to force a meeting. In any event, I thought, *this is it; it's up to me now to take the initiative.* I walked over to the front of their cottage and rapped on the glass door, startling a young girl dressed in tights who was doing ballet exercises on the floor. I held up the letter and gestured, but she darted from the room. At that point, I discovered that their mail slot was actually on another door and slipped the letter through. As I was again passing in front of the glass door, I saw Simon standing in the living room. I shouted that I had left a letter for him in his box. "Oh, are you the gentleman at Number 2?" he asked. I affirmed that yes, indeed, that was the case, and he responded that he would be coming around to introduce himself. "I look forward to it," I answered.

Bracken (he responds better to "Biscuit!") has become our closest new friend in England. He's scruffy, looks half-starved, and has a nasty grimace that Susan assures us is really a grin. He flies over fences and bushes with the ease of a leopard and butts his way through the door of our cottage given the slightest opportunity. He's certain he didn't finish all the biscuits we fed him while we were babysitting and he's determined to get back to them. Since Susan is a teacher, he's left alone all day and howls when he hears us in the cottage. If we are in the garden, he leans far out of a second-storey bedroom window, braying for our attention. All in all, he's quite a nuisance, but we find ourselves, nevertheless, growing fond of him, the way we did with Putchka at La Colla. Still waiting for Simon to call, but no longer with bated breath....

November

SUSAN KNOCKED at the door with Jason in tow, wondering if we could help him solve a science problem. We couldn't; but,

nevertheless, she invited us to join them for the fireworks on
Guy Fawkes Day at Bicton Gardens. We were non-committal.
We learned that she is, in fact, divorced and that the older boy
has now gone to live with his father. The next day there was a
note under the door, indicating the time for the fireworks, etc.
It was signed "Love Susan." Love?

The gentleman at Number 5 has still not paid us his call.
However, I have now had exchanges with him on two occasions
when we have been standing in our respective gardens. Each
time I have observed that it has been rather chilly; he has
concurred and added that, nevertheless, the weather has been
holding up quite well, and I, in turn, have conceded that that
is, in fact, quite true....

There is no longer any doubt in our minds that Number 1 is
being used for an illicit affair, but we have not yet established
which spouse is the guilty party.

December

SUSAN APPARENTLY has a boyfriend. We saw her strolling along
the road near Budleigh Salterton with a bearded and bespectacled
bloke at least twenty years her senior. Bracken was on a leash,
strutting proudly in front of them. Still no sign of Simon....

More cries of pleasure from Number 1. Well, the English always
have loved bedroom farces....

Poor Bracken is now spending even more time on his own what
with Susan's new love. In the mornings, he has taken to emitting
a forlorn wail rather like a foghorn out in the Channel. It's clear
he's entirely dispirited....

## January

THE COUPLE IN Number 1 have been back only once since Christmas. Her shrieks of delight were much more subdued and so far as we could tell they only made love twice. It's my view that they were just too played out because of Christmas, but Mom thinks their relationship has moved to a different, more mature level....

Simon has not been visible for some time....

## February

JASON AND SUSAN seem to be spending more and more time at her boyfriend's home. They were, however, here for two nights last week, and we babysat Jason one of them. Turns out he's a Man U fan. When the coal fire got hot enough, he took off his pullover and was wearing their jersey underneath. His favourite player is Ryan Giggs. I told him that in Canada that was like "rooting for the Pittsburgh Penguins and having Mario Lemieux as your hero." He stared at me blankly. "But the jersey all the kids wear has a big ninety-nine on the back. Any idea who that is?" I asked. No response. "Any idea what sport I'm talking about?" None. "What's the Number One sport in Canada, do you know?" "Haven't a clue."

Quite unexpectedly I ran into Simon late one evening along the lane as he was bicycling back from the railway station. We chatted for almost five minutes, breaking all previous records by a wide margin. Our exchange focused on thatching, as he is having his roof done. Ours was apparently done twelve years ago, but it looks as if it already needs rethatching. When I remarked to Simon that I was surprised by this, since I understood thatch lasted for at least twenty years, he allowed that there are several varieties of straw so the durability varies. "Ah, that's interesting," said I, and he added that dampness in particular shortens the lifespan, since under such conditions bugs get into the straw. "You seem to know quite a bit about thatch," I remarked, and he affirmed that he was learning a good deal because he has been doing a lot of work on their cottage. As we parted, he repeated once again that he would be coming to pay a call, and I assured him that he would be most welcome to stop in and take some refreshment with us....

## March

AWAY TRAVELLING.

## April

WE RAN INTO SIMON, walking up the lane with his daughter, Jenny. We had a rather lengthy chat — maybe six or seven minutes, in fact. Most of it pertained to Jenny as we queried her about her school, her thoughts on living in the country in a lonely row of cottages, etc. She is about seven, very fair hair and skin as white as chalk. A little wisp of a thing. She wears plastic glasses with round, mauve frames and purple stems. Her favourite food is tomato-paste sandwiches. Not exactly the sort of kid you run into every day on the school playground in Windsor.

Susan, we learned, is getting married! And we're to be invited to the wedding!

## May

JUST AS IT'S NEARING time for us to go, we're starting to feel part of the neighbourhood. The tenant farmer at the end of our track has taken to waving at us when he passes by in his truck or tractor. It actually started a few weeks ago when we encountered him along one of the narrow lanes at the top of the cliffs. He was driving a tankful of bovine diarrhea, in effect, to spray on his fields and we squeezed against the shrubs at the side of the lane to enable him to pass. He thanked us for our effort with a wave and a smile and now acknowledges us whenever he passes the cottage.

Susan's wedding has been a real social breakthrough. It was held at the little church in Bicton Gardens and was rather bizarre. The bride and groom arrived fifteen minutes late, and then the pianist got the music wrong for one of the hymns and we had to start it again. Afterward, at the reception in the orangery, we sat at the same table with Simon and his wife whom we'd never met and also the couple from Number 4. They live in Coventry and are here only every second or third weekend. It was, in fact, the first time we had met them as well. So it was very much a neighbourhood table. Everyone was there, except, of course, for the mysterious twosome at Number 1.

### June

EVER SINCE THE WEDDING, Simon has been quite chatty when we happen to be out in our respective gardens at the same time. In fact, one evening he even brought to my attention a cuckoo that was singing in a large tree between our two cottages. We still, however, have never been properly introduced.

» THE FIRST BED AND BREAKFAST I ever stayed at was in Stratford. Stratford, Ontario. The year Christopher Plummer played the king in *Henry V*. Funny, I don't really remember the place. Not the way I do The Black Swan (a.k.a. The Dirty Duck) in Stratford-Upon-Avon. It's not that bed and breakfasts aren't good in North America. They are: warm and welcoming, and often creative and health-conscious about food. I guess it's just that they lack the delightful idiosyncrasies of English originals. For instance, in Canada and the United States I've never had the landlady stand outside the loo shouting instructions: "Give the chain three short pulls, luv, and then a long one. Release it gently. Gently, dear."

At home the plaster has never felt damp to the touch; the carpets have never been a nauseating mix of mauve, red, blue, and yellow, matched with green curtains and pink towels; and rarely has there been a payphone in the hallway with incomprehensible instructions for its use. Nor have I ever had trouble taking a bath or shower in B&BS from BC to Rhode Island. On the other hand, I'm not sure I've ever had an entirely successful wash in England. On the ominous, alien bathroom panel, I pull switches, set dials, and turn knobs. I try them again, altering the positions. I swing the dials wildly, left and right. I cry foul and beseech the gods. Usually after great effort, I get a trickle of boiling water or a great gush of cold, but never a strong, steady stream of warm. However did there come to be so many different, so inept manufacturers of bathroom equipment selling their wares in Britain? Including the French! Now there's a reason for marching. "Once more unto the breach, dear friends, once more. Follow your spirit; and upon this charge cry 'God for Harry, England, and Saint George!'"

The precise etiquette of British B&Bs also sets them apart from ours. I love the way, when you enter the breakfast room, everyone looks up brightly from their tables and *Times* and there's a cheery round of "Morning! Morning!" *This is a friendly one*, you think. But then the room falls as silent as the gym at exams. I gaze awkwardly at the plastic flowers on our table, ruminate on whether the hideous floral wallpaper has ever been changed in this Elizabethan era. I whisper to Dot who whispers back to speak up, but already I feel ears straining to catch our exchange.

The landlady hurries into the room and stands before our table. The tension eases. "Morning!"

"Morning!"

"Full English breakfast?"

"Please."

An awesome stillness, amplifying the clatter of china and whispered exchanges at nearby tables. Students seeking clarification of questions or extra examination booklets.

Conversation, it seems, should be hushed and reserved, and *never* between tables until breakfast is finished. Then voices may be elevated somewhat, and it is not impolite to engage in a little exchange with strangers nearby. The topics must, however, be kept light, verging on the inane: the prospects for a sunny day after yesterday's rain, one's destination, the time. "Nine already, is it? By Jove! We must be on our way."

The breakfast options vary little. 1) Full English breakfast (i.e. fried eggs, toast, bacon, sausage, mushroom, and tomato); 2) toast and jam; 3) scrambled eggs on toast; 4) beans on toast; and 5) kippers. I'm tempted to play Jack Nicholson: "I'll have the full English breakfast. But hold the fried eggs. Just bring me the bacon, sausage, mushroom, and tomato. She'll have the scrambled eggs on toast. But put the scrambled eggs on my plate. Okay? Oh, and give her some jam for her toast."

I never do. Maybe they'd oblige. I like it the way it is. Inflexible. Resolutely British.

But B&Bs are changing. Not very often now do you see the sepia photos on the mantelpiece of uniformed husbands and sons lost in battle. It's a long time since a cat has curled up on our bed. Is there some new health regulation? The toilet paper is opaque and soft. Sometimes, even, all the guests eat at the same table.

That happened to us for the first time in 1994 at a B&B in Dartmouth in West Devon. Before we retired for the night, I noticed that, in the parlour, one long table had been set for six. I had a fitful sleep, anticipating long, awkward silences at breakfast, the sort of dead air that Brits are accustomed to but that makes Dot and me panic and babble recklessly. We were determined not to let that happen this time—to be appropriately reticent, reserved. I was right to have worried, however, because breakfast conversation with the other two couples from the midlands proved a daunting challenge. It was filled with deathly lulls in which all we could hear was the steady tick of a grandfather clock in the hall. Until, that is, one of the women asked us where we were from. When we answered Canada, she said excitedly, "Oh, you should go to Scotland. Foreign people really seem to love it. You run into them all over the place." On and on she nattered. "Americans. Italians. Greeks. Even Germans. We felt like we were abroad, didn't we, Harry?"

"In North America," I responded coldly, "we are always abroad." My turn to bring on an uncomfortable silence. A welcome one.

We shared a breakfast table again more recently, but this time with happier consequences. We were at a charming farmhouse in Winchcombe in the Cotswolds—on the lane leading to Sudeley Castle, once the home of Katherine Parr, sixth wife of Henry VIII, and of the unfortunate Lady Jane Grey, reluctant monarch for nine days before her imprisonment and eventual beheading. Across the dark, polished oak from us was a couple from Vermont. We'd eyed each other the evening before and each had assumed the others to be English. We all had the right gear: walking boots, waterproof jackets, and backpacks. Even ordnance maps of the area stowed in plastic. Alone at the table, normal B&B etiquette was unnecessary, and we fell into a lively conversation that never mentioned being foreign or whether it was a day for sunhats or brollies.

"I saw you at the bus stop yesterday," Norton said to Dot. "You were sitting on a bench with two backpacks."

"Terry was looking for a B&B," Dot replied sheepishly.

Our cover was blown. It had been our intent to walk the Cotswold Way from Chipping Campden to Bath, carrying all our gear but staying in bed and breakfasts along the route instead of camping. But the first day on the footpaths we had changed our minds. Hiking the Cotswolds weighed down by forty pounds wasn't as much fun as our walks of old. So we moved from village to village by bus or train and did packless circular walks at each stop. Dot guarded our gear and wrote postcards at the bus and train stations while I hunted down nearby bed and breakfasts for the night. Then we slung the packs on our backs and arrived each evening with the look of veteran ramblers.

The Vermont couple laughed at our confession. And then they told us theirs. Norton had not been able to cope with the thought of celebrating his sixtieth birthday at home where he would be depressed rather than buoyed by the well-meaning, but irritating, solicitousness of friends and relations. So they had decided to spend it in England where, like us, they had spent happy days as students in the sixties. Their plan had, however, been more ambitious than ours — to reaffirm their youthfulness by walking large sections of both the Cotswold and England ways. But that scheme they, too, had quickly abandoned in favour of weightless, circular rambles.

That night was to be their seventh or eighth in Winchcombe. But they had to move out of the B&B, for we had booked their room before they had decided to stay on still longer. We, too, were slowing down the rate of our progress through the Cotswolds. After we left, however, they were returning once more to the warm comforters and cheery decor of the well-appointed Almsbury Farm Bed and Breakfast.

B&Bs are changing. It's probably just as well. So, too, are the bodies that sleep in them.

Operating the MIRA 7-2 Supreme Electric Shower

1. Turn lower knob to position 2.
2. Wait for warm water to reach handset (5–10 seconds).
3. If necessary adjust temperature by turning upper knob in direction indicated on unit.
4. For a cooler or less forceful shower, turn knob to position 1 and adjust as in 3, above.
5. For a cool shower turn lower knob to cool position and adjust shower force using temperature knob.
6. After showering, turn lower knob to stop position.

NOTE: In winter conditions, when the incoming water is cooler, flow rates will be lower.

*Here's something different for breakfast:*

### BARB'S CRANBERRY SCONES

2 ½ cups all-purpose flour
1 tbsp double-acting baking
    powder
½ tsp baking soda
¾ cup cold butter
1 cup coarsely chopped fresh
    cranberries (if desired,
    fresh blueberries,
    chopped pecans, or
    grated orange rind can
    be added for variety)
⅔ cup sugar
¾ cup buttermilk

*Scones are great with cantaloupe quarters, filled with fresh blueberries, raspberries, or strawberries and topped with a scoop of fruit yogurt and pecan halves.*

» Sift flour, baking powder, and baking soda into bowl. With a pastry cutter or two knives, cut in cold butter until butter is the size of very small peas. Add sugar and mix lightly.

» Quickly add cranberries and blend in by hand along with buttermilk poured in gradually. Stop adding buttermilk before dough feels gummy. Dough should not be overmixed and should feel like short pie crust. Lightly knead on floured board until mixture is cohesive.

» Pat half the dough into an 8-inch circle about half-inch thick and cut into 6–8 wedges or 2 ½ inch rounds. Place on ungreased cookie sheet. Repeat with other half of dough. Sprinkle tops with sugar if desired.

» Bake in 400-degree oven 15–20 minutes or until tops are golden.

Ay, now I am in Arden; the more fool I.
When I was at home I was in a better place;
but travellers must be content.

*As You Like It,*
WILLIAM SHAKESPEARE

» I DON'T KNOW WHAT came over Dot. I had never seen her like that before. Nor have I since. Normally she is highly attentive to my needs and moods: feeding me what I crave on demand, responding to my wolf cries of pain as if her own, sympathizing when I am down, and up when I am up and she is really down. But it wasn't like that when Prime Minister Trudeau visited Indonesia in 1971.

Beforehand, she was too excited to focus on the tedious details that concerned me. She was busy getting her hair done just right and choosing the dresses she would wear for President Suharto's dinner in the prime minister's honour, and the return one to be hosted by Trudeau at the presidential guest house. And during the visit she was too anxious to see him — maybe have a conversation — to give much thought to what I was up to.

When Trudeau and his entourage arrived at the drab, over-crowded Kemajoran International Airport, adept in those days at losing luggage, the prime minister was introduced to the embassy staff and their spouses. To get his attention, Dot had all the kids in tow. Karen and Deb were in white cotton dresses, studded with red maple leaves, and Tim in white shorts and shirt with the same shower of red. A bit much, maybe. But, in '71, post-centennial nationalism still lingered. The prime minister did stop to speak to them, his sharp blue eyes focusing intently. "When you're back in Ottawa," he said, "you'll have to come and see me."

Dot was ecstatic afterwards. "Can you believe it? He actually invited me to come and see him?"

"Uh, honey, I think he was referring to the kids."

Dot wasn't listening. "Those eyes. It's incredible. They're so penetrating."

Me, I saw only the back of his head, hurrying from meeting to meeting, handing him the text of a short address on development that I had drafted, passing him a memorandum of understanding to sign, and blotting his signature afterward. Actually, my opportunity to touch the hem of his garment came before the visit. An Indonesian artist who was an acquaintance of ours wanted to make a batik sports shirt for the prime minister, but he didn't have his measurements. Since I had a similar build, he decided to cut it to fit me. During the visit, the shirt was duly presented to the prime minister. Later, he wore it during a visit to the Soviet Union, appearing in it, in fact, on the cover of *Maclean's* magazine. My fleeting moment as a fashion model.

Throughout the visit, Dot looked for seemingly natural opportunities to come face to face with Trudeau. "You keep popping up from behind every potted palm," he joked at one point. I think it was the only remark he directed exclusively at her.

It was because Dot was so distracted that I couldn't get her to focus on the seating plan I had drafted for the dinner party Trudeau was to host. And that almost led to a major botch-up for which I would have been entirely to blame.

Much care and planning went into the guest list for the dinner, and, in the usual manner for such occasions, it was sent to the chief of protocol at the foreign ministry for vetting and for him to provide us with the order of precedence for the Indonesian invitees. It was then my responsibility to work out the precise seating plan in the dining room and oversee the preparation of the name cards that would go at everyone's place, as well as the board at the entrance to the dining room that guests would consult to find their way to their seats quickly. This was not a task that came easily; diplomatic niceties didn't interest me. Still, I laboured hard to get the thing right, even remembering to omit several of the embassy staff, including myself, from designated places. Some guests who had accepted their invitations would not, in the end, show up, we anticipated, and this way there would be "spares" to fill what otherwise would be awkward gaps at the tables.

I went over the seating plan again and again looking for possible errors. Then I reviewed it with the ambassador, Tom Delworth, but he was too preoccupied with more important details of the visit to give the seating plan much thought. So I showed it to Dot. Her focus, however, was not on the essentials. "So where will I be sitting? Can't you get me any closer to Trudeau?"

Despite Dot's distracted perusal, I was, nevertheless, confident the seating plan was okay and that every detail for the dinner had been attended to. About an hour before the guests were due to arrive, I, half-dressed, did a final inspection of the large, functional dining room where visiting dignitaries did their entertaining. My mind was elsewhere, mulling over the text of the speech Trudeau was to deliver at the end of the meal. But then I froze suddenly and gasped for breath. "Oh, no! What's this?" I shouted to one of the embassy staff. "We've got the two middle tables reversed." I could feel blood surging into my head, my heart racing. "That means all the tables are wrong! Oh my God!"

I grabbed at some place cards frantically. "Come on, we've got to change everything! Hurry!"

"What do you mean? We can't change them; there isn't time."

"We have to. And the plan at the door. Here! You do that while I move the place cards."

"I don't see it? What the hell is the matter?"

There was a head table across the top of the room, covered in white damask and decorated with ornate candelabra, and then there were four long ones running at right angles to the head table the full length of the hall. One was directly in line with President Suharto's silk-brocade chair and another with Trudeau's. I had inadvertently reversed their order of precedence. Not that anyone in the prime minister's entourage would likely have noticed, but the protocol-conscious diplomatic corps and other local dignitaries would have. Some guests would have been miffed, and my gaffe would have been a delicious source of local gossip — to Canada's discredit.

Stripped to the waist, except for the suspenders holding up the trousers of my tux, I tore around the room on the edge of control, snatching place cards from the settings, dropping others in their places, and shouting the changes to my helper at the entrance.

Into this maelstrom, twenty minutes before the guests, strode the ambassador on his own final inspection. When he saw me, Tom blanched and his jaw dropped.

I raised my hand. "It's all right. Everything is going to be fine. Just don't talk to me. I've got to concentrate. And I've got to hurry."

We had an excellent working relationship. Tom had confidence in me, perhaps mistakenly. So he left without saying anything. But, returning to the guests who had now assembled for drinks in an ante-chamber, he spoke to Dot, suggesting that it would be a good idea if she checked on me. "What's up?" Dot asked me cheerfully as she walked into the dining room, looking ravishing in a long, silk evening gown.

"A problem with the seating plan."

"Oh." She sounded nonchalant. "Is it going to be okay?"

"I hope so."

"Good. Well, come and have a drink when you're free. The hors d'oeuvres are yummy."

She went back to the party and her tracking of the most eligible bachelor in Canada.

It was a close thing, but just as the guests were about to file into the dining room, we finished the rearrangement. Everything was in order once again, but still I glanced around anxiously as people took their seats, fearful there might still be a hitch.

Sure enough, there was one guest who didn't show, so I plunked myself at his vacant spot — at one of the central tables. The wife of an Indonesian cabinet minister was beside me, and she eyed me suspiciously, concerned that I had seated myself there in error. I was sweating and panting from the rescue operation and my hands were still shaking so I gulped down the glass of water at my place. And then, when the first of the wines was served—a Gewurztraminer—foolishly I drained it in one go, and had to wait impatiently for a refill. My dinner companion looked at me aghast, convinced now that there had been a terrible mistake in the seating plan.

"And what is your position in the prime minister's party?" she asked, assuming I had come from Ottawa.

"I'm first secretary at the embassy," I shot back defiantly.

"Oh!" She put down her soup spoon, dabbed delicately at her lips with her serviette, and turned to talk to the person on her other side.

I couldn't have cared less. Everyone but me, I knew, was where they were supposed to be.

The meal was rather disappointing. Several weeks before we had had a dry run at the official residence with Tom and his wife, Pamela. We had eaten our way through the entire menu and every course had been a gastronomic delight. But something happens to every recipe when you go from 4 to 140. And the ambiance, too, was entirely different at the staid state dinner than at the Delworth's boisterous practice party where we had been at liberty to give close scrutiny to the wines and champagne in particular. However, I didn't much care about the food at the presidential guest house. For me, the dinner was really over the moment it started successfully. My neck had been saved. By the paper-thin slice of a place card.

I've just found two of them, in fact, in our souvenir box. They're three and a half inches long and an inch and a half high and decorated with gold-embossed Canadian coats of arms. One says "Mrs. T.A. Keenleyside." And the other, taken at the end of the evening from the head table, "The Prime Minister of Canada." Snatched from behind a potted palm by an infatuated guest.

» I LIKE A GOOD SALAD anytime, but summer seems the season for making them a meal in themselves. That's when I most enjoy the crunch of a Spanish onion joined with the sweet juice of a stake tomato, the tang of feta cheese, and the mellow rub of black olives. Salads are good when you're sailing, too. Quick and simple. But they ought to be a little daring. Like sailing, they call for experimentation: tossing in different fruits and nuts, trying different oils and vinegars.

We had a lot of salads, sailing one spring in Greece. It was a bold thing to do, yachting there; even Karen wasn't an accomplished sailor at the time. It happened by accident—the way things often do to those who put to sea. We had gone to the boat show at Earlscourt in London just for fun, and at one point we climbed aboard a Sadler 32, belonging to a company promoting sailing holidays in the Greek islands—nine or ten boats cruising together along with a lead boat in charge of the fleet. "So, are you coming with us?" a company representative asked as we climbed down from the boat. "Why not?" I answered perfunctorily, laughing. We didn't think any more about it as we toured the rest of the show.

"Why not?" Karen asked that night. "It would be fun!"

"Yeah, why not?" Deb and Tim joined in.

We reviewed the pros and cons. The latter dominated. We were far from expert sailors. The holiday was expensive. It would mean curtailing other plans. Still, we put it to a vote—a secret ballot, our practice when faced with indecision and the prospect of one or other of us being swayed by someone else's openly expressed opinion.

Each of us anticipated a no vote, the sensible outcome. But flotilla sailing carried the day—five votes to none! We were on; there could be no turning back once the democratic process had spoken.

WE FILLED OUT THE reservation forms buried in the bag of enticing literature we had picked up at the boat show, deciding on a two-week trip in June from Corfu on Jaguar 27s rather than Sadler 32s. Better for novices, we thought. But acceptance was not automatic even if space were available. You had to submit details of your sailing experience; so we did that—not the details, just the raw facts. At eleven, I had crewed one summer at the Royal Canadian Yacht Club, the junior club across the lagoon from the real thing. We raced in what were known as Brutal Beasts, flat-bottomed tubs that needed someone up the mast on dry land to capsize them. I was on the *Bismarck*. We were dead last all summer until one race when, by accident, we finished in the middle of the pack. We were twenty minutes late getting to the starting line and had the advantage of a sudden change in wind direction. In the months before our Greek adventure, Karen had been taking lessons at a club in Surrey—in an abandoned gravel pit. She and her friend managed not just to dump their dinghy, but to get it to turn turtle—to flip right over so that the mast stuck in mud at the bottom of the pit. At her outdoor club, she had also learned to read a compass and navigate at night—on land.

That was the extent of our talent. Still, we were accepted. Maybe it was the "Royal" in "RCYC," or the words "navigation certificate" that we had craftily included on our application. Maybe it was just a slow season.

AS THE DATE FOR our departure for Greece grew near, I got nervous. Winches in particular bothered me. I'd never sailed in anything but a dinghy so I'd never seen the things up close and in action. So Karen and I went to another boat show—at Brighton

—to study winches. Our friend Roly invited us sailing at Bosham and we jumped at the chance to enhance our skills. Roly, a seasoned sailor, had a passion for "night crossings" to France and twice he raced from the Canaries to the West Indies. But an hour into our gentle sail in and out among the yachts in Chichester Harbour, he cried out to his wife, "Trish! I don't know where I am. Trish, where are we?" Navigation in Greece would be a good deal more difficult than off the English coast, I knew. There were shoals and they weren't all properly marked the way they were on Roly's charts. We flew to Corfu on a charter from Gatwick and then were bussed to Guvia, a harbour outside the city where the Jaguar 27s were waiting. The others in the group were mostly Scots, the men strapping giants with red beards and blue-and-white striped jerseys, their wives and kids sporty in red and yellow anoraks. They had binoculars and compasses dangling from their necks—ready to answer their skippers' commands. We were clutching *My Family and Other Animals* and *Six Poets of Modern Greece.*

We all checked out the gear on our boats, Karen and I concentrating on the winches. Then we walked into Guvia to buy some stores—ingredients for our salads in particular. I remember little of the town; I was too wired to take much in, though later in the trip, after I calmed down, I was struck by the lushness of the Ionian islands, especially Corfu, with its gentle green hills and rich vegetation. It was not at all the way I had imagined Greece—nor as we were to come to know it years later on the southern mainland and in the Cyclades where barren mountains of grey-and-black rock thrust precipitously from the sea and emaciated pines cling to narrow ledges, desperate for nutrients and water. No wonder Odysseus felt so comfortable on refreshing Corfu, although that had a lot to do as well with the warm welcome he received from the Phaeacians—warmer than tourists to any of the over-taxed islands of Greece encounter today.

WE WENT TO BED EARLY that first night, but despite the soothing rock of the boat, tied safely to the pier, we slept very little, anxiety mixed with excitement a reliable prescription for insomnia.

There was a skippers' meeting at nine in the morning to which Karen accompanied me for support. I noticed that most of the other boats were represented by more than one person, too. There also didn't seem to be as many rough, red beards and crisp, new anoraks covered in nautical equipment as I'd thought I'd seen the night before. Everyone was very quiet, none of the previous night's jocular talk from boat to boat. I could feel the tension as the leader of the tour explained our destination for the day — Stefanos toward the northern tip of Corfu — and the course we would be sailing. "The reading is 355 to the buoy you see marked on your charts, and then you will bear northeast to 30." The first mates, including Karen, all made careful notes on their pads.

Then we set off, with the lead boat away from the pier before the rest of us. We followed its tack precisely, and the other boats did the same. When it went about, we went about. If it set another sail, we set another sail. Karen put away her notebook and binoculars. We relaxed. Flotilla sailing was a cinch.

FOR MORE THAN A WEEK we lulled about the blue Mediterranean in light winds, calling at the picturesque ports of Stefanos and Kassiopi on Corfu; Lakka, Gaios, and Mongonissi on Paxos; and Mourtos and Parga on mainland Greece. This was not the time nor really the place for museums and archaeological sites, though Dot and I have done that since. Ancient Thira and Akrotiri — the lost city of Atlantis, perhaps — frozen in time 3,600 years ago by a massive volcanic eruption. Athens, escaping the in-your-face confusion of its dirty, crumbling streets and construction-zone squares to sit contemplatively in the National Archaeological Museum, the Roman Agora, and outside the scaffold-covered Parthenon. Tranquil Mycenae, legendary home of King Agamemnon, with its giant tombs and gold-filigreed treasures. Pine-shaded Epidaurus, where from the highest row in the almost perfectly preserved theatre you can hear the slightest stage whisper. Olympia and Delphi, the latter hanging on the slopes of Mount Parnassus like a goddess about to take wing. In their ancient stadiums, I couldn't resist the urge to drop into imaginary blocks and race the length of the track. "I'm the emperor Nero," I cried, finishing the course at Olympia. "I won!" No one dared to beat him, and none of the gawking tourists were exhibitionist enough to take me on.

In the Ionian islands with the kids it was a time for beaches, snorkelling, and windsurfing, and for sitting in tavernas overlooking harbours packed with fishing boats, cruisers, yachts, and our intrepid flotilla neatly tied in a row. There is little that surpasses the ambiance of such island settings at the end of long days on the water: a cobbled square of rustic, stone buildings, one side open to the zephyr blowing off the sea; shade trees with gnarled trunks and broad, drooping branches; white-washed walls spray painted in red geraniums; and tavernas with metal chairs, plastic seats, square, wooden tables, and broad, colourful awnings, pulled taught like our sails close hauled. A salt-cured sailor in a black cap sits on a bollard twirling his worry beads. Two Greek Orthodox priests with long beards, robes, and tall hats — four-star chefs in mourning — stroll by with practised dignity, as if leading a procession through a gilded church. An accordion player moves among the tables, wheezing a romantic tune.

*What's that I hear? Never on a Sunday. Again!*

Here in the islands, yes, I can imagine it. Melina Mercouri dancing the night away. But not in dirty, seedy Piraeus. Not any longer. Not with the sour Athenians, who have outlived their reputation for joviality, wearied by too many aliens, too much tragic history.

Taverna food, unfortunately, rarely matches the harbourfront settings. I like the way in Greece you can order a number of small dishes — *mezedes*, hot and cold appetizers. Brought to the table with a jug of cold wine, they look appetizing enough. But, in fact, they — and the main dishes that follow — are normally bland and vary little from place to place. Still, there is one item that is hard to beat: *loukoumades*. They have the shape and texture of doughnut centres and come drenched in honey and dusted with cinnamon. They pop in the mouth like juicy fruit gum, emitting a sweet, intoxicating syrup that arouses every drowsy muscle.

Here is the real, gritty Greece of today. You stand in Omonia Square in Athens drinking an espresso and munching on the *loukoumades* you've bought in a nearby shop. You don't do anything else. Just stand and stare. At the men reading the newspapers clipped to wires at the oudoor stands. At the druggies, sitting with their heads in their hands on the spit-splattered pavement, backs to the walls of decaying buildings. At the driver of a suddenly empty tramcar, using a long pole to once again attach his cable to the intricate net of wires running along Odos Panepistimiou. At the bus and truck drivers whose vehicles have reached an impasse. They are at right angles at an intersection where an illegally parked car and two long lines of traffic behind them have blocked any possibility of a solution. The drivers scream at each other long past the North American point of fisticuffs, then retreat to their respective cabs, light cigarettes, and wait. Wait for something to happen. Like the gawking crowd in Omonia Square. That is the real Greece.

Day by day our confidence in our handling of our Jaguar 27 increased. For practice, we'd take a reef in our sails, do some gybes in moderate winds, run up our spinnaker, and spin the winches like seasoned grinders in the America's Cup. Grasping a rope, Deb would dive off the stern and we'd tow her through the water. I put my first mate in charge, covered myself in suntan lotion, and stretched out on the small deck in the bow with C.P. Cavafy.

When you set out for Ithaka
ask that your way be long,
full of adventure, full of instruction....
At many a summer dawn to enter
—with what gratitude, what joy—
ports seen for the first time;
to stop at Phoenician trading centres....
to visit many Egyptian cities,
to gather stores of knowledge from the learnèd.
Have Ithaka always in your mind.
Your arrival there is what you are destined for.
But do not in the least hurry the journey.
Better that it last for years,
so that when you reach the island you are old,
rich with all you have gained on the way,
not expecting Ithaka to give you wealth....

The perfect recipe for travelling. Indeed, for living.

From the galley, Dot brought us plastic bowls of salad—an ever-changing mix of greens, fruits, nuts, cheeses, oils, and vinegars—so much better than the tavernas. To go with them, we tore off chunks of bread from huge, round loaves and passed around a bottle of cheap red wine.

We got so bold that one day we crossed the halfway point in the Aegean Sea, the dividing line between Greek and Albanian waters. The villages and resorts on the Corfu coast were splashed in cheerful reds, yellows, and blues, the sea a weaving pattern of masts and sails. But along Enver Hoxha's stark, silent coast, there was nothing.

"NAUPHUS TO THE BOAT heading toward Albania," the lead boat suddenly called us. "Would you go about, please?"

"Roger", I answered. "This is *Odysseus*. Going about."

Everything was fine until what was intended as a daylong race as we made our way from Kassiopi to Mourtos. It was a cloudless, breathless dawn, and a young couple with laser experience soon took a commanding lead. Looking for wind, Karen and I decided on a venturous move—a tack different from the rest, roughly in the direction of the town of Corfu. We were more than a mile from the other boats when we noticed dark clouds approaching us from the northeast.

"*Nauphus* to the boat heading toward Corfu," our radio crackled once again. "Would you go about please and rejoin the flotilla."

"*Odysseus* to *Nauphus*. Roger. Going about."

Very quickly, this was followed by, "*Nauphus* to all boats. *Nauphus* to all boats. Please lower your genoas and start your engines."

The order had come a little too late, however, for within moments the blanket of black clouds reached us. The wind climbed swiftly from two to ten knots, and then to fifteen, twenty, and twenty-five. By the time Dot, Deb, and Tim had climbed into our small cabin and huddled under the table, we were in a force 7 and Karen and I were being lashed by a mix of rain and hail, the hard, cold stones bouncing painfully off our sun-baked backs. The Greek gods thundered a reproach at our over-confidence and shot bolts of lightning across our bows. As they exploded, all that we could see in front of us was a sheet of white. With one flash, in fact, I could feel a surge of electricity run through the tiller, a fateful moment where, in the grasp of Zeus, my life seemed to hang in the balance and fear gave way to contrition. Through it all, Karen sat beside me, reading the chart and compass and guiding us, we hoped, in the direction of the flotilla.

Within twenty minutes, the rain and hail passed and the sky turned azure again; but the wind remained high. Miraculously, we discovered that we were back in the middle of the flotilla. There the damage was being assessed by the lead boat. There were two ripped mains and a torn jib, some broken stays, and a blocked head (there were always blocked heads). But our boat was untouched. Not only had we weathered the storm, we had safely navigated our way back to the fleet, and without a collision. The flotilla limped to Corfu harbour for repairs. Time to sit in a taverna again and rehash the drama of the storm with the other crews, a time-honoured tradition among sailors, live-released from Poseidon's rapacious net. Time to roam the streets of a town that pleasingly mixes its Greek, Italian, French, and British heritages, even possessing that most un-Greek of classical venues — a cricket pitch. Talking to the others about our adventure, we felt smug and triumphant. We had met the vagaries of the Mediterranean head on and overcome them. The Greek gods had shown us their wrath, but we had calmed them. True sailors, we!

WEEKS LATER, WE WERE travelling in England's Lake District. While Dot and Deb went horseback riding, Karen, Tim, and I decided to go sailing on Ullswater. At the sailing school, once again, they wanted to know about our experience before renting us a dinghy. That was easy this time. We were just back from two weeks sailing in Greece — and on a twenty-seven-foot yacht we told the instructor. We probably even mentioned the storm — now a force 8 — that we had weathered.

Off we set in a light breeze in a little dinghy. We can't have been more than fifty yards from shore, when a wind funnel, swirling between the fells, hit us like a forest fire. Abruptly, we healed to a precarious angle. I let go of the main and headed into the wind. We all hiked frantically to windward. It was enough to keep us from capsizing, but water poured in over our decks and, as the sudden gust passed, we were left wallowing helplessly in the lake like an abandoned wash tub. Our sails luffing in irons, we hastily baled out the dinghy with a large plastic bucket. All the time, red-faced and sweating, we glanced over our shoulders toward the sailing school, wondering if the quality of our seamanship had been noticed.

*Sailing can be a humbling sport. It also requires a little daring.*
*So does a good summer salad:*

## BEST-EVER SUMMER SALAD (FAT FREE)

### SERVES 4

any mixture of leafy greens, but
    mesclun is especially tasty
2 green onions, chopped
6 or more fresh mint leaves,
    snipped, or 1 tsp dried mint
1 pear, cored and cut into
    bite-sized pieces*
10 strawberries, whole or sliced
1 tbsp red-pepper jelly
1 tbsp balsamic vinegar
purple chive flowers, separated
    into individual petals

*\* kiwi, apple, melon, raspberries,*
*  and blueberries also work well.*

» Toss greens, onions, mint, and fruit together in salad bowl. Put jelly in the palm of your hand and rub hands together. Toss ingredients gently using jellied hands until jelly is distributed somewhat evenly among greens and fruit. Sprinkle vinegar on salad and toss with salad servers. Top with chive petals.

» THERE IS ALWAYS so much happening in Europe, so much to
see and do. In North America it often seems as if everyone is
locked inside—at shopping malls or in front of televisions and
computers. But not in Europe. Wherever you go, people are out
and about pursuing their own special interests. Walk across a park
or drive down a country lane, you can always find something to
amuse you.

I suppose it is usually that way in Ireland, too, but it certainly
wasn't when we went there with the kids. I think the weather had
something to do with it. Two weeks of rain, interspersed with
drizzle and fog. "Soft," the Irish kept saying to us. "It's soft today,
isn't it?"

We rented cottages in counties Cork and Clare on bluffs overlooking the sea, the same bluffs, we were told, blue eyes watering,
where, during the potato famine, bonfires were lit to bid farewell
to loved ones sailing away to a better life in America . "Ye come
from Windsor, did ye say? I've relatives in Sarnia. O'Reillys. My
great-grandfather lit a fire for them on the very cliff you can see
from here. O'Reilly is the name. I don't suppose you know them."

"I knew a Dennis O'Reilly when I was a boy at camp,"I
answer encouragingly.

"Aaaah!" The old man cries. "Those would be the ones.
There's a Dennis in the family, I recollect. Aye, for sure, for sure."

Looking out the casement windows of our white-washed cottage
at Toe Head, we couldn't see the cliff of which he spoke. In the foreground, through the mist, we could just make out a patch of yellow

bracken and a swirl of heather, covered in droplets like a bather who had emerged from an extralong shower. And once in a while a gull would appear out of the gloom, shriek madly, and disappear again like a ghost vanishing effortlessly through a grey wall. But that was all. In fact, on neither the south nor the west coast did we ever catch a glimpse of the ocean. It was soft that fortnight, very soft. And nothing much seemed to be happening, not outside at least.

We drove about the countryside, stopping in villages and towns looking for things to do—looking for "Irish experiences." Even the local markets were, however, practically deserted, and the produce appeared stale and uninviting. At one stall, two small heads of lettuce, a dozen hard tomatoes not much bigger than golf balls, broccoli with yellowing flowers, and okay potatoes. Several anemic mackerel and maybe one small cod at another, lying uninvitingly on a slab of scale-encrusted wood.

To lift our spirits, we picked up young hitchhikers and chatted with them about Irish schools. "I've a cousin in Winnipeg," one would say. "I've an aunt who lives in Saint John." On an almost-deserted beach, much to our surprise, we came upon some college students practising the sport of hurling. They handed us their hurleys—like fieldhockey sticks—and we batted the hurl back and forth among us. We also visited Doneraile Court, the Georgian manor home of my ancestors, the St. Legers, where in 1710 young Elizabeth St. Leger inadvertently overheard the secret proceedings of a Masonic meeting. Rather than putting her to death or taking some other dire action, the compassionate brethren who included her father, brother, and future husband, took the most practical course available. They initiated her into the order—the first lady Mason. Of the varied personalities on our family tree, she certainly had one of the more interesting Irish experiences— apart, that is, from her brother, John, who was killed in a duel in 1741. "So you're related to the St. Legers, are you now? Well, welcome back to Doneraile."

Most days, we stopped for lunch in a pub. They were always crowded, but we very much doubted that had anything to do with the weather. They were mostly simple places with cheap fittings and little character. Not like England. More like home. But always there was an effusive welcome. We knew it was not uncommon to get involved in a round of singing and to be asked to do a ditty. So as we drove over the slow, rough roads on the fog-bound Ring of Kerry, we practised our party piece. *Dangerous Dan McGrew*, we decided we'd give them — Irish at least in tone. Fortunately, we never had to perform. "My sister lives in Moose Jaw," someone would say. "I've ancestors who went to Montreal in the middle of the famine." A tear brushed from the eye. "We've lost all touch. Terrible, isn't it, how time goes by?"

Never in England has anyone ever demonstrated to us the slightest interest in their North American connections — in what happened to the youngest son of landed gentry who set off for the Yukon because for him there was no inheritance, or to the northerners who, with the closing of factories and mines, put their pennies and their fates in the hands of Cunard. Not so the Irish. For them the transatlantic tie is important, and they relive those sad departures as if they happened yesterday, and you are a distant relative "come home" who will surely understand their grief and pain.

When we checked into our cottage in County Clare for our second week, it was still soft, and, desperate for more Irish experiences to keep the kids amused, I asked the landlord what, if anything, was going on in the vicinity over the ensuing week.

"Ah, you're in luck. There's a ceremony tomorrow right here on the beach. They're unveiling a monument in honour of Matt McGrath."

"Matt McGrath?"

"Yes. He won the gold medal in the hammer at the 1912 Olympics. This is his village, you see. The plaque is to commemorate the hundredth anniversary of his birth."

So on a blustery, showery afternoon, we gathered with the villagers on the beach—an assembly of fifty maybe, mostly old and middle-aged men with flushed faces and purple, bulbous noses. There was a large van parked at the edge of the beach. One of its sides folded out so that, together with the floor of the truck, there was a platform for a small, roving, string orchestra—all violins.

The ceremony commenced with the playing of the *Star Spangled Banner*, although it had the lilt of an old Irish ballad. *Why the American anthem?* we wondered. But then the nephew of Matt McGrath was introduced. He had flown over from the States especially for the occasion. Matty, we discovered, had indeed been born in the village. He had, however, as a young man, emigrated to New York City where, appropriately, he had become a cop. The gold medal that he had won, it turned out, was not for Ireland but the United States. Still, no reason not to celebrate.

Matty's nephew brought greetings from Matty's son and his apologies for not being present in person. In a New York accent that, in that little Irish village, jarred like cheap whisky, the nephew explained that Matt McGrath's son was recovering from a hip-replacement operation, providing more details of the hospital procedure than the occasion seemed to warrant. Still, no shuffling of feet, no murmurs among the polite Irish audience.

He was followed by the former parish priest—a young, red-haired man with a happy, freckled face—who received enthusiastic applause. Then came the final speaker, the current priest, Father O'Leary, an older, dark-haired man with sharp, pointed features and a dour manner. He was accorded, we thought, a rather cool reception. There was only light applause when he concluded his speech with a familiar quotation, but one that did at least seem appropriate to the event:

For when the one great scorer comes
To write against your name,

He marks — not that you won or lost —
But how you played the game.

The shamrock-green cloth was removed from Matt McGrath's plaque, the little orchestra struck up another Irish ballad, *My Country, 'Tis of Thee,* and the ceremony was over. As the gathering dispersed, we walked over to the plaque and read Matty McGrath's dates. Born in 1878. But hold on! This was 1980. They'd missed the centennial by two years.

Another delightfully Irish experience, we thought. But that was not the end of it.

That evening we went to the village pub for dinner. Through wreathes of blue-grey smoke, we could make out many faces that were familiar from the afternoon ceremony, now ruddier still. One voice, however, rose above the others in that merry throng. One person in particular was determinedly circling the room, encouraging, commanding, and cajoling like a director on a film set. He was sombrely dressed in a dark suit and he was wearing a stiffly starched clerical collar. It was none other than Father O'Leary, the parish priest. But he was no longer sober-looking. Indeed, he seemed to be the life of the party. *Now this is truly an Irish experience!* I thought excitedly.

I can't recall very clearly much about that evening at the pub — how long we were there, who we talked to and what about. But well into the night, while we were standing near the rear, there was a commotion by the main entrance. The police had apparently arrived. Because it was past closing? Seems improbable. To break up a fight? More likely. Whatever it was, the efficient Father O'Leary shepherded us, along with several of his flock, out of the pub through the back door, apparently anxious that we (and he) avoid an unseemly incident.

"Now, we'll all go over to the rectory for a nightcap," Father O'Leary exclaimed once we were out on the street.

"Ah, Father, I can't make it," one person apologized. "I've an early morning."

"We'll try, Father, we'll try," others said. "But we have to look in on the wee ones first."

He turned to me. "You'll come, of course."

*Fantastic!* I thought. *We've actually been invited into the home of a parish priest. What more could you ask for?* Without checking first with Dot and the wilting kids, I eagerly assented.

"Here," he grabbed Karen peremptorily by the arm. "You come with me in my car, and the rest of you follow us. It's not far."

It was only when we piled into our red, fifth-hand Ford that I discovered the others didn't share my enthusiasm for this particular experience. "How could you let Karen get in the same car with that old drunk?" Dot chided me.

I leapt to Father O'Leary's defence. "He isn't drunk. He's the parish priest, for God's sake. He's just a little high."

"I'm tired," Tim complained.

"Me, too," said Deb, whose inquisitiveness rarely flags. "It was smoky in there."

"We can all sleep in," I retorted. "The forecast is for more rain. This is an opportunity we can't pass up."

When we arrived at the rectory, Father O'Leary instructed Dot and me to sit in the parlour while he steered the kids into his Spartan kitchen. From a bare cupboard, he pulled down a jar of instant coffee, plunked it on the table, and put a kettle on the stove.

The parlour had a turn-of-the-century look. Victorian lamps with large silk-fringed shades, garish china figurines, big stuffed chairs, and a red velvet loveseat. Black-and-white family photographs lined the fading yellow walls, including several of Father O'Leary at various stages in his career. But what particularly caught our attention was a long, knitted banner hung high along the rear of the room and running its full width. Immediately, our eyes were drawn to its solemn dictum.

He marks—not that you won or lost—
But how you played the game

We were thankful that on Sundays we were spared sitting through Father O'Leary's sermons.

"Right, then!" The parish priest strode into the parlour with a large, full bottle of whisky tucked under his arm. "I've locked the children in the kitchen. Let's have a drink."

Dot jumped from her seat, but Father O'Leary raised a hand to restrain her. "Sit!" he ordered sternly. "They're fine. They're fixing themselves some coffee."

"Coffee?"

"Where are all the others, then?" I asked innocently.

"It looks as if no one else is coming." The priest's lips curled into a thin smile. "We'll have to take care of the bottle ourselves."

"Father, we really must be off," Dot said, rising again. "It's very late for the children."

"Sit!"

*Leon Uris's Trinity*, I mused. *So it's still like that in the isolated parishes of Ireland. Fascinating. And to think we're witnesses to it!* I tried to give Dot the *relax; it's okay* signal. "So where did you study theology?" I inquired, eager to milk the situation for every drop I could.

"Stand up!" Father O'Leary turned his authoritarian voice on me, and I immediately did as bid.

"Walk over to that photograph on the wall."

I peered at a photo of a graduating class from Trinity College, Dublin.

"Where am I in the photograph?"

I searched in vain and Father O'Leary had to help me, spilling whisky on the carpet as he lurched toward the wall.

"So that's you. Well, well, you—"

"Sit down."

Dot excused herself to go to the bathroom, but with the intent of surreptitiously checking that the kids weren't really locked in the kitchen.

Father O'Leary, however, followed her out of the parlour. "The bathroom is at the top of the stairs. I'll show you."

Now, instead of heading straight for the kitchen, Dot had to make a detour and climb to the second floor. But she could sense Father O'Leary following her up the stairs — hear him breathing hard, smell his fruity breath. "Here, let me show you the upstairs," he said lecherously. "My bedroom is particularly nice. You'll like it."

Dot wheeled to face him, forcing him to halt on the landing halfway up. "No thank you, Father. I don't want a tour. I just want to go to the bathroom."

He stood on the stairs leering. "Ye sure, now? Ye sure? I'm quick, ye see. I'm quick and I'm good."

Dot turned abruptly, raced to the top of the stairs, and slammed the bathroom door behind her.

Unaware that anything untoward had happened, when Father O'Leary returned to the parlour I continued my innocent interrogation, probing as deeply as I thought I dare into this strange priest's psyche. "So what do you think of the new pope?" It was less than two years since John Paul had ascended to the seat of St. Peter.

"That bastard!" shouted Father O'Leary derisively. I gulped at my drink to hide my shock, and he lapsed into a semi-coherent tirade against the church, its preoccupation with ecclesiastical issues and lack of attention to contemporary social concerns.

It was interrupted by Dot appearing at the door, holding Deb and Tim by the hand and with Karen standing close behind her. "Father, we must be off," she said curtly. "Thank you for inviting us into your home. But it is very late."

The priest protested, but Dot was adamant. "Come," she said to me with a firmness that surpassed even Father O'Leary's, and reluctantly I rose from the loveseat.

"Aaah! Have one more drop," the priest pleaded. "We've hardly touched the bottle."

I held out my glass, but Dot and the girls glowered at me and I set it down. Some authorities are higher than the church.

Then Dot turned to Father O'Leary and addressed him the way his parishioners had, using one of their lines. "I'm sorry, Father, we really can't stay. We have an early day tomorrow." And at last he relented.

Over those two wet weeks in Ireland, our old car was almost impossible to start whenever the engine was cold. In the mornings, we had to lift the hood and dry out the sparks before we could induce it into a hacking cough. Would that be our fate late that cold, damp night as well? As we climbed hurriedly into the car, I knew that the others were crossing their fingers hoping that the Ford Motor Company would not let us down. It did not. The engine, like Lazarus resurrected, sprang to life, and we escaped from the clutches of the Catholic church.

As we sped away, the kids explained the scheme they had been hatching in the kitchen to fell the prodigal father had things got particularly ugly. "We knew the three of us could take him easily from behind," Deb said with a hint of disappointment that in the end it hadn't happened.

At last, with visions of the banner headlines such an end to the evening would have invoked, I, too, was glad to be safely away from the rectory.

Looking for Irish experiences. It was a game worth playing. Indeed, it is in any country. Sometimes you win, sometimes you lose. But the important thing is how you play. And here my children admonish me, "with a little bit of caution, Dad, a little more prudence, please."

*It's quick and it's good!*

## IRISH SODA BREAD
### MAKES 1 LOAF

1 ½ cups all-purpose flour
1 ½ cups whole-wheat flour
2 tsp baking powder
½ tsp salt
2 tbsp brown sugar
1 ¾ cups sour milk
  (add 2 ½ tbsp vinegar
  to fresh milk)
1 tsp baking soda
2 tbsp vegetable oil
1 cup raisins
1 tbsp caraway seeds

» Sieve flour, baking powder, and salt into a large bowl. Tip in bits of wheat that won't sieve. Add brown sugar.

» In a smaller bowl, combine sour milk, baking soda, and oil, and stir until baking soda has dissolved. Pour into flour mixture and, using a strong wooden spoon, stir until blended. Mix in raisins and caraway seeds.

» Pour into a greased 9 × 5-inch loaf pan. Bake at 350 for 50–60 minutes. Remove from pan and cool on a wire rack.

» THE ASCENT FROM the narrow, rock-strewn road that twists through the mountains west of Ste Agnès is steep but relatively easy. We climbed it one autumn Sunday with our English friend, William, and a French family — to a place called Pic de Baudon.

It's incredible how quickly the scenery changes as you drive into the mountains behind Menton. At first the vegetation is lush and green as you rise gently through the ambrosial lemon groves that yield a bountiful harvest, thirty thousand fruit to the acre. According to local legend, the trees all stem from the seed of the lemon Eve, on expulsion, plucked from the Garden of Eden and, after wandering the unfriendly earth for years, planted in Menton, the closest thing she and Adam found to Paradise. After the orchards, you twist through terraces of old, gnarled olive trees, their green and black fruit shining against the small, silver leaves. Then the terraces give way to steep hills dotted with pines and finally scrub oaks still higher up.

Leaving the road and starting on foot toward the Pic, it's not long before there is nothing but bare white rock, clumps of dry grass, and herbs. The path is rough, and little clouds of white dust settle on your boots and pants as you scramble over loose rocks and jagged hunks of limestone firmly embedded in the hard, parched earth. It's not beautiful like the high Alps or the Vallée des Merveilles, much deeper into the Alpes Maritimes where Riviera hikers go on more arduous expeditions. But after the coast, it is refreshingly cool and the scent of rosemary and thyme sweetens the air.

At the summit, we lazed in the sun and ate a light picnic of cheeses, prosciutto, and baguettes. I had brought a bottle of white wine, but surprisingly, with a French family in our company, it was the only one. So Dot passed around small plastic cups for everyone to share.

"*Je ne bois jamais de vin blanc,*" William's friend Rolland sniffed. He had lived his whole life in the region and he swept his swarthy arm around the rocky promontory on which we were perched, admiring the snow-capped peaks to the north, and then, as if connected to what he had just said, he added, "France is my home. But I love all of Europe. I have been to North America." He paused for a studied shrug, worthy of Trudeau. "I don't much care for it. No, I need only France and occasionally other corners of Europe."

It was perfect. Said with supreme arrogance and indifference. Flare. As only a Frenchman could do it. It was Rolland's version of the headline for a story on Canada-France relations I had read in *Le Monde* at about the same time. The article was on the fisheries dispute over the waters off St-Pierre and Miquelon and the headline read sardonically, "D'abord La Pêche, Ensuite La Pêche, Tojours La Pêche." *Le Monde*'s version, perhaps, of Innes's staples theory of Canadian economic development. There was nothing to write about but fish.

After lunch we descended quickly back to the road. Rolland was in a buoyant mood and most of the way he cheerfully whistled popular French tunes. Despite my poor choice of wines, he had, nevertheless, drunk his share. More, in fact. As we stood by the cars, he wrapped his arms around his wife and suggested that she drive down to his cousin's place in Gorbio while the rest of us walked there along a valley path. Then he would drive me back to get our car for the return trip to Menton.

France — it was a popular name for babies born during the occupation — agreed. And so we set off along a marked route below the road, with Rolland booming patriotic songs down the mountain.

This was his family domain and, after a while, he decided we should leave the main path and take a shortcut to the left along a narrower track that he knew would take us directly to the village. But some forty minutes later, it petered out and we found ourselves hacking our way through tangles of bushes from clearing to clearing, looking for a continuation. Rolland stopped singing and reverted to whistling — at first steadily and cheerfully, but then only intermittently and softly. At last we were clear of vegetation for some distance and the situation looked more hopeful — except for a steep descent ahead of us that required bracing ourselves with our hands to prevent an uncontrolled slide over outcrops of limestone rock to a line of trees below us. But when we got to them, we discovered we were at the edge of a perpendicular drop of several hundred feet and that the gorge below us ran as far as we could see to the left and right. It was one of the four parallel valleys that run from the mountains to the sea at Menton, separated from each other by white, rocky ridges.

There was no alternative but to scramble back up the slope and then cut our way wide to the left or right of our current route. Panting when we reached the top, we paused to fan our flushed, perspiring faces. Rolland decided that we should have quit the main path earlier in the walk, so he opted to go left. Again, clawing our way through bushes and brambles and covered in burrs and scratched by thorns, we worked our way across the valley for some time. Rolland stopped whistling altogether. Shafts of light from the setting sun burned patches of gold in the intermittent clearings, but they failed to arouse him from an enveloping gloom. The prospect of spending the night lost in the silent valley of his ancestral home was clearly looming.

Once more we reached a steep descent — this time over scree — but we could see beyond the bottom and knew that immediately we would have to climb another high ridge. Still, Rolland was sure we were heading in the right direction and that, rather than a path, the road to Gorbio could not now be far away. So we slithered down the rocky slope, unleashing streams of smooth pebbles and stones that clattered into the dry valley bed. And then we picked our way up the ridge opposite. We were sweating profusely when we reached the top, but within moments we were cold and shivering. The sun had now completely left the valley and it was almost dark.

"How cold is it, these nights?" I asked Dot. "Do you think exposure will be a problem?"

She just shrugged and said nothing. When Dot loses her optimism, it's not a good sign.

Tim, who was the only one of the kids with us, sensed her sagging spirits. "I'm starving already," he complained. Out of sight of a refrigerator he was always fretful, and the prospect of missing a meal was like watching a blueberry pie splatter on the cottage kitchen floor when it was your sister's fault.

From the ridge, Rolland's son, Frederic, scampered ahead of the rest of us — up a gentler incline in what Rolland believed was the direction of the road. Moments later, we heard him shouting excitedly, "*Il y a une piste.*"

We quickened our pace and joined him at a path at right angles to the direction we were moving. Straight ahead was another hill that Rolland was confident led to the road. But he was also convinced that to the right this path would take us to Gorbio. Indeed, it was, he said, the very one he had intended us to be on all along!

Making for the road seemed a safer bet, so it was with considerable trepidation that we yielded to Rolland and set off down the path in almost total darkness. Frederic ran ahead out of sight to scout the way. Rolland was whistling again — at first tentatively, but as the path widened and looked more worn, his cheeks pumped harder and faster and the tunes became livelier. Soon, Frederic came running back up the path, "*Oui, c'est la! C'est Gorbio!*"

At last Rolland broke into song again, his rich tenor voice resonating proudly and confidently through the valley. Then, as we crossed an uneven stone bridge over the gorge that earlier had blocked our way and reached the edge of the village, he switched to a loud and joyful rendition of the *Marseillaise*. Within minutes the atmosphere had been totally transformed. It was like Napoleon meeting the French forces at Auxerre on his return from Elba, the troops suddenly swinging to his side.

An anxious France was at the front door of his cousin's simple bungalow to greet us and there were hugs with everyone, together with the mandatory three *bises* on alternating cheeks. The cousin's home was, in fact, a restaurant as well, a modest one with white-washed walls and a red-tile roof. It was closed on Sundays, but that didn't matter. Immediately, we were invited in, the lights were turned on, and china jugs of young red wine were brought to us at a large, circular table. We were urged to take off our boots and socks and rub our aching feet and legs. At first the conversation was too fast for us to follow, although we knew that it pertained in part to food. Rolland's cousin was clearly being insistent about something, but if Rolland was protesting, it wasn't vigorously. Then the cousin left the room briefly, returning with a young man in a white shirt and pants, who was tying on an apron. There was more double-quick discussion in French. But now we understood what was happening. The chef was explaining what, under the circumstances, it would be possible to serve us for supper.

While the meal was being prepared, Rolland drove me up the mountain to get our car. The drive back to Gorbio, following him around the horseshoe curves of a dark, narrow road, where going out of control meant plunging into a wall of rock or the valley below, was one of the most frightening of my life. The French always drive fast and dangerously, but at no place and time more so than on the Moyen Corniche between Roquebrune and Nice in the week following the Monte Carlo Grand Prix. That's when the men test their skills as Formula One drivers on the tight switchbacks blasted from the face of the cliffs along the Mediterranean coast. And that's how Rolland drove that night on our own terrifying race course. Rapid-fire gear shifts up and down. Foot hard on the gas pedal at every possible moment. Tires screeching. Car swaying. Horn blaring. Rolland was anxious for more *red* wine, and supper.

As it turned out, it was a hearty rather than a gourmet meal, prepared without firing up the grill — almost as quickly as Dot can do it. Ravioli in cream sauce, followed, as I recall, by *le pan-bagnat* — in effect, the ingredients of a salade niçoise stuffed into a loaf of French bread, dusted in flour. Midi midday food, really. Still, it was one of the most memorable meals we have ever eaten.

As we finished, all of Rolland's relatives joined us at the table. Jugs of red wine kept arriving from behind a polished wooden counter, and voices rang higher and higher in jubilant song — in a spontaneous celebration of our deliverance from the dark and impending cold. Rolland even recalled from his youth some French-Canadian ballads that he sang especially loudly and especially for us — *"nos cousins d'outre-mer!"*

It was an unforgettable evening. Exhausted and hungry when we had at last reached Gorbio, our next meal had seemed a long way off. Then suddenly we were in a bright, warm room, devouring an assuaging supper that had the zing and kiss of the south — dripping extra-virgin oil over the troubled waters of the day. And we were eating in a restaurant that had been opened exclusively for us and in the company of its smiling owners who had welcomed us, as Rolland's friends, with weathered, outstretched arms. The weary traveller cannot ask for more.

We raised our glasses in countless toasts. I'm sure that, much to Tim's embarrassment, I was responsible for most of them: *"Vive nos nouveaux amis! Vive Gorbio! Vive La France! Vive Le Canada! Vive l'amité entre nos deux pays!"*

Even *"Vive le pan-bagnat!"*

## PAN-BAGNAT

SERVES 4

1 loaf French bread
4–6 medium, top-quality
   tomatoes
1 cup best-quality extra-virgin
   olive oil
⅓ cup white-wine vinegar
½ tsp sugar
1 clove garlic, minced
½ tsp fines herbes
2 tins solid white tuna
2 shallots or 4 green onions,
   chopped
10–15 Greek olives (Kalamata),
   pitted and sliced
½ red and ½ green bell pepper,
   sliced in very thin rings
2 hard-boiled eggs, thinly sliced
6–8 fresh basil leaves, chopped
salt and pepper to taste

» Cut loaf in half length. Remove some of the soft white middle from each half.

» Chop the tomato, sprinkle with salt (about ½ teaspoon) and set aside in a strainer to drain for 20–30 minutes. Meanwhile, whisk oil, vinegar, sugar, fines herbes, and garlic together in a small bowl or shake together in a lidded jar to make a dressing.

» Drain tuna and mash it with a fork in a bowl until evenly shredded. Mix in chopped shallots or onions. Add enough dressing to moisten well.

» Drizzle a little additional dressing on both bread halves. Distribute tuna, drained tomatoes, olives, eggs, and pepper slices evenly on the bottom half of the loaf. Sprinkle with chopped basil, salt and pepper, and a little more dressing if desired. Cover with the top half of the loaf and slice into four portions.

» I'M NOT SURE it's a good idea to hear a lot about a place before you visit it. Not that you shouldn't read about its history, get a sense of the things to see, learn the dos and don'ts. That can be useful if what you are exposed to is objective, dispassionate information. What I'm talking about is the effusive lauding of a town or country's beauty and charm by a smitten colleague, friend, or relation who may have visited the place only once or approached it with distinctly different tastes and expectations.

I'm especially wary of recommendations about accommodation and restaurants. Conditions change quickly and, in any event, it is often ephemeral circumstances that determine whether or not a room or meal is enjoyable. Was the desk clerk from *Fawlty Towers* or *Pretty Woman*? Did the distant strains of a violin float through the French doors at bedtime or the discordant din of a garbage truck at 6:00 AM? Was I starving after a day's trek or still coated with clotted cream from tea at four? Did the conversation bubble like the chianti or collapse like a failed soufflé? These are the shifting ingredients of the travel recipe unrecorded in guidebooks and differently experienced and reported by those returning from the same destination. So, by and large, I think it's wise to treat their recommendations with caution. Besides, half the pleasure is making discoveries oneself—in being the one to tell others where and where not to sleep and eat, though woe betide those who don't follow *your* advice!

Don't get me wrong, I like Bermuda despite what happened to Tad and me. What Anglophile wouldn't, with its tidy lanes and manicured gardens aflame with bougainvillea, oleander, hibiscus, and frangipani, its cream teas, tartans, scarlet tunics, and cornucopia of outdoor and indoor pursuits? For the sports-minded, there's golf, tennis, hiking, biking, horseback riding, swimming, sailing, snorkelling, fishing, and spelunking. And when the less active tire of stretching out on Bermuda's scores of soft-sand beaches, there's shopping in stylish Hamilton and quaint little St. George's. There are also galleries, museums, trust houses, gardens, a perfumery, aquarium and zoo, theatre and music. The Brits brought it all. Even rugby and cricket. No, I like Bermuda. But in many respects, it was different from what we had expected.

There aren't, for instance, the long swaths of deserted beach framed by swaying palms that I recall others raving about. There are some beautiful ones, to be sure, with firm, pink-sugar sand and clean, aquamarine water. It's just that they are all quite short — investigated from end to end without wearing off breakfast or lunch.

There also aren't the quiet roads circling the island that we had expected — the sort that one can laze down on a moped, stopping every so often to admire the stunning views of the ocean over the white, stepped roofs of pink and yellow villas, their walls constructed from native coral. Rather, the traffic on all but a few connector roads is heavy, noisy, and noxious, and the quaint stone walls that line them come perilously close to your handlebars as passing lorries press you to the curb. Driving a moped in Bermuda is youth-restoring, it's true, but it's not apt to extend your life expectancy.

My image of Bermuda was also of bountiful, gourmet meals served on patios bedecked in flowers overlooking sail-streaked harbours. It is that way if you are on a big budget and staying at one of the many fine hotels or eating in the upscale restaurants. This, after all, is the place where a prime minister was forced into resignation by his decision to allow McDonald's onto the island. But fine dining isn't easy if you choose housekeeping accommodation and do your shopping in the local grocery stores. We found them drab, expensive, and poorly stocked.

The golf, too, was not what we had expected. But for that we can't really blame Bermuda. Just as we had been told, it has several excellent courses with spectacular views of the sea, and there are more of them per square kilometre than in any other country. They have been laid out by such master craftsmen as Robert Trent Jones, so we anticipated that the challenge they offered would raise the calibre of our neophyte games.

Deb and Tad, who were living in Japan at the time, joined Dot and me in Bermuda for Christmas. We rented two tiny cottages in the parish of Southampton on the north shore. It was a perfect location because we could quickly scooter across the hilly centre of the island to lovely Horseshoe Beach to swim (Canadians only), body surf, and play tennis. And, afterward, we could climb Gibb's Hill to the lighthouse for the best view of the island and tea and scones. We were also close to the Southampton Princess Hotel, which has an attractive par-three golf course where Tad and I honed our skills over the first week of the holiday, preparing ourselves for more taxing exploits.

The best thing about our accommodation (we *thought*) was that it was on the property of the secretary of the Bermuda Golf Association. "Anytime you want to play one of the top courses, just let me know and I'll arrange a tee off for you at a good price," he told us. We demurred at first, indicating that we needed to work on our games.

So Tad and I played a few rounds at the Southampton Princess, with its enthralling views over the sapphire sea, and then we tried the government-owned Ocean View course in Devonshire Parish. Tad looked pretty good. I was still shaky, but on our second-last day in Bermuda we decided it was time; we didn't want to miss a crack at one of Bermuda's finest. So we studied the guidebook on

Bermuda's courses, selected the Port Royal, and revisited our obliging landlord.

"I've got you a tee off time at 9:05 AM," he told us. "And it will be at half price."

The time should have alerted us to the fact that trouble lurked along the fairways of the Port Royal, but we didn't twig it the next morning when we hauled our golf bags onto the bus and rode westward to the entrance to the course, nor as we walked the long road winding up to the clubhouse, taxis and limousines dusting us as they streaked by.

We got there early with enough time to practise on the driving range. After a few swings, Tad was stroking the ball well. I was still wobbly, but passable if, as we expected, it would just be the two of us hacking our way around the course together.

But that was not to be. We checked in at the desk and, golf bags over our shoulders, walked to the first tee where a long line of gleaming carts and neatly tailored golfers was assembled. There the starter indicated to us the two retired executives from Dupont who would make up the rest of our foursome. Our optimism sagged, but we bravely introduced ourselves and chatted amiably as the queue slowly advanced. One of the gentlemen, we learned, had just returned from a two-week golfing holiday in Ireland. We looked at the shiny, woollen-capped clubs resting expectantly in their cart in burgeoning leather bags, at their polished brown-and-white leather golf shoes, at their freshly pressed slacks and shirts emblazoned with country-club crests, and at their tanned, relaxed faces that said, "been there, done that, no big deal." Then we looked at ourselves. Two half sets of second-hand clubs (circa 1975), a couple of thirty-dollar drivers purchased on sale the preceding autumn, wrinkled pants, muddy running shoes, beer-stained, logoless T-shirts, and terror in our eyes. In addition, we had no cart. We had opted to walk the course — not only to exercise and save money, but also because we anticipated spending a lot of our time at right angles to the fairways. As a final touch, Tad was clutching two ham sandwiches in a brown paper bag, a snack for the back nine. A motley pair we were next to the well-healed duet from Dupont — like immigrants at Ellis Island suddenly anxious about the choice they had made.

If you've ever played the Port Royal, you will know that the first tee sits on a promontory with a drop of about one hundred feet to the fairway. As we moved into position, a milling mass of impatient golfers watching our foursome get under way, I whispered to Tad that there was no way I was teeing off under these circumstances and he'd have to drive my first ball for me. Tad is not always straight, but at least he's long, *most* of the time — a John Daly sort of player — and length was what I was looking for. Anything to get us away from the gawking crowd at the first tee. Confident about his driving at least, he agreed to hit for me — our own variant on a Mulligan.

The first of the Dupont dandies — the one who had *not* just returned from Ireland — led off with a respectable drive of maybe 170 yards, but he hooked it slightly into the rough. We relaxed a little; this was well short of Tad's normal range. But then the second one drove his ball straight down the fairway some 275 yards (he eventually finished the eighteen holes just four over par). Maybe that got Tad a little anxious, I don't know, but he didn't really look it as he strode onto the launching pad, a couple of tees in his mouth, and took several, mighty practice swings.

He teed my ball up first and attacked it with tremendous force. The impudent ball, however, disregarded his exertion and squirted off the tee along the ground. Then it dribbled down the hill, landing in a flowerbed at the bottom, still short of the fairway. We could sense a collective groan from our Dupont companions and those in the gallery waiting to start behind us. But undaunted, Tad teed up the second ball — his this time — and took a couple of extra practice swipes. Again, he curled his driver hard behind his neck and bore down with all his power on the tee. But the result was the same. The recalcitrant ball spun off the tee through the grass and bounced down the hill to the flowerbed.

We urged the Dupont duo to go ahead, saying that we would play at our own pace behind them. But they would have none of it. The fates had joined us for the day and so it would be.

Thus began some four to five excruciating hours of golf and one of those embarrassments you feel will never end, and yet when it does, you never cease talking and laughing about it. Tad got better as the day wore on, even birdied one of the late holes. But I never found my composure and hardly ever even lofted the ball into the air. Humiliated, I finally called it quits after the sixteenth hole where the green is breathtakingly perched at the edge of a cliff that plunges abruptly into the ocean, an enticing thought for harried golfers. "Shot your limit for the day, huh?" Mr. Dupont II quipped. To be fair, they were perfect gentlemen throughout. We had good conversation and never an angry word was spoken. Wherever they are, whatever course they are parring, I thank them now for their forbearance.

We liked Bermuda. But it wasn't the way we envisaged it.

» I'M A BIT BAFFLED by tourists who circle the globe in Hilton hotels, those glass-and-concrete enclaves in every major city on every continent that epitomize the remorseless spread of North American culture—the gradual, insidious homogenization of the world. They may be a sort of ubiquitous oasis for anxious couples, carrying their own instant coffee and facial wipes. But for those who believe differences should be nurtured and those who delight at watering holes with a look and feel never encountered before, they are at odds with the preservation of the infinite variety of the planet that makes travel so rewarding. Why go abroad if you need every-one you encounter to speak English? Why choose to be hermetically sealed off from the local environment? Why visit only the famous sites listed in Fodor's or Frommer's and viewable, at any rate, in magazines, on the Internet, or compact discs? Why, for that matter, choose burgers and fries when shwarmas are tastier and healthier?

Maybe it's a good thing, though, that so many people like Hilton hotels and that they stick to well-marked routes when they travel. That's what makes it still possible to find out-of-the-way places where tourists seldom go and to share precious times with trees, totems, and local tribes. In 1994 we had a scary but awe-inspiring moment on an out-of-the-way path in the Middle East, albeit one that has been trekked for centuries—the famous cara-van route from Wadi Rum to Aqaba.

Dot and I were travelling with our old friend Sepp, at the time the Austrian trade commissioner in Damascus. Sepp doesn't have the bearing of the typical diplomat. He's short and stocky, his suits are crumpled, and his hair is long, dark, and matted. But, as befits his profession, he's adept at getting the feel of the places to which he's posted — at fitting in — and he prefers the enigmas and challenges of developing countries to the familiarity and ease of the industrialized West. For Sepp, it was nothing to race hundreds of kilometres a day in his white Mercedes across the naked landscapes of the Middle East to show us his favourite places. Sepp never does things in half measures, never by the book.

We approached Wadi Rum from the north along the dangerous Desert Highway that snakes down the valley from Ras an-Naqb. It's like driving into a giant gravel pit, only larger than rapacious man could ever conceive of carving. As you near Rum, the high, jagged cliffs on either side of the valley of sand and rock gradually close in upon you. This is how Lawrence of Arabia described the experience in *Seven Pillars of Wisdom*, coming the other way by camel:

> We looked up on the left to a long wall of rock, sheering in like a thousand-foot wave towards the middle of the valley.... The hills on the right grew taller and sharper, a fair counterpart of the other side which straightened itself to one massive rampart of redness. They drew together until only two miles divided them: and ... ran forward in an avenue for miles.... The Arab armies would have been lost in the length and breadth of it, and within the walls a squadron of aeroplanes could have wheeled in formation. Our little caravan grew self-conscious, and fell dead quiet, afraid and ashamed to flaunt its smallness in the presence of the stupendous hills.

The road ends abruptly just past the headquarters of the desert patrol, and from that point on there are only tracks across the sand to Aqaba and the sea. But our little caravan of one, with the redoubtable Sepp at the wheel, decided to carry on across the desert for a picnic, though we lacked the aid of four-wheel drive. After skidding and sliding from track to track as Sepp sought a firm route, his ever-reliable Teutonic camel with the specially reinforced chassis finally packed it in. Several kilometres into the desert, it went down on all fours, deep into the red sand. We climbed out, unloaded the trunk, and started pushing. But all we succeeded in doing was burying our mount deeper and deeper until it came firmly to rest on its stomach. Clawing at the sand with a large bleached bone lying nearby, we tried to dig the chassis free, but the sand poured back in almost as quickly as we dug it out. At the same time, the heat generated by revving the engine caused the clutch to give out. "No problem," Sepp said cheerfully. "We can get it fixed in Aqaba."

"Aqaba?!" I snorted. "How the hell are we going to get there?!" It was more than thirty kilometres ahead of us across the desert.

"We might as well sit down and have our shwarmas and some wine," Sepp responded, "while we wait for someone to come."

I pulled a scarf over my nose and mouth and, squinting (I hoped like Peter O'Toole), surveyed 360 degrees of vacant desert under a clear blue sky. The churning dust and sand had transformed the receding ridges of the valley behind us into dark shadowy mounds of uneven rock, like stark sets lowered from wires onto the stage of a sombre, surreal play. Ahead of us, there was nothing but drifting sand, sagebrush, and sky. It looked like we were in for a long wait, and a glass of water seemed more appropriate. How far were we, I wondered, from the famous spring where Lawrence bathed and watered his camels? Worth making for it? But I said nothing to Sepp. Lawrence would have been forbearing, and I tried to act the same.

As always, Sepp was right about our predicament. Things work out for him. Before we even got the shwarmas unwrapped and the wine bottle uncorked, we spotted a Land Rover following another track through the desert several kilometres away. We waved wildly and it turned in our direction. The driver was a Jordanian guide with a load of English tourists, excited at having to make a desert rescue. While the guide attached a line from our chassis to his hoist and pulled us free, we were apprised of the weather in England when the rescue party had left three days before: high winds and heavy rain. Immediately, the desert at Wadi Rum seemed once again a good place to be. Miraculously, too, the clutch was functioning again, so we made our way more carefully back over the tracks to the road and thence northward, messily devouring our shwarmas as we drove. Late the following night, we were pounding along the desert highway toward Damascus at 130 kilometres per hour when we were swiftly passed by a car with no headlights. It was, however, being led by another with functioning lamps. Mindful of the piles of rubble and other hazards that suddenly loom out of the dark on the highways of Syria, Sepp had been taking it easy. But now he had an opportunity and he brightened. These two vehicles could run interference for us. So he cranked up to their speed, staying at sufficient distance, however, that should they hit something, he would have time to react. The desert tracks of the Middle East are, I reflected, much safer than its highways, even on a camel with four wheels. "*Al-hamdu lillah a la Salaam!*" Dot and I exclaimed when we reached home. Thank God for our safe arrival.

There's an amusing travel biography with the ominous title *Holidays in Hell*. It's interesting reading for those enticed by toughing it out in the worst of conditions, living on the edge. But that is not to everyone's taste, nor does it have to be that way to have unique and memorable moments. At Rum, at least we abandoned our itinerary and left the main road. For a few fleeting minutes we were alone and at risk — with Lawrence in the desert. Whatever else, we had not "gone Hilton."

## SHWARMA ALARMA

» Unless you have a vertical
roasting spit, a shwarma is
harder to make than a Big Mac,
but you can get a reasonable
facsimile by filling pita bread
with slabs of barbecued lamb
and stuffing in lettuce,
tomatoes, and parsley, and then
lathering the whole thing in
tzatziki sauce. You don't have
to eat them alone in the desert,
but they are best outside with a
bottle of dry red wine.

» VERDANT HUMPS pushing out of the water like giant dorsal fins. Catamarans chasing over turquoise seas. Coral reefs sheltering gleaming schools of iridescent fish. Snow-white beaches backed by gently swaying coconut palms. Glossy-painted fishing boats tilted in the sand. Pina coladas resting on umbrella-shaded tables. The relentless throb of drums — of creole, callaloo, and calypso bands — loud, rhythmic, and mesmerizing. That's what springs to mind for most people when they think of the Caribbean.

Banana groves and gently sloping *mornes* covered in sugar cane. Tulip trees aflame in green, dripping forests where *lianas* stretch for sunlight. Cascading waterfalls, rock pools, and hot springs. Showers of red and pink bougainvillea, yellow hibiscus, orange immortelle, passion flowers, orchids, and heliconia shaped liked lobster claws. The fragrance of jasmine and frangipani, the mellow odour of ripe and rotting fruit — mango, soursop, and sweet banana — the pungent scent of curry and coriander. The hot, humid feel of a greenhouse — of lazy sensuality, fertility.

Shantytowns where chickens and barefoot kids wander the dusty, unpaved streets. Rows of simple, wooden shops with hand-made, peeling signs. Inside, the latest fashions from Paris, London and New York. Tax-free perfumes, jewelry, and watches, cheap wine and liquor. Plump, easy-going mothers in bright-cloth prints, babes on hips, swaying to the beat of booming stereos. Young men in dreadlocks loping market squares as if walking on old bedsprings. Everything rubbery, relaxed, gliding in slow motion. That's how people see the Caribbean.

But not me. That's not my image.

I hear rigging whining and clanging. I hear sails, taught in a stiff wind, flapping along the edge, the explosion of waves against a fibre-glass bow. I see wisps of low-flying clouds racing across a darkening sky. I see an unending expanse of heaving, foaming sea with two-metre swells. And, every so often, bobbing forlornly on top, I see a little dinghy — our tender. A rope, frayed by the force of the sea, has set it free. And, as the skipper maneuvers us toward it, I see myself standing on the deck, mouth dry, heart pounding, waiting for the instant when, with luck, the tender and the Sweden 38, each rolling to a different beat, will be close enough for me to drop cleanly and safely from the railing of one to the floor boards of the other, line in hand. I see death staring me in the face — by concussion, drowning, or mauling in shark-infested waters; or, adrift in a lost tender, by exposure or dehydration. That is my Caribbean.

WITH FOUR ENGLISH friends, we sailed first from Le Marina du bas de Fort on Guadeloupe along the eastern wing of that butter-fly island — past rain forests and volcanic peaks. Our destination was Les Saintes, charming, unspoilt bumps in the ocean just eleven kilometres to the south, but so distant in spirit that, there, to refer to "*le metropole*" is as likely to mean the main island of Guadeloupe as it is France itself. Terre de Haut, the principal mound of Les Saintes, was never planted and never had many slaves. Most of the population is descended from French immigrants from Brittany and Normandy: people with blond hair and blue eyes whose skin doesn't tan, but who mingle easily with their nut-brown confreres. Bourg, the principal settlement on Terre de Haut, is a miniature in many ways of a seaside village in France. School children, cheap plastic book bags over their shoulders, scamper laughing and shouting from open-air classrooms onto lanes of white-washed houses with red-tin roofs. Under palm trees, fishermen sit on wooden crates mending their nets. In the central square, adjacent to the ferry wharf, old men in black berets suck thoughtfully on their pipes, engrossed in dominoes. Nearby, lovers share a tryst and an espresso in an outdoor café. The Saintes are a happy, care-free place, free of the social conflict that sometimes afflicts the larger islands.

But that is not principally the way I remember them. I remember anxiety and tension. Sleepless nights checking our anchor to see if we were dragging perilously near to others in the flotilla of yachts and cruisers sharing our little crescent-shaped bay on Terre de Bas. Our propeller tangled in the line of a lobster pot as we limped from one anchorage to another. Chest-aching dives under the hull to slash away the twisted rope with the aid of borrowed knives and waterproof flashlights. A tube of lip cream slithering through the narrow aperture at the base of the toilet, and an all-day operation to repair it. A 9.9 outboard engine that, every time we went ashore, had to be lowered awkwardly from the deck of our yacht and attached to the tender. A petulant 9.9 that was resistant to starting so that once, after a particularly hefty pull, my right elbow flew squarely into the face of my old friend Eric, knocking off his glasses and jack-knifing him to the bottom of the dinghy, groaning.

I remember, in one isolated harbour with absolutely no one about, going ashore with the skipper to investigate what appeared to be an abandoned marina. Two scavengers, we picked our way along a crumbling concrete pier, strewn with empty oil barrels, tires, and rusting cables like fish guts scattered on a rocky shore. Our failed objective: to find a source of fresh water and a hose so we could fill the almost-depleted hold of our yacht. And I remember once again the anchor dragging. As Eric and I, the grinders of the crew, hauled it up, the chain suddenly jerked forward, driving my right hand fiercely against the brass anchor runner. I have a permanent lump on one forever-bent and crooked finger to remind me deck hands must be quick with winches, ropes, and chains.

From Les Saintes we sailed up the western coast of Guadeloupe to a remote cove with golden-brown sand and a thick, lush forest that rose steeply behind it. A scarlet ibis, half hidden by a spray of palm fronds, glowed like a little campfire in the brush. But it is not so much the Robinson Crusoe setting that I recall as playing the adventurer himself — scrubbing and sponging our tender until it gleamed, so that when the heavens mercifully unloaded that night, we were able to collect rain water for the long sail the next day to Antigua.

When we set off at dawn, the wind was blowing at twenty to twenty-five knots. But the skipper was reluctant to reef the sails. We needed to get as much distance out of the wind as we could in case it dropped later in the day and we had to motor. Now it wasn't just fresh water that was a concern; we were low on diesel fuel as well. By the time we reached the northern tip of Guadeloupe, the wind was just as high, but we no longer had any protection from the coast, so there was no choice but to take a reef. We started the engine and while I, at the helm, desperately tried to hold us into the wind, the skipper and Eric rolled in the main. We crashed and wallowed for half an hour, the yacht drifting ever nearer the rocky coast of Guadeloupe, before the job was done. And in the commotion Eric lost his prescription sunglasses overboard and someone else their Tilley hat. *Okay. Smaller calamities. Maybe the worst is past,* I thought to myself as the sails billowed again and the yacht charged toward Antigua somewhere beyond the horizon.

It was a long, rough crossing with most of us battling seasickness. Yet at the same time it was exhilarating. With the mainsail reefed, we seemed in control and making good time, sufficient to reach English Harbour and drop anchor before dark. In the afternoon, some distance to port, we passed Montserrat, smoke rising into the azure sky from its peak as if from the stack of a luxury cruise ship, slipping off the edge of the earth. It was on the first of July, 1995, that the volcano had erupted, spilling rivers of lava down the southern third of the island, and leading it to be abandoned as Montserrat's population dwindled to five thousand from twelve. Yet how peaceful it looked now from afar, an old *soufrière* enjoying a leisurely afternoon smoke, as I, at the helm while the skipper and Eric dozed, revelled in my first real experience of sailing by compass.

But that teasing interlude of calm and mastery is not what I principally remember. Rather, it is the moment, late in the afternoon, when suddenly and instinctively I looked behind me at our wake — at the spot where our tender, our lifeline to the shore, usually skipped happily behind us, securely tethered to the transom. It wasn't there.

"The dinghy's gone! The dinghy's gone!" I shouted.

"What?" The skipper clambered on deck, hauling up his trousers. "Oh, God! That's the worst possible thing that could happen."

I glanced at the cleat to which I had attached the tender that morning and, to my relief, the end of the painter was still there. This was not a calamity for which I was personally responsible.

"We're going back for it. What's our bearing?" the skipper asked as he took over the helm.

The wives protested. There was no telling when the dinghy had broken loose and the chances, in any event, of spotting it in a high sea seemed slim. Besides, it had been a long, tiring sail and it was important to get to Antigua before dark. Still, the skipper was adamant; so, with the main and Genoa still up and the engine started, we began retracing our route across the restless, rolling Caribbean.

Amazingly, within ten minutes the tender was spotted, and the Sweden 38 closed in on it.

"Okay, I'll bring us alongside. Terry, you try and drop in and attach a line."

I'm not sure I would have been particularly worried about my assignment had we not faced so many little misadventures over the preceding days. But I was anxious — anxious that the skipper with all his skill and experience might not be able to maneuver us in the two-metre waves close enough to the dinghy for me to jump in safely. I knew that if I missed, I would never reach the dinghy; the wind would take it away faster than I could possibly swim. Then my fate would be relatively swift. I knew that if I landed successfully in the tender, but somehow lost or could not attach the line and the dinghy slipped away, it was possible, in the heavy sea, that I would drift out of sight and not be found again. A slower end. I was anxious, too, about the commotion on deck, the uncertainty, as everyone debated how best to attempt the rescue. And I was concerned that we were all so focused on the gap closing between us and the dinghy that we had forgotten about our rigging. As we motored toward the dinghy, we kept crossing the path of the wind and the boom would fly across the deck each time almost clipping Eric on the head. He was, I was beginning to realize, prone to accidents.

On the first pass, we didn't get close enough to the tender for me to leave the yacht. And as we went about for a second try, we lost sight of the dinghy in a trough. Then we spotted it again and made another run. This time, for an instant, yacht and dinghy were side by side, and in that second I leapt over the rail and dropped into the tender.

On deck, Eric and Dot were tightly holding one end of a long rope, and at the other was a shackle in my hand that I had to attach to an eye near water level at the base of the dinghy's bow. The shackle, however, was not the type you snap on; it was an old one with a cotter pin that had to be screwed into the shackle. Leaning over the bow of the tender and trying to thread the pin as the dinghy heaved crazily in the waves, I dropped it. Involuntarily, I shouted, "I've lost it! I've lost it!"

Dot thought that the rope was gone and that now I was adrift at sea without a lifeline to the yacht. She began to scream.

In fact, everything was really all right. Forgetting about the shackle, I looped the rope through the eye on the tender's bow, knotted it, and pulled myself back to the yacht along the line.

"Well done," the skipper said quietly as I scrambled over the yacht's railing.

Breathless, dry, and shaking, I nevertheless felt proud of myself. I was maturing as a grinder. Good enough now to make the B team for a challenge for the America's Cup, by Liechtenstein maybe.

THE INTERIOR OF Antigua is uninteresting, undulating scrub land that was once completely covered in cane fields. Crumbling, cone-shaped windmills mark a region where 160 plantations flourished until late in the nineteenth century when European beet sugar replaced Caribbean cane. But the coastline of Antigua is magnificent. Wide, curving bays of gleaming white sand. A beach for every day of the year with some to spare. English Harbour is the centrepiece. In the seventeenth and eighteenth centuries, it was the principal British naval and military base in the Leeward Islands. Nelson was stationed here from 1784 to 1787, and his dockyards, abandoned late in the eighteenth century, have now been tastefully restored. The brick and stone warehouses, workshops, and living quarters house swanky hotels, gift shops, bars, restaurants, and a museum; but there are active chandleries and repair shops as well, for this is one of the busiest sailing harbours in the Caribbean and home of the famous Antigua Race Week.

From the fortifications at Shirley Heights above the harbour, there is also one of the most spectacular views in all the Caribbean, especially at sunset. On the horizon, silhouetted against the burning sky, you can see the volcanic peak at Montserrat, symbol of nature's destructive power, and below you the myriad masts of yachts in English and Falmouth Harbours, sheltered now from the capricious wrath of the sea.

But that view is not my most vivid recollection of Antigua. It is of the evening we safely arrived in English Harbour. After cocktails on deck, we crowded into our little dinghy, now more cherished than ever before, and in the dark of night we motored the length of English Harbour, weaving around other tenders doing the same, past ferries and tugs, and two- and three-masted schooners. It was probably a passage as dangerous as any we had taken at sea, but I don't think anyone noticed. Then we walked along a short, rough road to Falmouth Harbour to the Mad Mango, where we dined on barbecued shrimp and a rice pilau. The restaurant was packed with other sailors — mostly Brits, Aussies, and Americans in moccasins, khaki shorts, and white T-shirts emblazoned with the names of their yachts. Unlike us, they were mostly young, blond, and well tanned, but, like us, they were loud and boisterous — ready to "jump up" — as they, too, relived the highs and lows of the day.

That was the moment I finally understood what only began to dawn on me years before in Greece, the allure of adventure travel, whatever the challenge: trans-ocean single-handed sailing, polar crossings, isolated mountain climbs, off-piste skiing, hang-gliding, jungle hiking, or simply ignoring consular advisories. It is the high people experience from risk-taking — perhaps not so much at the moment when their lives are most in danger, but immediately afterward. The sudden release of tension when, at last, for the present, survival seems assured. And especially it is the exhilaration afterward of eating and drinking with friends who have shared your trauma. It is the delight, in comfort and safety, of reliving what happened, laughing about it, sharing different perspectives and feelings. It is experiencing the renewed sense of bravado that envelops a boisterous table after the danger has passed, and relishing the special bond that triumph over adversity forges.

It was at that moment, too, that Eric offered his own low-key, Englishman's analysis of the rescue of the tender. "I thought this is *not* good. But it's not *that* bad, either. Terry is a strong swimmer. If he misses the dinghy, he should be able to swim to it. And if we lose sight of him and the tender, Search and Rescue should reach him within twenty-four hours!"

The world is a perpetual caricature of itself;
at every moment it is the mockery and the
contradiction of what it is pretending to be.

*Soliloquies in England,*
GEORGE SANTAYANA

» ONE OF THE REWARDS of travelling and living abroad is being able afterward to picture far-off places and events. It gives them relevance wherever one is and whatever the time. When I see a TV image of peasants in loincloths gathered around a village pump on a sun-baked desert, I have a vague idea what they are feeling. On the hard, dusty plains of Uttar Pradesh, the five of us once consumed a case of Coke, hurtling between Delhi and Agra in 120-degree heat. When I listen to a symphony orchestra on our stereo, I can imagine I'm in the Great Hall of the Concertgebouw in Amsterdam, a gilded jewel box with almost-perfect acoustics, and my appreciation of the music I am listening to now is immeasurably enhanced as a result.

I felt that way recently visiting the Art Gallery of Greater Victoria on our way to Deb and Tad's home on Vancouver Island. My interest was augmented by my connection with some of its works in a different place many years before. The gallery houses a large and important collection of Chinese artifacts, a number of them, interestingly, gifts of Canada's former ambassador to China, Arthur Menzies, and his family in memory of the Rev. James M. Menzies, Arthur's father, a Presbyterian missionary in China from the 1910s to the 1930s. The first substantial donation, however, was the Chen King Foh Family Collection. It was critical in launching the gallery on the development of what is today "one of the most distinguished Far Eastern art collections in Canada." Acquired by the Chens over a period of more than a century, it includes ceramics and textiles dating from around 200 BC to 1790.

Browsing through the gallery's Chinese collection, I was disappointed to discover that none of these particular items were currently on display, for at one time I had felt very close to them, almost as if they were mine. Yet, afterward, I realized that it was only appropriate and also ironic that they were all stored away just as they had been back in 1970 when I saw them in crates at a Catholic orphanage in Jakarta. In one of my less noble acts as a Canadian diplomat, it was I who devised the means by which more than three hundred pieces in the collection were spirited away to Canada — in a move that missed an exceptional opportunity to foster closer Canadian-Indonesian relations.

Diplomacy, like politics, is, as Otto von Bismarck remarked, "the art of the possible." Grab what you can, to put it bluntly, when you have a chance. Don't expect too much, but be alert to every opportunity.

One day, not long after we arrived in Jakarta, a Canadian woman of Chinese origin who was a former citizen of Indonesia visited me in my stark embassy office. She was short, stocky, and middle-aged, a no-nonsense matriarch accustomed to running both her private and business affairs. She had in her hand a cheque for several thousand dollars made out to the embassy, and she wanted our assistance in arranging for a large proportion of her family's art collection to be shipped to her home in Canada. There, by prior arrangement, it was to be placed on extended loan in the Art Gallery of Greater Victoria.

"Can't do it," I told Mrs. Chen King Foh. "Not for a private collection. We can't just tell the Indonesian government it's a bunch of old embassy furniture we're shipping back to Canada. Some other countries might do that, but not us."

Not used to encountering obstacles, she looked displeased, her jaws clenching like a porcelain dragon, and we sat there silently while I mulled the matter over. I started thinking about the Trudeau government's foreign-policy review, published just that year. One of its six principal themes was more esoteric than the others, visionary in a way, an echo of Camelot. It was the notion of enhancing reciprocally the well-being of Canadians and other peoples through such things as cultural, educational, scientific, and industrial exchanges. The quality-of-life theme. As I saw it, I had a responsibility to breathe what air I could into this rather deflated aspect of the review. Bringing the remainder of the Chen King Foh collection to Canada would qualify.

"You know, there is one way we could help you," I said at last. "If you're willing to make your collection a gift to Canada, then we would be in a position to approach the Indonesian government for an export permit. We would be asking, in effect, for permission to ship to Canada property of our own government. The Indonesians might find it hard to refuse. Think it over. Discuss it with your lawyer."

Mrs. Chen called me back a few days later to confirm she was agreeable to the plan. So I advised the ambassador of the discussions I had with her, and he agreed to my nefarious scheme. A deed of gift was duly drafted and signed, donating the Chen King Foh collection to Canada on the understanding that the works would be housed permanently in the Art Gallery of Greater Victoria. Then I prepared a formal note to the Indonesian foreign ministry, requesting an export permit for the collection — for these valuable works of art now owned by the government of Canada.

Not long after, I was summoned to the cultural-affairs branch of the foreign ministry, where I drank a glass of that ubiquitous orange soda with a kindly civil servant nearing retirement age. He looked at me with a wry, knowing smile unlike any I had experienced in Bangkok. Even though I knew a confrontation loomed, I felt comfortable in a way I never did in the offices of Thai officials. There, bureaucratic faces — even smiling ones — were always inscrutable, and it unnerved me to watch assistants, ordered brusquely by their superiors to fetch files, back out of a room crouching, bowing, and *wai-ing* all the way to the door. Indonesia was different. There was a relaxed openness dealing with official-dom even in the face of disagreement, a subtle understanding — the product, perhaps, of the country's colonial past.

"You Canadians make things very difficult," the foreign-ministry official shook his head slowly. "Why didn't you deal with these artifacts the way the French would?" He meant, of course, why *didn't* we just say we had old embassy furniture we wanted to ship home. "There may be important works of art in this collec-tion that should never leave Indonesia. We can't let it go without an inspection."

"That would be difficult," I responded. "Everything is already stored in crates at an orphanage, ready for shipment. It would be very expensive to have to unpack and repack everything."

He poured me another glass of soda. "I'm sorry, we must do an examination."

"Suppose," I responded, "you do just a spot check of a few crates. We'll also give you a complete inventory you can go over."

Again, he flashed that knowing smile as if to say, *Your approach is different. Ingenuous. Superficially honourable, perhaps. But at heart you're no different than the rest.* But then to my surprise he nodded his assent, and we arranged a date and time to meet for the inspection.

WANDERING THROUGH the cheery Art Gallery of Greater Victoria, discussing the Chen King Foh Collection with Barry Till, the gallery's curator of Asian art, I felt I was back again in the bleak courtyard of that orphanage in Jakarta. I could see Mrs. Chen, the foreign-ministry official, several people from the department of cul-tural affairs, and myself all clustered around a huge stack of heavy crates, fastened with thick bamboo straps. Randomly, the govern-ment officials chose cartons to be opened, and with much sweat and exertion, the bindings were cut away, the tops of the crates pried loose and the packing paper removed. Out poured delicate figurines, vases, bowls, cups and saucers from the Han to the Ch'ing dynasty. Then, from the largest of the containers, they carefully removed long, elegant black screens — room dividers made of ebony with chunks of polished jade liberally embedded in the panels.

I studied the men from cultural affairs closely as they ran their hands over some items and carried others for a closer inspection into a shaft of light that streaked across the flagstone courtyard. Mrs. Chen was impassive but tense. It seemed like more than an hour went by on each crate, but I suppose it was only minutes. Then, at last, miraculously, the foreign-ministry official snorted, "There's nothing here of interest to us!"

Mrs. Chen and I relaxed. The game of Russian roulette, it seemed, had worked. But then the officer rummaged in his pocket for his copy of the full inventory. "There are, however, two stone Buddha heads listed here that we would like to see. They may be very rare."

I shook my head. "We can't do that without opening all the crates. We don't know what is in each one."

"We do need to examine them," he said gently, but insistently.

*Trouble,* I thought. It wasn't so much the time and expense of opening everything as it was the risk of exposing valuable works the Indonesians would not let us have. But my diplomatic training had made me persistent. "Suppose you let the collection go. Once it's unpacked in Victoria, we'll have the stone Buddha heads photographed and the prints sent to you. Then, if you decide you want those pieces back, by all means, they'll be sent. We can draft a written understanding."

Once more the comprehending smile. *This is the price we have to pay for your economic aid.* "I'll let you know," the ministry official responded at last, and we all left the orphanage.

Several days later, my friend at the foreign ministry phoned to say he had secured agreement to let the collection go on condition the stone Buddha heads were returned if requested. There was, however, one remaining hurdle before an export permit could be issued: a security clearance had to be conducted on Mrs. Chen King Foh.

"A security clearance?" I was momentarily surprised. How could that in any way be germane? But this was Indonesia. And it was only five years since the country had been wrenched by what was alleged to have been an abortive communist coup surreptitiously supported by the Chinese Peoples Republic. In the aftermath, thousands of Indonesians of Chinese descent had been massacred. Suspicion of the Chinese community was still endemic. Besides, I knew that Mrs. Chen's late husband had been a friend of the recently deposed president, Sukarno. If there were to be a security check, the situation was hopeless, I thought. We would never get the export permit now.

Throughout this affair, we had been keeping Ottawa informed of our progress with the Chen King Foh collection. Only now, with this news of a sudden snag, did there come any response. Someone — frustrated ambassadors always envisage a lowly, probationary desk officer with time on his hands — had suddenly remembered the quality-of-life theme of the Trudeau review. It was *supposed* to be reciprocal. Of course! What we needed to do was sweeten the Indonesians' disposition by offering them a collection of Canadian art in return. By telex we were instructed to advise the foreign ministry that, in exchange for the precious Chen King Foh Collection, Indonesia was to receive the following donation of Canadian art: two dozen Inuit soapstone carvings and a contemporary replica of a British Columbia totem pole. Total estimated value: $3,000. The art of the parsimonious.

Much to our amazement, before we even had an opportunity to advise the Indonesian government of Canada's munificence, a formal note arrived from the foreign ministry authorizing export of the Chen King Foh collection to Canada. Somehow, Mrs. Chen had managed to sail through the security check. Helped, no doubt, by the persuasive powers of my wise old friend in the cultural-affairs branch, conscious of his country's developmental needs.

Duty-bound, we telexed the good news to Ottawa.

I still can't believe it. But it is true. Almost immediately, we received back a telex advising us that if we had not yet notified the Indonesian authorities of the gift from Canada, then we should "NOT REPEAT NOT" do so. The government, we were told, had very limited funds available for artistic exchanges.

I LEFT THE ART GALLERY of Greater Victoria with considerable reluctance. It had transported me back in time to a notorious moment in my diplomatic career—to a perfidious deed—and the memories, while not altogether pleasant, gave added meaning to the Chinese collection I had just admired. But it was after 2:00 PM and the others were hungry.

We went for lunch in the city's pristine Chinese quarter. It smells of the sea rather than garlic and rotting vegetables as if created by an edict of Singapore's Lee Kuan Yew. "So what happened?" Tad asked me, sucking back the noodles in his soup. "Did the Indonesians get our stuff?"

"Yes," I said. "We never told Ottawa we hadn't yet informed them about the gift when the telex came withdrawing the offer."

"Good."

Dot and Deb weren't listening. They were dissecting the contents of their bowls, comparing them with Dot's Stuffed Cucumber Soup, adapted from one Jaraway used to make for us in Bangkok. "Still, I've always wondered where our pieces ended up. The public galleries were in terrible shape and lacked space as it was. The last thing the Indonesians needed was a token donation of Canadian art, especially a fake totem pole."

"Who knows? Maybe it's in a rice paddy somewhere," Tad joked as he raided Deb's noodles. "I'll bet it's enhanced some farmer's quality of life!"

"That's possible," I laughed. "Just possible."

## STUFFED CUCUMBER SOUP
### SERVES 4

4–5 cups pork stock*
½ pound lean ground pork
½ tsp basil
½ tsp oregano
⅛ tsp salt
4 gherkins (small, fresh
    cucumbers)
2 cups roughly broken rice
    vermicelli noodles
4 oyster mushrooms, sliced
2 whole cloves garlic
2 tbsp crudely chopped fresh
    coriander leaves, plus
    extra to garnish
¼–½ tsp chopped hot red chili
    pepper, plus extra to pass
20–25 snow peas, trimmed
    and stringed
salt and paper to taste

* Pork stock can be made by
    simmering spareribs or pork
    hocks in 5–6 cups water to which
    have been added: 1 onion,
    chopped; 1–2 bay leaves; a few
    dashes of Tabasco sauce, and
    1 tablespoon white vinegar.
    The resulting stock can be chilled
    to facilitate removing excess fat
    and frozen until required.

» Combine pork, basil, oregano, and salt. Peel cucumbers and cut in half crosswise. Gently scoop out seeds and a little flesh to form a deep cavity, being careful not to pierce casings. Stuff with pork mixture. Form extra stuffing into small meatballs.

» Heat stock in a medium-sized pot. Add noodles, mushrooms, garlic, coriander, and chili pepper. Stir briefly. Add meatballs. Carefully add stuffed cucumbers, meat end up.

» Simmer covered very gently for 20–30 minutes until vegetables are tender and pork is cooked. Add snow peas for last 5–10 minutes of cooking. Pass extra chili peppers and coriander.

TIM » I'VE NEVER LEARNED how to make a proper crêpe, although I do remember my first crêperie experience vividly. We'd taken the ferry from Newhaven to Dieppe on a school break. Dad had one of those *France on Five Dollars a Day* guide books. He took the title literally. It was his bible.

Looking back, I realize that we experienced French cuisine the way everyone should for the first time. The great French steak frites after all is overrated. We ate picnics. Bread and cheese and pâté and, if lucky, a roasted chicken. But the crêperie was a turning point. A rare restaurant moment and a lesson in the true metaphysics of a simple meal—the dance of life between appetizer and dessert.

The crêperie of note was in Britanny, near the end of the trip. I had become difficult to deal with by this point, constantly complaining about having to put up with the same old picnic lunches and dinners every day. I hadn't learned to appreciate the delicate simplicity of a fresh French baguette, jam, and hot choco-late for breakfast or pâté and bread, camembert, and apples for lunch. But I was young and innocent and thus forgivable. I wanted sustenance. I wanted hot food.

Any meal in my family is preceded by a walk. I have learned over the years that it is the most important part of the meal. It is the real *soupe du jour*, and it is particulary important when preparing to eat in a foreign country. There should be a recipe for the walk. It must be a significant outing. The pre-lunch walk should focus on the city or village in which one plans to dine. The after-lunch walk, which, in many ways, is equally important, can focus on the outlying countryside if one exists. But the pre-lunch walk should take you through the heart of the community — the back alleys and residential areas. It should take place at a low simmer for about thirty minutes to an hour. Be careful: with youngsters it's easy to overcook. Dad was a disastrous chef in this regard.

As a kid, I always hated the pre-lunch walk. I'd be too hungry to pay attention to the things that mattered around me. But I know now that there was logic in my father's single-mindedness. The walk heightens the senses. It prepares the nose, the taste buds, and the mind for the meal ahead. It is during the pre-lunch walk that the true flavours of a region come out. Even the unsavoury things are important. Open sewers. The little *amuse-gueule* left behind in a country overrun with dogs. There are also the pleasant odours. The locals preparing their own foods. Garlic wafting through open windows, fresh bread cooling on the window sill.

There is one critical ingredient that must never be left out of a pre-lunch walk in a foreign country, and that is conversation — not just conversation among the members of your party, but with the locals. Dad has an unwritten rule when travelling. Contact with at least one local must always be made before lunch. Language barriers are part of the fun. Mom, Karen, Deb, and I once had a two-hour conversation with a German hotel owner who didn't speak a word of English. We didn't speak a word of German. We recognized the word Babylon.

On this particular day, our walk took us through a small fishing town on the Brittany coast — a sunny, warm spring day. In the harbour, people were out working on the boats, or heading off for an afternoon of sailing. The smell of the sea was strong on the air as fishermen unloaded their morning catch. Seafood crêpe. I remember the clanging noise sailboats make as the ropes hit the mast. Waves breaking. People calling to one another. The occasional motorboat.

Before long, my father approached a man in his early thirties who was working on his sailboat. "Beautiful day," he started off with a recognizably non-French accent and the banality of some-one attempting conversation with a stranger in a foreign language. After answering the obvious questions about where we were from and what we thought of France, the conversation turned to the man's boat. He had bought it only a few days earlier and was fix-ing it up, leaning precariously over the water to paint a new name on the stern, *Esperance*. The day is fresh in my mind years later.

THE MAIN COURSE was nothing spectacular, but I can still taste it. I had a ham-and-cheese crêpe. Maybe it was because we were near the end of the trip and were under budget, or perhaps it was because, for once, I hadn't complained when my father muttered his obligatory "one more block before lunch." Whatever the reason, on that particular day I was told I could order dessert.

Now this was no ordinary dessert. It was a baptism. Never before had I experienced or appreciated such a subtle balance of flavours. Chocolate, ice cream, crêpe, and fresh fruit, all height-ened by the strong yet pleasant shock of Grand Marnier. It came to the table on fire, which made me feel like a child millionaire. I was transformed. I shared. I offered suggestions as to the route for our after-lunch walk. It left me with incredibly clear thoughts, a sense of balance—harmony. I lingered over the last mouthful, soaking up every ingredient, aware of my breathing, of the way the afternoon light was poised at the edge of our table. The cheque came. My father paid. I thanked him. We stood. We made our way to the door.

FORTUNATELY, I DIDN'T see him clearly through the commotion —only his wet hair as an ambulance attendant pulled the blanket over his face. Little about the day had changed. A crowd had gathered, and the sun was a little lower in the sky. Boats still came and went. We stood together, silent for a moment in the ethereal space between delight and despair. And then we walked.

## DESSERT CRÊPE

» The Bretons might not agree, but making a great dessert crêpe doesn't have to be an elaborate enterprise. Ready-to-use crêpes available in most grocery stores will do.

» Throw one in a frying pan — no oil — and heat quickly, 20 seconds a side, max.

» Put the warmed crêpe on a plate. Place a scoop of vanilla ice cream in the middle. Ladle on some maple syrup — maybe 3 ounces. Add one shot of rye whisky.

» Gather the crêpe over the mound of ice cream. Garnish with fresh fruit such as blueberries and raspberries. To fancy it up, sprinkle on some sifted, powdered sugar. Serve immediately.

---

## SEAFOOD CRÊPES
### SERVES 4

*Crêpes*
2 eggs, beaten,
2 tbsp vegetable oil
1 cup milk
½ cup all-purpose flour
¼ tsp salt
butter to grease pan

» Combine wet ingredients. Gradually beat them into dry ingredients until batter is smooth and creamy (or blend all together in blender).

» Heat a lightly buttered small non-stick frying pan or crêpe pan until the butter is hot but not burnt. Lift the hot pan from the heat and pour about 3 tablespoons of the crêpe mixture into its centre. Quickly twist the pan so that the batter runs to thinly cover the bottom.

» Cook the crêpe over medium heat, carefully flipping once so that both sides are golden but not brown. Gently lift crêpe onto bread board or plate to cool. Lightly rebutter pan and repeat process. Makes about 12 medium-sized crêpes. Stack between wax paper.

## Filling

1 can flaked crab meat, well-drained (squeeze liquid out by hand)
½–¾ pounds salad shrimp, cooked and peeled
¼ pound mushrooms, sliced and lightly sautéed
1 tsp fines herbes
scant ½ cup sauce (see below)

» Mix above ingredients together in a medium-sized bowl. Evenly divide filling among 8–10 crêpes and roll them up.

## Sauce

2 generous tbsp butter or margarine
5 tbsp all-purpose flour
1½ cups milk
1 cup light cream (half and half)
1 tsp Dijon-style mustard
½ cup freshly grated Parmesan cheese, plus extra for topping
1 egg yolk
2 tbsp dry white wine or sherry
1 tbsp chopped fresh parsley, plus extra for topping
2 green onions, chopped
salt and pepper to taste

» Over low heat, melt butter or margarine in a saucepan. Gradually add flour, stirring until blended. Add milk and cream, gradually stirring with a wire whisk over medium-low heat until sauce is thick and smooth. Stir in mustard. Add cheese and blend until melted. Whisk in egg yolk, wine, parsley, and salt and pepper. Heat but do not boil.

» Arrange rolled crêpes in an oven-proof dish. Cover with sauce, making sure sauce runs under crêpes as well as over. Sprinkle with extra cheese, parsley, and the chopped green onion. Heat in a moderate oven (350) until bubbly and brown (20–30 minutes).

» DESPITE WHAT TIM SAYS, I don't always force march the family for an hour before lunch. They can play tennis, go skiing, skating, swimming, ride a bike. I'm really very flexible.

But Tim's right. When we're travelling, the usual option is a walk. The necessary gear and conditions are often not available for other pre-gastronomic pursuits. And walking is the best way to get to know a new patch of countryside, a village, or even a city. Many of the latter, after all, are really only clusters of towns that sprouted over a long growing season, and during an extended stay you can pick them off one by one before lunch.

There are, I contend, only three choices when it comes to food, travelling, and the body. You can eat and drink whatever and however much you want, not exercise, and get fat. In that case, before long, the legs won't take you comfortably up the stone steps of Petra or Machu Picchu and the will to wander the world will languish. At the same time, it may take culinary masterpieces, probably served up at exorbitant prices, to really whet the appetite. Second, you can worry through life on a strict, boring diet, eschewing every tasty temptation, not drink, not exercise much, and stay thin. But then half the pleasure of travel — searching out (usually by foot) and experimenting with the local produce — is lost, and one becomes a miserable wretch that no one wants to go anywhere with anyway. Or finally, I submit, you can eat and drink within reasonable limits, exercise vigorously, and stay fit and slim enough to please anyone but the editor of *Vogue* or *Cosmopolitan*. Then the joy of travel never dissipates and even simple meals, prepared creatively with fresh, local products, have the potential for greatness.

By and large our family has pursued this third option, with only occasional digressions by some of its number to the other two. These have never lasted long, however. An imperious father's call to "lace up" has generally carried the day.

Several times in the past, we had gone for short walks with friends in the same area of the Ligurian Alps in northern Italy. At a point where two paths crossed and we always took the one that led to a good place to swim in a stream, you could see in the distance, peeking out from a heavy green blanket of forest the cupola of a church and the orange rooftops of a small village. It was at the top of a V-shaped valley several hundred feet above us, and it seemed clear that the path we never followed would wind its way around the valley and eventually climb to the village. I asked the person who organized these outings if he knew its name and had ever hiked to it. He didn't and he hadn't. But each time we returned from our picnic and swim in the stream and reached the fork in the paths, I looked longingly toward that village and I knew someday we would have to mount an expedition to it.

The moment came when Tad was travelling with us, early in his courtship of Deb. I told them about the village deep in the hills and the little trattoria that would be in its central square — no Italian community worth the name was without one. It would have simple wooden chairs and tables under the shade of two olive trees or a trellis smothered in grape vines. A man with hunched shoulders, blue overalls, and a black beret would welcome us, and when he learned that we had come by foot from the valley floor and that we were Canadians, the greeting would take on extra warmth and energy. China jugs of the *ristorante*'s own wine would immediately be placed on our table, and a short, round lady in a black dress, her grey hair tied up in a tight bun, would peek through the plastic strips of curtain at us as we settled expectantly around the table.

There might be a menu, but more likely the old man would ask us what we would like and then suggest what we should have and we would defer to his judgment. Fleetingly, we might suspect that there really wasn't a choice. But no matter, with what the old lady had on hand, she would prepare the perfect, simple feast for four hungry trekkers. There would be an antipasto of various salamis, anchovies, olives, pickles, and local vegetables, followed by ravioli in a rose cream sauce, perhaps an escalope of veal parmigiana, and finally a huge bowl of fruit — red and green grapes, oranges, pears, and plums. The jugs of lively red wine would never empty. Then, as at Gorbio, at the end of the meal, the old man and his wife would sit at the table with us and, using a mélange of Italian, French, English, and gesticulations, we would tell them where we were living and how we happened to come to their village, and we would learn about the sister living in Toronto and the cousins in New York.

Tad was already salivating as we struck out along the right fork in the path. Tall, broad-chested, and muscular, he is never off his feed. The rooftops of the distant village burned bright orange in the morning sun like markers in a channel, guiding us safely to sustenance. Soon we discovered, however, that the direction of the path was almost at right angles to the village. We were moving up the valley toward it — sort of — but at an excruciatingly slow pace, and we were getting more and more to starboard of that splash of orange. It was as if we were in a dinghy close hauled to the wind, trying to tack around a buoy, but our centreboard was up and we kept sliding away from the marker.

We were about an hour into the hike, negotiating our way along the edge of a terraced olive grove, when I suddenly pulled up with a jolt. I slapped my left hand on my pant leg and felt nothing where my wallet ought to have been. I had left it in the glove compartment of the car!

Dot stared at me in disbelief and Deb let out a long, forlorn, "oh, nooooooooo." Tad looked at me disgustedly, "You did *what*?"

He said it with an emphasis I'm used to now, as when we're paired in tennis and I make a bad shot. "*What* was *that?*" he'll jeer. Only at tennis, never golf where he harbours no illusions. But then Tad chortled at our predicament and everyone began to laugh.

We sat down on the white, stony edge of a terrace to decide what to do. We had gone too far to return to the car for my wallet, yet we appeared to be only about halfway up the valley to the village. Pockets were searched for loose change and the sum total counted. Lunch was clearly out of the question, but there might be enough for a glass each of wine or cassis. The deceptive route of the path had made me even more determined to explore that village and Deb at least wanted to see the trattoria where we would have lunched. She has a determined streak; I can't imagine where she gets it. So we pressed on.

For a while, it was as if the wind had changed direction and we were able to head toward the marker with no slippage. But then the valley narrowed and took a sharp turn to the right. Now, between us and the village there was a deep gorge, presumably with a river at the base. The path was taking us almost 180 degrees away from the village and it was sloping downward toward the river bed. We had to follow it until the valley narrowed further and there was a bridge across the river.

Once we had crossed, we knew we were far to the right of the orange marker, but we couldn't see it any longer. It was hidden in the trees above us. In the descent to the river, we had lost most of what we had gained in our earlier slow climb up the wide middle of the valley. So now the path headed back to the left and it rose steeply toward the village, which we calculated was still at least two kilometres away.

The scout leader sensed a frostiness in response to his efforts to bolster the spirits of the expedition. For Dot, I knew, it was all too much like the descent from the Pic de Baudon. I, on the other hand, was still optimistic that everything would turn out okay. Just as at Gorbio, we would find a wonderful trattoria; probably they would even give us lunch on a promise to pay them later. The Italians would never let us go hungry.

When we finally got to the village, it was well past lunchtime and the town was deep into its siesta. Shutters on the peeling grey walls were pulled tight against the hot white light in the azure sky. The children and dogs were silent. From one window, there issued the scratchy voice of a tenor—on an old wind-up record player, it seemed—singing a mournful aria from *Tosca*.

We trudged silently into the centre of the village—a dusty square of houses, maybe five storeys tall, the same as on all the streets. There *was* a curtain of orange, white, and blue strips of plastic on a hole in a wall that led to a small shop where we were able to buy two bottles of water. But there were no olive trees in the square. There was no vine-covered trellis, no wooden tables and chairs in the shade. No jugs of cool, young wine. No trattoria! No Gorbio!

"*What* is *this*?" Tad sneered in my direction. "*This* is Italy?"

"I can't believe it!" Deb said with some sympathy. She was more inclined than the others to my view that *no* Italian village could be without a place to eat and drink.

"Oh, I can believe it, Deb!" Dot said with the conviction of years of tramping the countryside with me.

Leg-weary, we made our way back to the bridge across the river. There we sat dangling our feet over the edge while we had our lunch—two bottles of Evian water. I tried a feeble toast. I think it was to Tim who'd presciently passed on this particular pre-lunch walk. But the reception was cooler than the water that had by now warmed in our backpack.

There was no conversation as we climbed out of the narrow section of the valley where the river flowed. But a little later, when we were on more even ground, Dot finally said, "So what do you guys want for dinner?"

"What have you got in?" I asked.

Dot went over the stores and the various possibilities.

"What do you feel like cooking?" Deb inquired.

"I don't know." Then a little later she smiled, "I know. How about veal spaghettini?"

"Sounds great!" we all concurred.

The remainder of the trek back to the car was on a downward slope and went very quickly. Dot was preoccupied visualizing the meal she would prepare. Deb and I were deep into an analysis of how it might have come to pass that the village had no *ristorante*. Tad was alone in the lead and setting a torrid pace. Another swig of water had soothed his scorched throat and dry tongue. He was salivating again.

---

*Since that infamous hike, we've called it "Pissed-Off Pasta," and it can be made with whatever is on hand. It's surprisingly quick to prepare and gourmet enough to woo wounded appetites. Vary quantities as desired, but use lots of garlic and crunchy vegetables:*

**VEAL SPAGHETTINI**
SERVES 4 TO 6

4–6 pieces veal or pork scallopine (thaw quickly from the freezer)
garlic powder
breadcrumbs
salt and pepper to taste

» Sprinkle veal with garlic powder, dredge in breadcrumbs and set aside.

3–4 slices of fried bacon (set aside to crumble and add at the end)
4 tbsp extra virgin olive oil
1 onion, coarsely chopped
4–6 cloves garlic, chopped
½ pound mushrooms, sliced

Some or all of as available:
1 head broccoli, broken into flowerets
1 zucchini, sliced
½ green and ½ red and/or

yellow bell peppers, chopped
   or sliced
½ cup frozen green peas
a few snow peas, trimmed
   and stringed
1 thin stick pepperoni, cut in
   bite-sized pieces and/or bits
   of dry salami, prosciutto
10–15 Greek olives (Kalamata),
   pitted and sliced
2 green onions, chopped
¼ tsp hot red-pepper flakes
freshly grated Parmesan cheese

spaghettini pasta

» Stir-fry vegetables, garlic, and dried meats in 2 tablespoons olive oil, adding items that need little cooking last. Vegetables should be crunchy.

» Add bacon and hot red-pepper flakes. Toss with cooked pasta and 2 tablespoons olive oil until well mixed. Add more olive oil as necessary to moisten pasta. Remove to serving dish.

» Quickly sauté veal in frying pan used for stir-fry, adding oil, if needed. Veal should be just pink inside and golden outside. Serve immediately with pasta.

» Pass cheese, pepper grinder, and olive oil.

» WHEN YOU TRAVEL mainly "no star," one of the great pleasures is to have dinner at a really ritzy hotel to observe how the rich and famous are doing it. Maybe that sounds excessively lavish even as a one-time splurge on a tightly budgeted holiday. With wine, dessert and liqueurs at a five star, wouldn't the bill be $300 or more?

Not so. It is doable, and for as little as $50 a couple. Indeed, that is one of Dot's and my favourite ways to end a day of sight-seeing, in London in particular. We love to go to Brown's, Claridge's, the Connaught, or the Ritz for dinner. However, you can do it anywhere in the world for about the same price.

It means having dinner in the lounge or bar instead of the cav-ernous, half-empty main dining room with its too-stiff chairs and waiters, tables set so far apart that it's hopeless to eavesdrop.

The lounge is best if you are dining early. It is likely to be packed then, stylish women in their latest outfits from Harrod's surveying all the tables, suited business executives from the City earnestly assessing how the merger talks went that afternoon. There will probably be one or two tweeded tables of country gen-try — in London to take in a play or ballet. Especially at Brown's or the Basel. I didn't mention the Basel. That's an old family favourite, and dinner there runs less than $50. The glassed-in lounge on the second floor is very private and it's tastefully deco-rated with oriental paintings and carpets, a tiled fireplace, chintz curtains, and matching chairs. Besides, it's close to Harrod's, so if you've been there to gawk at the shoppers, you can spy on them again at the hotel.

Yes, the lounge is best early, and you can't beat it for eaves-dropping.

The Ritz has a great lounge, elegantly appointed in cream and gold. It's up a few steps from the foyer and gives you an excellent view of everyone passing through the hotel. The main dining room is off to the left as you look out so you can keep an eye on those with the means to go there for a more elaborate meal. And the Ritz's lounge is always crowded so there are lots of conversations you can attempt to follow unobtrusively.

We like hotel bars if we're dining late. Brown's is a favourite. It's swanky but intimate. It's fun to sink back into the soft chairs when the room is almost deserted, resting before the arrival of the post-theatre crowd or the stragglers from the dining room coming for a liqueur or Irish coffee. It's a good time to chat with the bartender and learn a little about his clientele, maybe get a tip on the Derby.

Oh, yes, and what to have for dinner? We always have Manhattans on the rocks. I suppose they're best in New York—the Oak Room bar at the Park Plaza was tops— but they serve an excellent Manhattan in all the great hotels of the world. The first course comes with the cocktails. A big bowl of nuts. Sometimes classy potato chips. But usually not on their own; they come along with the nuts. And I don't mean peanuts like you'd get in some ordinary bar. Mixed nuts, or maybe a straight bowl of cashews, almonds, or pistachios. Sometimes, other hors d'oeuvres may even be passed around on silver trays.

We empty our bowl or bowls with our first cocktails and then order another Manhattan to split. Depending on the predilections of the bartender, that might mean that we are served just one Manhattan full to the brim. If we are lucky, however, we'll get two, poured to just a shade below the top. With the drink or drinks come fresh bowls of chips and nuts. Indeed, the waiter will probably have noticed how we attacked them the first time and ensure that he doesn't skimp with the refills. These are classy hotels, don't forget. They want their patrons to be happy. Sometimes Dot will boldly ask the waiter to be liberal with the cashews and he will dutifully oblige.

To enhance the occasion, we give the dishes the names they might be given in the dining room: *un panier de fruits à écale salés et panachés*, or *noix de cajou dans un bol d'argent*. By the time we are nearing the end of our second helpings, we are stuffed and have easily exceeded our daily caloric limit. Besides, we'll look more stylish, we know, if we leave a few scraps in the bowls. So we do that, and we lean back in our chairs as content as we would be after a rack of lamb, spiced with sage and rosemary, or a bouillabaisse with delights from all the seven seas.

NOT LONG AGO, at Brown's, we watched a waiter carefully arrange champagne glasses at a table near us. Later, he brought a large bottle of Paul Roger, decorked it, and set it in a silver bucket. No one came. The waiter returned, fluffed up the chairs, and fussed over some flowers. Still no one. Intrigued as to who these important patrons might be, we ordered another Manhattan and went on staring at that empty table and the tall bottle of champagne slowly losing its fizz. We had almost finished our drinks when the waiter returned once more. This time, he whisked away the champagne bottle and glasses, quickly brushing the table and chairs at the same time as if they had been occupied all along. For us, of course, it was as if they had been. We'd passed a happy hour speculating excitedly about the occupants who would have entertained us— lovers forced to abandon their plans due to a suspicious spouse, MPs delayed by a late vote in the Commons, perhaps, or a wealthy heiress locked in her suite in depression over the styling choice of her venturesome hairdresser.

We were by then rather mellow and, as the waiter passed our table, it was hard to resist stopping him and asking if he would mind topping up our glasses with a little of the neglected bubbly, and, at the same time, inquiring about the identity of the guests who had appeared as apparitions only. But conjecture was richer in possibilities than reality so, instead, I simply motioned with my hand for the bill, signed the chit, and we left.

"Taxi, sir?" the doorman asked.

"No, thanks," we responded cheerfully and headed contentedly to the tube.

» WE FOUND FLORIDA pretty much as expected. None of us was particularly enthusiastic about going there, but we knew we had to try it one winter. Everyone does; it's really a requirement of being Canadian—like going to Niagara Falls, and just as predictable.

We envisaged an unbroken chain of highrise condominiums and hotels—a coastal Great Wall of China, unvarying in character from end to end. And that is what we found. Just back from the shore along a dusty, well-travelled road, we anticipated a tawdry strip of bars, restaurants, souvenir shops, bowling alleys, and miniature golf courses with forest-green carpets for grass. Anastasia Island outside St. Augustine had all that. We were prepared for fish, burgers, and ribs, served with greasy fries to porky people in shorts and flapping, floral shirts. Florida would not, we knew, offer a varied international cuisine, and it did not. We expected the air to be hot and humid, restricting our tennis to early mornings and evenings, and the weather, too, did not surprise us.

It did, however, come as a shock to discover that on our strip of beach—as well as others—cars were permitted to cruise the shore and park wherever they pleased. Thus, by mid-afternoon, the Great Wall of highrises appeared reinforced by a long, thin line of tanks between the ocean and the grassy dunes behind the beach, their turrets pointing menacingly seaward. The cars were particularly disconcerting at night, we found, when, strolling the almost-deserted shore under a canopy of stars, we had to shield our eyes from the glare of their headlights as they advanced toward us along the beach. It required faith in the sanity of their drivers—a faith not deeply held after all we had read about drive-by killings in the Sunshine State—that they would not mercilessly mow us down, innocent infantry in a nasty, mechanized war. What bizarre thinking on the part of municipal councillors, what ineptitude in the departments of tourism and highways, or what arcane clause in the United States constitution allows for this right to take tanks onto the beach? And in a state whose citizens by all appearances would clearly benefit from the exertion of walking from parking lot to shore! This was one thing about Florida for which we were not prepared.

We walked the heart of St. Augustine, an attractive city of gracious mansions and gardens that retains a Spanish flavour from the days of Ponce De Leon. And we did the standard sights — Marineland and Disney World. And they were as predicted. But for all Tim was primed beforehand for the latter, he still didn't handle it well on the big day. He was never one for Donald Duck or Mickey Mouse on a Saturday morning in front of the box, preferring to make up his own characters in his own stories. He was also never readily cowed into going along with the crowd — by parent, teacher, or huckster with a mic or megaphone. So I'm not sure it would have been better if we had taken him to Disney World when he was tiny, but it was certainly too late at twenty-five.

As we sped down the 195, gazing skeptically at the solid phalanx of motels and hotels from Orlando to Disney World—a second line of defence behind the coastal Great Wall—he started shaking his head. When we exited at the Disney turn, finding ourselves still on a four-lane highway into Walt's Wonder, and tuned into the radio frequency for Disney info, he cried, "I'm not ready for this, guys, I'm not ready!"

Eventually, massive parking lots fanned out from the highway like vast expanses of hard sand beach, though more densely packed with vehicles than the strip on Anastasia Island. An attendant waved us into a rapidly filling section and, as we alighted, a loud voice bellowed over a microphone: "You are parked in Goofy 26 to 32. Remember, you are in Goofy 26 to 32 or you will not find your way back to your car. Goofy 26 to 32." Tim ducked his head as we walked quickly to the line of trains waiting to take us to the entry gate, afraid, perhaps, that someone might recognize him — some erstwhile friend from Grade 5 at Princess Anne. Climbing onto the train, another voice spoke to us through a speaker on the ceiling: "Five people to each row. Please move together. Five people to each row." Involuntarily, we stiffened.

At the entry gate, we waited patiently in a long line while we continued to be bombarded with amplified instructions. Everything was repeated over and over again; at Disney World they expect short attention spans.

For our day excursion, we had selected — perhaps wrongly in hindsight — the Magic Kingdom. For a first or only visit, it was the best thing to do, we had been told. But our choice meant that, after the entry gate, we had to line up yet again to take a ferry across a lake. Then we had to pass through yet another gate before we faced the option of queuing up in any one of a number of daunting lines for "rides" to magical places: the jungle rivers of the world, 20,000 Leagues Under the Sea, Mars.

Apart from Tim, we all flung ourselves into the experience as optimistically as we could, determined to extract as much perverse pleasure from our day as possible. We chatted amiably with our fellow queuers. We admired the cleanliness of Disney World, the efficiency with which garbage was removed, the feel of its recon-structed turn-of-the century Western main street, the attractive designs of its shops and restaurants, its pretty flowerbeds and ponds — its utter artificiality. For Tad, the essence of the Magic Kingdom was food and he launched himself on a feeding frenzy the likes of which I have seen only in pie- and pancake-eating con-tests. From noon to five, he consumed three hamburgers, two hot dogs, two boxes of French fries, three soda pops, two ice-cream waffles, a box of popcorn, a candy apple, and God knows what else I missed. For Deb and me, it was the rides. We ooohed and aaahed at the paper mâché animals that loomed before us. When every voyage reached the inevitable moment of crisis — the submarine, *Nautilus*, in trouble on the seabed; the spaceship losing its protective outer skin as it hurtled bumpily through the atmosphere to earth — we screamed. And, afterward, as we disembarked from each ride, we exclaimed, "Phew! That was a close one!"

But not Tim. He never got into the spirit of Disney World. Like most Canadians, the most important thing to him about a Florida vacation was soaking up the sun. So every time a line in which we were standing moved from sunlight to shade, he gave up in frustration and searched out another. So, for much of the day, we parted ways, though periodically we would run into him wandering aimlessly through the kingdom, a fallen knight in plastic armour without a ride. "I'm not having fun, people," he moaned, "not having fun." Around four o'clock, he gave up altogether and announced, "Time to go, everyone, time to go." All he had got out of Disney was a predilection for repeating himself.

When we announced we couldn't leave before we had seen the parade of Disney characters, which wasn't for another half hour, he groaned and collapsed on the castle steps at the centre of the parade route. "Meet you here," he commanded. "Meet you here for the parade."

Tad, however, was a long time getting his last ice-cream waffle, and by the time we returned to the parade route, there was too large a crowd for us to push our way to the castle steps. So we watched the parade from a different vantage point. Afterward, as the happy crowd thinned, we sought out Tim. "Where have you been?" he snarled. We explained what had happened, but he didn't really listen. "Been waiting here for over an hour. We're going. We're going right away."

On the drive back to St. Augustine, the rest of us chatted noisily about Disney World, marvelling at its drawing power. But not Tim. He sat glumly throughout, never mouthing a word. I'm not sure I've ever seen him in so dark a mood for so long.

By and large, Florida was as we expected to find it, and so, too, was Disney World. So Tim's little display of temperament was really our fault. We should have anticipated that he would lose it at Walt's and never have dragged him along. Sorry about that, Tim. Disney World is not your sort of thing. Not your sort of thing at all. No, definitely not at all.

*Here are a couple of fast-food meals you can't get at Disney World:*

## MAGIC WINGS
### SERVES 4

4 pounds chicken wings
    (about 60)
2 tbsp oyster sauce
1 tbsp lemon juice
1 tbsp sesame oil
1 tbsp hoisin sauce
1 tbsp soy sauce
1 tbsp vinegar
4 cloves garlic, minced
1 tbsp dark brown sugar
½ hot chili pepper, chopped

» Mix all ingredients. Add wings and toss. Put in shallow, oven-proof dish and bake at 350 for 30 minutes. Grill briefly at end to crisp the skin.

## GOOFY BURGERS
### SERVES 2–4

1 pound minced chicken or
    extra-lean beef
1 small onion, chopped
¼ cup chopped fresh coriander
    leaves
2 tsp soy sauce
¼ tsp Tabasco
juice of ½ a lime
3 tbsp coconut milk
3 cloves garlic, chopped
1 tsp chopped ginger
salt and pepper to taste
1–2 tbsp olive oil
hamburger buns

» In a large bowl, mix first 10 ingredients together by hand until well blended.

» Shape into patties and fry in oil until meat is cooked through but not dry. Pour pan juices over patties.

» Serve on buns with a variety of toppings such as sautéed onions and mushrooms, sliced tomatoes, grated mozzarella cheese, yogurt, sliced cucumbers, and pickles.

» GOING BACK TO OLD haunts can be chancy. If as a youth you embraced a lover on the banks of the Seine on a warm summer night, best choose a restaurant in Montmartre the next time; it will likely be cold and raining in Paris. If you sang and drank the night away at the Red Ox around the time *The Student Prince* hit the screen, you'd be disappointed today by the way the pedestrian zone has transformed the feel of central Heidelberg. It made good sense to ban vehicular traffic there, I'm sure, just as it did to surgically alter the hearts of so many other European cities. But the result, almost invariably, has been transplants that are uncomfortably artificial — municipal organs that function efficiently but have rejected the vibrancy that was a product of their disorderly pasts. If you once stumbled upon the Royal Oak Pub in the village of Winford in the middle of Exmoor and you were enchanted by its rustic wooden floor, bar, and casement-window seats, you shouldn't try to find it again because you'll be appalled by the plush red carpet they've tacked to the floor and the matching upholstery on the seats. Now it has the same, safe decor the big breweries have urged on all their clients.

Conscious of the risks in retracing one's steps, I don't know why it is I'm so often tempted — to a degree the rest of the family finds obsessive. I'm afraid they've had to walk many an extra mile as I've tried to find that hostel I stayed at in '58 or the restaurant where I was first introduced to *moules marinières*. Attempting to experience again favourite digs and dinners is one thing; it's quite another to push your wife and kids up a mountain or urge them along a muddy river bank to see a view that's been with you for forty years. Especially if they're acutely suspicious that you have them on the wrong mountain in the right season or the right river bank in the wrong month. My family are a tolerant lot; they've endured much pain and tedium to assuage my need when usually nothing worthwhile has come of it.

Why do we insist on going back? Are we trying to recapture lost energy or the wonderment of youthful discovery—of an aesthetic world beyond the functionalism of North America or the way the senses are heightened when travelling: the thrill, for instance, of a soft cheek brushed in an Alpine or Venetian gondola? I don't know why, but I, for one, am forever doing it.

Sometimes, it is true, retracing steps is not disappointing—things are the same as you remembered them, maybe even better. For forty-five years, we've revisited the Lamb in Sheep Street, Burford, and it's always looked the same—no carpets on its uneven stone floors, no upholstery on its polished wooden benches and chairs. Place du Trocadéro in Paris, waiting for the lights and fountains to come on across the river from the Eiffel Tower, has never disappointed. The activities change, but there is always something intriguing happening. In '63 Dot and I watched a gendarme parade imperiously along the terrace above the gardens that lead to the river. At each turn, he stopped, leaned over the balustrade and, lifting his great blue cloak, took a swig from the bottle of wine hidden under it. In '86 we were transfixed by the skateboarders flipping and jumping for coins on the terrace and down the steps to the gardens, in 1999 by the live gold-and-silver-painted "statues" on the terrace, repositioning arms and legs only when adequately rewarded, and in 2004 by photojournalists' gripping portraits of the ravages of recent wars hanging from the surrounding buildings like massive Nazi banners.

There are, of course, some places that even a nostalgia buff would not be so foolish as to revisit. I was in Phnom Penh before

Pol Pot and the Khmer Rouge, when it was a happy, sleepy, French provincial town of wide crushed-stone avenues, pedal-taxis, and jubilant showers of bougainvillaea. The five of us spent three days in Teheran, before the Ayatollah Khomeini and the revolution, wandering the carpet bazaar and gawking at the Shah's palace. Deb and Tad were living just outside Kobe, Japan, during the earthquake of '95. There is no incentive to revisit such places — those you liked that you know have been irreparably changed by political or natural disasters. Or by the steep price of progress. That is why Dot and I will never return to Menorca — not even for a zesty omelette on a sunny, seaside terrace.

We visited it in a different era in a different way, at a time when there were practically no flights, no grand hotels, no packaged tours. On Majorca and Ibiza, yes, but not Menorca back in the early sixties. We took the boat train from London to Paris, the *métro* to Versailles, and hitchhiked from outside the palace gates to Barcelona. The slow route, the student route to the Balearics.

From Barcelona, we took the overnight ferry to Menorca. It cost a dollar to sit up all night in a deck chair. In the morning, porpoises played in the wake of the ship and then left us as we started the passage into the long, natural harbour of Maó (Port Mahón), perhaps the finest in the Mediterranean. At the dock, we slung our backpacks over our shoulders and walked the harbour front, looking for a suitable, cheap pension. We chose the Rocamar — long since replaced, no doubt, by a highrise resort or condominiums. It was a two-storey, white stucco building with green shutters, and we were given a large, airy room on the second floor, overlooking the harbour. The dining room was at the front on the main floor, its big, wooden shutters always open to the happy, unhurried life of the street, and there were tables and chairs outside as well. We often sat there over a gin before dinner and Chartreuse afterward. Both made locally and about five cents a glass.

We rented bicycles and our routine was to take the box lunch the hotel prepared for us and cycle to a different beach each day to swim and explore. The roads were virtually deserted — just infrequent trucks carrying produce to Maó and Ciutadella, and mopeds and bikes, like ours, heading to and from the beaches. The water was warm and the sky invariably blue. Even the box lunches were tolerable, though I don't have the same nostalgic feelings for our daily squid sandwiches that I do for everything else about Menorca.

Cycling home one evening, I punctured a tire. But we weren't at the side of the road more than ten minutes when a Spaniard on his moped stopped and went to work with his little repair kit. When he'd finished, along with effusive thanks, I tried to press some *pesetas* on him — to pay for his supplies at least. But he brushed me off, shouting as he sped away, "*Manana! Manana!*" Spain as it was supposed to be!

Maó was so quiet that we started seeing the same locals at bars and restaurants. Soon we were invited to join them in songs and toasts, raising glass beakers of sherry high above our heads and letting the amber streams splash off our cheeks and lips and slide into our wide-open mouths.

The day before our departure, one of our new friends "borrowed" my bicycle and didn't return it before it was due back at the rental shop. I was upset, certain its absence would raise some consternation just as it would have at home. Earnestly, I explained to the shop owner what had happened, but he just shrugged and waved his hands. "*Manana,*" he said. It will turn up tomorrow.

When we left, many of the friends we had made gathered at the ferry dock to see us off. They brought us little presents, and there was much hugging and kissing on the cheeks. White handkerchiefs were still waving on the pier as the ferry sailed out of sight. What a wonderful holiday it had been, we thought, such a beautifully simple and innocent place. May it never change.

We've thought often of returning. Whenever we're looking for a sunny destination for an early spring vacation, one of us will say, "How about Menorca?" Over a nostalgic omelette breakfast, we'll each quietly reflect for a while on our holiday there in '63 and what the island must be like today. Then we'll shake our heads and agree, "*Manana*. Maybe *manana*."

---

## YESTERDAY'S OMELETTE
### SERVES 4

8–10 eggs
1 tsp fines herbes
1 cup leftover pasta (chicken, shrimp, etc., cream or tomato based)
salt and pepper to taste
1 tbsp butter

» In a medium-sized bowl, beat eggs until light and frothy. Add spices and leftover pasta and stir gently into eggs. Melt butter in a hot, non-stick frying pan. Pour in egg mixture and cook quickly over high heat. Tip the pan frequently to let raw egg run toward the edge of the pan, pushing it back toward the middle as the outside edges begin to firm. Keep the pasta evenly distributed.

» Flip the omelette over while the top is still a little runny. Cook briefly until this side is just solid, but not dry.*
Serve immediately

*It is difficult to flip a moist omelette in one piece. I usually flip it in smaller portions, such as four (to serve four as in this recipe). It's worth sacrificing style for texture!*

Hermit hoar, in solemn cell,
Wearing out life's evening gray;
Strike thy bosom, sage! and tell
What is bliss, and which the way?

*In Ridicule of an Author,*
SAMUEL JOHNSON

1

TIM » DON'T EVEN TRY THIS RECIPE. It doesn't exist. It is a state of mind. A place in time. There's a restaurant on Bourbon Street in New Orleans, I forget the name, that comes close to making it, but they Cajunize it too much and the mix of hot spice and garlic doesn't quite work. There's a deli on Bathurst Street in Toronto that has a similar-looking meal roasting in the front window, but it's an impostor. You must just accept it. This meal does not exist. If you believe it does, you will only be disappointed. Imagine going through life always aware that there is something better. A common question in our family has always gone, Is the person who has not experienced the world beyond a quiet suburban street and a nine-to-five job better off than the one who travels the world and experiences life in all its rich variety? Isn't the fortunate adventurer destined to be eternally restless — always searching for more and better experiences — a little unsatisfied? Isn't it better just to be content with a well-manicured lawn and Monday-night football? I won't even attempt to create a recipe. I can only tell a story about the best roast chicken known to mankind. It existed once in the countryside of France. Forget it, that's all there is to tell.

2

» IT WAS ON APRIL 18, 1980, and we bought it on the central boulevard of the provincial town of Libourne. We had spent the night there on the return leg of a holiday in the Dordogne. We slept in a one-star hotel nearby. Rather, we dozed. All five of us in one long room above the bar, jolted by late-night bursts of laughter and shouting as someone played a winning hand of bezique. The bill: 80 francs.

It was in a roasting pan that the proprietor of the *charcuterie* had just pulled from the oven: a huge, battered, black-encrusted pan that might have seen service at a desert encampment of the French Foreign Legion. There was nothing extraordinary about the bird's appearance, however, nothing in particular that hinted at orgasmic pleasure. It was average size, quite plump, but otherwise presumably *très ordinaire*. It could have been in a supermarket in Burlington or Buffalo. But the proprietor shoved it into a brown paper bag and over it ladled pan drippings that oozed fresh buds of garlic.

We bought our baguettes at the *boulangerie* in the same square, still warm from the oven and earnest negotiations of early-morning shoppers. The loaves had brown, brittle crusts like the stooped ladies in black with bulging net bags in line in front of us, but centres soft and white as only in their dreams.

The wine—it must have been a Bordeaux red—we purchased in a little shop with dusty bottles in wooden racks and bins.

We headed north from Libourne, and in the early afternoon pulled our car to the side of the D 731 four kilometres from

Cognac. We carried our picnic along an embankment behind a vineyard just beginning to powder itself green. In the distance, above the vines stirring in the sun, glistened the church spires and rooftops of Cognac. There, later in the afternoon, we planned to visit the cellars of the Otard Cognac Company in the Château Valois, birthplace of François I. It was there also that Richard the Lionhearted was married and English prisoners from Canada, captured during the Seven Years War, etched their names and drawings on the grey stone walls.

We spread our morning purchases out in the grass and unwrapped the brown parcel from the *charcuterie*. A passing Citroen on the D 731 tooted approvingly. A jealous "bon appetit!"

We tore the beast apart with our hands and feasted on its pungent, juicy meat and crisp, golden skin. We were crusaders to whom a culinary truth had suddenly been revealed. Oil and garlic dripped from our fingers as we desperately picked for every remaining, delectable morsel. The baguettes doubled as sponges. The cool wine kneaded our palates and the spring sun licked our pink, Canadian faces.

Heaven.

## STATE-OF-MIND CHICKEN

DEB » It can be replicated — or at least an approximation. But it's not quite the same without all the original ingredients: the young grape leaves, the poppies I swear were scattered among the vines, the crisp taste of my first apple cider, and my family. I remember emotion. I remember love. And I remember all of us sprawled in a rough circle almost completely concealed by goldening grasses the colour of my brother's hair, eating the best chicken in the world.

When I feel lonely, and BC seems especially far away from the rest of the family, I buy a plump chicken and fill the cavity with lots of garlic cloves cut in half lengthwise (cut garlic is more flavourful). I make slits in the flesh of the chicken and slide in more cloves. When I think I've added enough garlic to the chicken, I stuff in some more. You can never have too much garlic.

I place the chicken, breast down, in a roasting pan so that the white meat will be juicier.

I cover the chicken with aluminum foil and cook it at 350, basting it occasionally, for 1 to 1 ½ hours, depending on its size.

Then Tad and I carry our succulent French impostor outside and are transported to wherever we want to be: the vineyards of Bordeaux or back home in the East.

» IF YOU'RE EVER IN NEED of great nuts, the place to go is Choucri Hamasni.* It's in Lebanon, not far from the Syrian border. A modern, nondescript building surrounded by others typical of the Middle East: concrete blocks with cement pillars and steel rods protruding from their unfinished top floors, a tangle of wires strung among them in a desperate effort to keep everyone electrified. Choucri Hamasni itself, however, is different. A little more upscale. It's like an extra-large convenience store with all sorts of luxury items not readily found in many parts of Lebanon and certainly not in neighbouring Syria. Most of all, however, it specializes in nuts. There are big bins of all kinds. Pistachios. Almonds. Macadamia nuts. Cashews. Walnuts. You name it. All fresh, unblemished, and delicious. We went there with our old Austrian friend Sepp. It was a weekend at the very end of Ramadan, and the store was crowded with Syrians loading up before returning to the austerity of their homeland.

Funny to think of Lebanon as a tourist destination, especially that soon after the war. But that's what it was for Syrians prosperous enough to go there to shop. For us it was mostly depressing—shocking, in fact, driving through southeastern Beirut and across the infamous green line, walking through silent Martyrs Square in the centre of the city. Block after block of flattened buildings. Families living in the still-standing shells, front walls blasted away, others forlorn piles of rubble except at ground level where small shops had reopened. At Byblos, north of Beirut, the oldest continually inhabited city in the world, we had drinks at Pepe's Fishing

Club, once a fashionable bar where the rich and famous gathered from their yachts. Bardot, Brando, Niven. Empty now. It was disheartening looking out from there at the Roman ruins of a city that dates back to the Phoenicians, millennia of old devastation on top of the havoc so recently and insanely perpetrated. Even the cedars —in the mountains leading to the Syrian border—failed to boost our spirits. The most famous grove, above Bcharré, is actually pretty puny, and there was a tank at the side of the road, its barrel pointing menacingly toward a ski lift. *Why is there a cedar tree on the flag of Lebanon when there are so few?* we wondered. *It ought to be a steely-eyed guard with a rifle slung over his shoulder.* That was the dominant image wherever we went.

Crossing the border back to Syria that day was quite a feat. A long queue of vehicles from loaded limos to limping, listing Ladas was jammed motionless at different angles in the direction of the bleak customs and immigration offices. Sepp groaned; he had seen tie-ups like this before, and friends who had left Beirut two hours before us were still waiting to cross. I was instructed to get out and guard the rear of the Mercedes to make sure that no one got too close to our bumper in the event we had to try to back up, turn around, and retreat into Lebanon.

While we waited, Sepp told us that, once, at this particular crossing, the tie-up was so bad that it took three days to disentangle all the vehicles; a number of people perished during the cold, winter nights. *What's this? Another Wadi Rum?* We sat patiently and reflectively, nibbling on our newly purchased nuts, knowing that the supply would last us for some time.

Sepp has never been particularly respectful of diplomatic formalities. It wasn't long before he got out of the Mercedes and had a tete-à-tete with the embassy driver who had tortured us with his middle-of-the-road driving and loud Arabic music. They huddled together thumbing through an enormous wad of faded, soiled bills, evaluating what it would require to get through quickly. As always, they got the sum right, and an armed guard quickly waved us into another, shorter line. Impressed, we munched happily on our pistachios, tossing the shells out the window the way the locals did.

The Arab Middle East is a fascinating place, full of surprises, and Syria, despite its many faults, has a remarkable appeal. Travelling there is like visiting Europe before the Second World War — before the inundation of tourists. It is laced with Roman and other ruins — too many to be adequately maintained and supervised, yet spectacular in their breadth and completeness: Palmyra, 125 acres of layered history; Apamea; Cyrrhus; the Crac des Chevaliers, the best-preserved Crusader castle in the Middle East; the desert ruins of Rasafeh, Hala-biyyeh; and best of all Qasr al-Hayr Ash Sharqi, which requires a bold thirty-five-kilometre detour off the desert highway along unmarked twisting tracks that often lead nowhere. Sepp's kind of road. And there's Qalat Seman, where the northern Syrian shepherd who became St. Simeon spent the last thirty years of his life perched upon a pillar, preaching to pilgrims, an iron collar around his neck chaining him to his post.

At most sites, apart from Palmyra, there are hardly any visitors and at many none at all. At Cyrrhus, in the Kurdish hills near the border with Turkey, we picnicked high in the mausoleum of its Roman remains. The only other person there was a shepherd, tending a herd of goats below us, kneeling eastward in prayer. We scrambled down and Sepp asked him if many people came by bus to see the ruins. But he looked confused. Apparently there was no word in the local vocabulary for such a means of transport!

Except for the armed guards at every important building and the secret-service agents at the Damascus airport (eight or nine branches), people were friendly everywhere we went. In Jordan, high in the stunning ruins of Petra, carved by the Nebateans from the rainbow rocks — above the monastery where we watched the sun set over Wadi Araba — we were invited by Bedouins to spend the night by their fire. We couldn't, but riding horseback out of

Petra later that night I beheld an equally warming scene, typical of the Middle East. It was a clear, sharp night and we were moving slowly through the deep crevasse in the sandstone rocks known as the Siq — the narrow passage through the Shara Mountains that more than 2,000 years ago enabled the clever Nebateans to stop the camel caravans trekking the Incense Road in order to collect their taxes. Sepp was on the horse in front of me, as always looking the part — as if he had spent his life in the saddle not on skis. Our guide was sharing his mount, snugly perched behind Sepp, arms wrapped around him for security. In the darkness, I could see a small red glow as they passed a cigarette between them.

A shaft of moonlight carpeted the canyon floor and the rough walls reverberated with the hollow clicking of the horses' hooves on the uneven, rocky ground. There was no other sound — except every so often I could make out the hushed voices of Sepp and the guide in earnest conversation. Sepp had made special arrangements with the authorities for us to stay in Petra after the usual closing — after all the tourists had left for the hotels newly sprouting in Wadi Musa beyond the canyon walls. And now he and the guide were amiably arguing over the size of the surcharge for being so late — late leaving history behind!

In the *souqs* in central Damascus and Aleppo, the bustling covered markets where women in skimpy dresses, high heels, and makeup walk beside others totally covered in black burkas, shopkeepers regularly invited us to stop for tea. So few tourists ambled their colourful, twisting passages that on our return visits, they greeted us, "Hello. Ah! Mr. and Mrs. Canada. Come to my store. Yesterday you say you come. Not buying? Okay. Have some tea."

Another welcome discovery was that theft hardly seemed a matter for concern. Wandering the dusty streets of Damascus, lamp posts and telephone poles lying across the sidewalks, slabs of concrete heaving, and trees uprooted, we happened upon the Commonwealth War Graves Cemetery. On several benches, visitors had left purses and books unattended as they strolled the grounds. It was the same, we found, in the courtyards of mosques, despite the old destitute men propped against stone walls. Once, on a business trip to the Arab emirates from Beirut, Sepp left a dispatch case with all his important papers on a counter at the Amman airport. Returning two weeks later, it was still in the same place, covered in a thick layer of dust.

Though bombarded with anti-Western propaganda, most people seemed tolerant if not always open-minded, and that, too, was a pleasant surprise. Israelis were not generally spoken of negatively, only their government. At the Omayyed Mosque in central Damascus, Muslim worshippers stooped to kiss the tomb of John the Baptist. St. Paul's Chapel, where the disciples lowered St. Paul out of a window in a basket to flee from the Jews, is a respected tourist site. Today, however, if you were lowered from the chapel to the street below, you would feel at risk — of being run over by a bus with faulty brakes speeding round the ring road that circles the old city. High in the mountains of Lebanon near Beiteddine, we also learned new respect for Kamal Jumbladt, one-time socialist and maverick leader of the Muslim Druze, a person often reviled in the Western press. He was not only a powerful political figure during the civil war until his assassination in 1977, but a Sorbonne-educated philosopher, historian, and humanist. Mukhtara, his palatial home, now a museum, is full of fifth- and sixth-century mosaics he rescued from derelict Christian churches in Tyre.

One thing that was disappointing about the Middle East, however, was the food. We didn't have many memorable meals, although one does stand out, another moment bored forever into memory. It was at Apamea in northern Syria, a Roman city founded by Seleucus I in the second century BC. At its peak it had a population of 500,000. Antony and Cleopatra visited it once. And we did, too, by a full moon. There was no one there, and Sepp left the route designated for visitors to drive down the *cardo* or market area. The uneven stone road stretches for two kilometres and along large sections fluted, Roman columns adorn each side. We stopped after a short distance to walk the rest of the way in silence, each of us thinking our own thoughts: about history, development, the tragedy of poverty and war, and our own good fortune.

The majestic columns and dusty road surrounding us were splashed in moonlight, the pillars spreading a zebra-skin cover over the ground. You could feel a Roman centurion hurtling over the stones in a chariot bound for distant Damascus, or gossipers in togas whispering at the base of a pillar. We, too, sat beside a crumbling column. Sepp uncorked a bottle of good Austrian red and we opened up the ever-present bag of nuts from Choucri Hamasni. We sipped the wine. Only the muted sound of cashews crunching disturbed our communion with the ancient past.

* *Choucri Hamasni — since 1880, "finest roasted and salted nuts" — is in the Kob-Elias quarter of Chtaura. It's across the road from Modern Conserves. If you ask for Modern Conserves, they'll tell you it's across the road from Choucri Hamasni!*

» INSIDIOUSLY, TEA WORKS its way into everyone's life. In the forties, when we were recovering from upset stomachs, it was the first fluid we were allowed to drink. Weak with lots of milk and sugar and a slice of dry toast. We had it by the fire on Sunday evenings in the fifties with crab and salmon sandwiches while my mother read us English adventure stories, especially Arthur Ransome: *Swallows and Amazons*, *Winter Holiday*, *We Didn't Mean to Go to Sea*.

Desperate to stay warm in our damp Clapham flat in the sixties, we consumed more tins of tea than our grate bags of coal — along with biscuits from the bakery. On breaks from the library at the Commonwealth Relations Office in Whitehall, I'd buy a current bun and tea from the café in St. James' Park and have them sitting by the pond, watching old ladies with string bags and long woollen coats feeding sparrows that alighted on their shoulders. Tea — in glasses with silver handles — often greeted us when we arrived somewhere on official business in Southeast Asia, with a rice cake circled by a swarm of flies. In the seventies and eighties we drank it with Dot's father in his study in Toronto while we watched Sunday football. It came with Bath Oliver biscuits. Now there's a combination for buffs of the bland!

On sabbatical in the nineties, we'd have a pot with scones, clotted cream, and strawberry jam, of course, in Exeter, Exmouth, or Sidmouth. I love English tea shops almost as much as pubs. The lace curtains and doilies on the tables, the polished oak smelling of lemon oil all remind me of visiting old aunts in Napanee who sat on velvet divans and crocheted. Especially, I like the way ladies in flowered frocks and gents in heavy woollen jerseys, their socks tucked into their leather walking shoes, look you over when you enter, smile, maybe nod, and return their gaze to their leaves. It's impolite to talk above a whisper and disturb the clink of cups against saucers.

Have you ever noticed how rarely people drink tea alone? It's always tea and something. Tea and a book. Tea and scones. Tea and a crossword puzzle. Once, when we were in Indonesia, Karen was invited to the home of an eccentric lady for "Tea and Snakes." The hostess greeted her wearing a "necklace" that, to Karen's horror, suddenly arched toward her. I remember that year in Devon, there were so many rain delays during the first test match between England and New Zealand that on several occasions "tea was taken early." How unnerving! Tea and a rain delay.

Tea and something. It says a lot, I guess, about the versatility of tea.

For tea and really something, you can't, of course, beat high tea at one of the great hotels of London. It's expensive, but so is every show. Besides, you get a lot: pots and pots of tea; cucumber, egg, and smoked-salmon sandwiches on thinly sliced bread; cakes with thick, rich icings; scones with clotted cream and jam, all elegantly presented on multi-tiered silver servers.

Not long ago, Dot and I had high tea at Claridge's with our friend Trish. While they shopped on Oxford and Regent streets that afternoon, I had business to attend to in Kensington; so we arranged to meet at Claridge's at four. I had a lovely walk back across Hyde Park, stopping to watch old boys sailing their handmade yachts in the Round Pond, yet I still managed to get to Claridge's quite early. Oddly, it wasn't until I was standing outside its front door — face to face with the doorman in his black top hat and gold-braided coat with brass buttons — that I thought at all about my attire. I had on a pair of grey flannels, a white shirt, and a sweater. Pretty good for me, but not, perhaps, it suddenly occurred to me, for Claridge's.

By this time, people had for years been breezing into London theatres, fancy restaurants, and hotels in jeans and New York Yankees wind breakers. But not, I feared, into Claridge's for tea. Not without a jacket and tie. Claridge's is, after all, sometimes referred to as "the annex to Buckingham palace." Guests of the Queen are moved there after the third day of an official visit, and it is at Claridge's that visiting heads of state reciprocate for her hospitality by hosting dinners of their own. All of its suites are individually decorated in late-Victorian or Art Deco style by leading designers. A decent one runs a least $1,500 a night. On any given day, Claridge's is likely to have a number of distinguished patrons so that it is no wonder that when someone once called the desk and asked to speak to the King, the desk clerk politely responded, "May I ask, sir, which king?"

Suddenly mindful of Claridge's pedigree, I did an abrupt about-face at the door and shuffled off, fretting about what to do. It hit me that it was some time since I'd been inside the Connaught, another of London's fashionable hotels, maybe half a rung below Claridge's. So I decided to walk over to Carlos Place and have a peek — see what people were wearing there for tea. As I walked in, out of the corner of my eye, I could see that my dress had set off the doorman's sensitive alarm; he was following me into the lobby. "May I help you, sir?" He approached me politely but swiftly.

"Ah, yes," I said confidently. "I'm meeting some people here later for tea, and I was just checking to see where it would be served."

"In there, sir." Then he lowered his voice and said sternly, "but you know you will require a jacket and tie."

"Of course," I retorted indignantly, and retreated from the Connaught.

Now I knew I was in trouble. If the Connaught required a jacket and tie for tea, there was no question about Claridge's. *This could be embarrassing*, I thought, as I hurried back to our rendez-vous. *What if Dot and Trish are already there, waiting for me in the lounge? What if I can't get to them? Will the doorman at least take in a note, telling them to go ahead and to meet me later for a cup at Waterloo Station?*

Bravely, I approached the doorman. "I have a bit of a problem. I'm meeting two very attractive ladies here for tea who will be much more elegantly dressed than I. Could you tell me, will I need a jacket and tie?"

"Yes, sir!" From his cheery reply, I knew he took delight in protecting the classy from the classless, and I frowned. "Hmmm."

He kept me waiting several seconds, shuffling awkwardly like a new boy before a sadistic prefect. Then he added, "But if you go inside to the cloakroom, I'm sure they can fix you up."

There I was greeted with unexpected warmth and civility and shown what, to my untutored eyes, was a rack of jackets as large and fine as any in Saville Row. The attendant appraised me carefully. "Ah, this one should fit you perfectly, sir." Enthusiastically, he helped me into a dark-blue blazer. "And this tie will be a lovely match. Oh, yes, smashing! It's just the outfit to go with your flannels."

Enjoying the flattery, I admired myself in a floorlength mirror. "Thank you. I do think I am a credit to my tailor."

"Happy to be of service any time, sir."

Into the large, bustling lounge of Claridge's I confidently strode. Dot and Trish were not yet there, so I sat poised in a plush red-leather chair near the entrance, awaiting their arrival, impatient to show off my new wardrobe. When at last they hurried in, I immediately stood up, and, smiling smugly, gave them each a little bow and a kiss on the hand. And then I stood back beaming, expecting the plaudits to descend.

But they said nothing. Their eyes circled the gilded lounge, taking in the Regency-style footmen in their red britches, white stockings, and black and gold-braided jackets, pushing carts among the tables. They closely scrutinized the self-conscious ladies in Liberty's latest and smiled affectionately at the unconscious Harris tweeds behind the *Times*. They soaked in everything about the room. But they never noticed that I was in any way different from when we left home — that I, too, had gone shopping — that I was sporting a jacket and tie from Claridge's, no less.

"That's because you look just right for the place," Dot tried to console me after I told them about my new clothes.

I was not appeased. Never mind, I thought to myself. *I* know I've never looked better. *I* know I look terrific.

I'll never forget that tea at Claridge's. Tea and sartorial splendour.

## CUCUMBER SANDWICHES, AFTERNOON-TEA STYLE

### MAKES 4–6 SANDWICHES

2 cucumbers, peeled and
    thinly sliced
1 tsp salt
½ cup water
¼ cup white-wine vinegar
¼ cup powdered sugar
2–3 sprigs fresh dill
fresh white bread, thinly sliced,
    crusts removed
2 tbsp snipped fresh dill
parsley for garnish

» Place cucumber slices in a colander. Sprinkle with salt and set aside to drain, tossing and pressing down occasionally (4–5 hours).

» Mix water, vinegar, and sugar together in a small pot and stir over low heat until sugar dissolves. Remove from heat, add dill sprigs, and allow to cool.

» Rinse cucumber, drain, and add to cool syrup. Refrigerate for 20–30 minutes. Discard dill sprigs. Drain cucumbers and squeeze out excess syrup by hand using paper towelling.

» Butter bread for sandwiches. Arrange 2 layers of cucumber neatly over bottom slices. Sprinkle a little snipped dill over cucumbers and close sandwiches. Cut into neat squares or triangles. Arrange attractively on serving plate and garnish with parsley.

*Afternoon tea is a fiddly affair!*

» MORE THAN BERMUDA, the Caribbean, and the Great Wall of Florida, I like South Carolina for a winter getaway. It's close at hand for eastern snowbirds, and it's great 'cuing country. Now what's a better way to cook when it's blizzard season back home?

I love those vast marshlands along murky rivers and inlets leading to the open Atlantic. Long wooden docks on tall stilts protrude from their banks like centipedes idly floating on the tidal waters. Flocks of shorebirds do the Charleston on the muddy banks, picking for insects among the oyster and crab shells. Snowy egrets, so still they seem the work of taxidermists, cling to stalks of grass, looking for prey, while turtles doze in the afternoon sun on half-submerged rotting logs and pelicans drift nonchalantly on little puffs of wind. Out on the open ocean, silhouetted against a red-beach-ball sun, shrimp boats rock in a gentle swell, nets swinging from their hulls like the wings of gypsy moths, and a line of sailboats parades toward harbour.

South Carolina wouldn't suit everyone for Christmas or a midwinter break. The average high is only around 60 degrees, dipping to the low 40s at night. But sometimes the temperature climbs to the 70s, and, when the sun is out, even the cool days are comfortable—often warm enough for shorts and T-shirts, especially if, at midday, you are sitting on the wooden steps of a walkway across the dunes to the beach or lying in the sand by a cluster of swaying pampas grass.

In fact, for an active vacation of tennis, golf, bicycling, Roller-Blading, and hiking, the winter temperature is just about perfect for comfortable exertion. And the facilities are first class at places like Kiawah Island and Hilton Head. Massive live oaks, dripping Spanish moss, shade the lush, challenging golf courses, and towering loblolly pines and quivering palmettos shield the clay courts and bicycle trails from the wind. Winter is off-season, too, so bargains are plentiful, especially for housekeeping accommodation. The beaches, trails, courts, and courses are also uncrowded, and there's a quiet, unhurried feel to all the coast that puts you in harmony with the birds gliding gracefully over the salt marshes and the dolphins cruising the shore, blowing softly as they surface and dive in unison.

Having beautiful cities nearby such as Savannah and Charleston is another plus. The latter has more than eight hundred buildings dating from the first half of the nineteenth century or earlier. They're painted in every shade of the palette and their long, high-ceilinged piazzas look out on gardens blooming with orange and red camellias even in mid-winter. There are also the plantation homes along the Ashley River: Middleton Place, Drayton Hall, and, my favourite, Magnolia, with the oldest major garden in the Western Hemisphere, particularly noted for its azaleas and camellias. Beside it is a pea-soup swamp, covered in duck weed and ringed with live oaks, sycamores, tupelo gum trees, dogwoods, and red maples. Like deadheads on a northern pond, alligators float near the surface, bulging eyes protruding through the scum; or they imitate landing barges, dragging themselves onto wooden platforms to sunbathe and listen to the birds chattering in the dead branches of bald cypress that have waded into the swamp like old men reluctant to bathe.

I think of the food, too, as better than at other winter destinations. But that's probably because it is in South Carolina that Tim perfected the art of cooking shrimp and swordfish on the barbecue. Most of our days are filled with activity, and at lunch we usually pause only briefly, maybe just for a bag of chips and a beer, catching the sun on our deck at its peak. So by the time Tim lights up the barbecue in the evening, everyone is ravenous.

I pour a scotch and soda and join him outside in a sweater or winter jacket. He's a temperamental chef and it's important not to leave him on the deck or in the driveway while everyone else gathers in the living room. He likes to have someone to complain to — about the coals or cooking utensils — someone to fetch and carry, bring him nuts. Tim's foot jiggles impatiently as he watches the barbecue, the same way it does when I'm too long making a point in an argument. He sees things quickly — including the irony in images we pass walking or driving, and he's frustrated with Dot and me when we stop and dwell.

It's amazing to watch him cook; his style is so different from the others. He doesn't have their range, but he never looks at a recipe. Never measures. He cooks the way he writes poetry, creating an original dish on the spot that fits his mood and the requisites of the focal point of the meal: the fish, the poultry, the meat, or shellfish. He works with boldness and flare. An array of spices, sauces and juices are sprinkled, shaken, and squeezed over the barbecue at carefully determined intervals. A corner is carved off a fillet or a scallop is skewered and tasted. A dash of this and a splash of that is urgently added and then I am sent to warn the others to be ready. Tim grows tauter and ever more focused as the moment of decision approaches — in fact the moments, for different items must be plucked from the grill at different times. I stand by as each in turn is dropped onto a platter and I rush the dishes one by one to the dining room. After we are all seated and enjoying our first delectable bites, Tim slips into the room and asks anxiously, "How is it, guys?"

It's always great, always a little different. We analyse the tastes, compare them with the last barbecue, discuss what other vegetables you could grill with grouper, what would be the best wines. Once we even talked about writing it all down. And thus the evening passes in a happy buzz of voices over voices.

I like South Carolina, but by the end of our holiday I'm usually ready to go. Places like Kiawah and Hilton Head are gated communities; sometimes there are two or even three between you and the outside world. In a sense you do pass through them to an earthly paradise — secure from poverty, crime, violence, and the disparities and contradictions of most of North America. Perfection, however, can become tedious. You feel cut off from the clutter of the real world with all its scars and injustices — from the incessant tussle between good and evil. You want to be engaged again. You crave stimulating conversation, culture, and diversity. You long for news of the rest of the globe, let alone of that blank space above the US weather map where, apparently, nothing exists but icy currents to disrupt the balmy conditions of the South. No, I like the Carolina lowlands, but not for the long haul. After all, you can always barbecue on a deck at home — even in the middle of a blizzard. So as we start to pack our things and I accept we've had our last barbecue for this holiday — with the yeasty excitation of everyone together around the table — I think, *It's okay. It's really okay. We've had some great times. Heaven can wait.*

TIM » FISH. FISH. FISH. Say the word in your head softly. Repeat it. Form the coals into a perfect mound. Add the lighter fluid. Light the coals in four places. Wait. Timing is critical. Express doubt publicly. Be confident inwardly. Embrace ritual. Fish. Breathe. Flame. Breathe. Clear your head. Slow your thinking down to the molecular level. Inhale. Exhale. Open your senses. Go quantum. Become ritual. Spread the coals. Forget ritual. Everything is connected. The universe is self-actualizing. You are perfect. The fish is perfect. You are fish. You are fire. Time is changing. Become.

I HAD MY FIRST Zen Buddhist experience before memory. It happened to me in Thailand, during my first haircut. I was about fifteen months old. Obviously I can't give you much in the way of details—it's more of a feeling, a deeper understanding, a connectedness. Sitting there in my high chair I stumbled across an interesting paradox, a sort of koan, if you will. My fear of the scissors gave me an overwhelming urge to squirm. The more I squirmed, however, the greater my fear that I would lose an ear or some other facial appendage. My fear grew proportionally with my will not to squirm. I eventually transcended fear and discovered an inner peace I haven't fully reconnected with since. I became still— Buddha still. In my stillness I realized that barber, scissors, hair, chair, ears were all connected in a beautiful and magical dance. We were all in this together. We would all get through this together. And whatever the outcome, it would be perfect. Enlightenment at fifteen months. I guess you could say I peaked too soon.

Which brings me to cooking fish, or any other food for that matter. I choose to focus on fish because, in my opinion, it takes the greatest amount of Zen to get it right. Beginners can start with beef or chicken. Cooking fish gets me closest to the state I achieved during my first haircut. There's something about fish that sets it apart from other foods. It lies in the size of the region between too done and not done enough. For most foods, there is a rather forgiving range of doneness on either end of the scale. With fish there is no range at all. There is only one precise point in the cooking process, one state only at which the fish can be truly said to be cooked to perfection. Even the slightest effects — an unexpected breeze, a subtle drop in air pressure — can change the outcome. Cooking fish requires at least a basic understanding of chaos theory, general relativity, and quantum mechanics. Cooking the perfect piece of fish forces you to enter a state of higher awareness.

First, your heart must be in it. There must be total commitment. Go back and read the first paragraph. Think about it for a while. You can make your own variations of the process, but the driving force behind your cooking, your total commitment and concentration, is essential.

What I say about timing is important. If you think I mean the time it takes for the fish to cook you are lost. Timing is much more than that. It involves when you decide to light the barbecue, when you decide to put the fish on, when you decide to take the fish off, when those sharing in the meal should come to the table. It involves your understanding of time. Remember the fish does not just cook. You are cooking the fish.

Now, another note about timing. Do not rush into things. Spend some time with the uncooked fish. Smell it. Touch it. Understand it. Think of what it means, where it came from. The more you appreciate the fish, the more you will care about what happens to it — and to you.

Try to stay aware of your surroundings while simultaneously losing yourself in your task. Study the air temperature. Take note of the bird that flies overhead. The slower you think the more you will notice. At the moment you stop thinking and begin simply doing a task that feels completely natural and connected to the world around you, you will know when the fish is done.

DOT » I'M KIND OF INFAMOUS in this family for *not* remembering things—like the names of places we've been and the details of things we've done. To any question that begins, "Hey, remember that place where we…?" I invariably answer "uh, no." It drives everyone crazy, especially Terry, who has a prodigious memory. But I insist it keeps life interesting; everywhere we go, whether we've been there before or not, it's all new to me. I'm ready to be delighted. Who could ask for a better travelling companion?

I wonder if my parents recognized my memory deficit at an early age and planned our family holidays accordingly. Higgins Beach, Maine. We spent every two weeks of my father's summer vacation there in the old inn, its corner bay windows streaked with salt, offering tantalizing glimpses to Ocean Street and the sea. I could count on it, look forward to it, know it, just like I could count on Dad's walking in the front door at 6:00 PM, Jack Benny on the radio on Sunday night, or mashed potatoes and gravy with our Christmas turkey.

I remember the trip, especially Route 20, with names like Canandaigua, Skaneateles, Cazenovia. I remember the I-think-I-can hills the old Buick struggled to climb, the elevator dips in the road, the red barns and silos, the sweet perfume of clover, and the advertising signs strung along the edges of fields: "Spring has sprung. The grass is ris. Where last year's careless driver is. Burma Shave."

I remember the cabins we slept in on the way, with their warm dusty smell of summer secrets. We never had to worry about reservations when I was a kid; Mom always booked the same place every year, right down to the same cabin number, and she booked it well in advance. Predictability, what a great mnemonic device.

Most of all, I remember the sea and Higgins Beach, with its hard-packed golden mile of sand. It seemed endless then, a little diminished now. And I remember the barnacle-encrusted ribs of the shipwreck near the dangerous tidal river, the rock pools, full of Velcro-limbed starfish and the stench of decay. We collected sand dollars and Chinese hats and brought them home in empty yellow tins of Will's Gold Flake Cigarettes to sit forever in the hall cupboard along with the unopened Wamsutta sheets that Mum bought in Saco and treasured for their superior cotton weave.

Always there was the power of the sea, the exhilaration of being carried to shore by a wave, the tinge of fear as waterfalls of foam crashed over you—a tiny taste of the edge where power and pleasure hang. At the end of a day surfing in the numbing waters of an offshore breeze, everyone but me had an ounce of Teacher's Highland Cream. I ate Len Libby chocolates.

Fog for days, salty lips, drive-ins, and, once a summer, Valle's Steak House. I even remember what I ordered: filet mignon, french fries, salad, and Indian pudding for dessert. I remember ecstasy. So there.

## INDIAN PUDDING

4 ¾ cups milk
scant 1/2 cup corn meal
1 cup sweet molasses
2–3 tbsp butter
¾ tsp cinnamon
1 tsp ginger
½ tsp salt
2 eggs, well beaten

» In the top of a double boiler*, whisk together 4 cups of milk and the corn meal and cook over boiling water, stirring until mixture is smooth (about 20 minutes). Stir in molasses and cook gently, 3–5 minutes. Remove from heat and stir in butter, cinnamon, ginger, salt, and eggs.

» Pour into a well-greased casserole and pour the remaining ¾ cup milk over the top. Bake uncovered in a medium oven (350) for 1 to 1 ¼ hours or until the top is golden brown.

» Serve hot in bowls with a scoop of vanilla ice cream on top.

* *This recipe really does call for a double boiler. Otherwise, the corn meal settles and sticks to the pan.*

» WE HAVE CAVIAR very rarely. I guess that's the way it ought to be. For special occasions only. Caviar and champagne.

The first time I went to Europe — at eighteen on a student tour — we crossed the Atlantic on a liner, and some in the group ordered pink champagne and French pastries for breakfast in their cabins. The height of decadence, it seemed. At least for sweet innocents for whom caviar was dark and menacing like old age.

We drank Singapore Slings then, too, not whisky and water, in the taverna where we stumbled across the dance floor, pretending it was the swell that was the problem not our ineptitude. I'd gag on the sugar in a Singapore Sling today, but in '58 the name alone conjured exotic and worldly sophistication — all we wanted sailing away from home on our first big adventure. On *The Homeric*.

They're all gone now from regular North Atlantic crossings. All but one. *The Caronia*, *Queen Mary*, *Queen Elizabeth*, *Queen Elizabeth 2*, the *United States*, and the *France*. The lesser ships as well that did the trip from Montreal: the *Empress of Canada*, the *Saxonia*, *Ivernia*, *Carinthia*, and *Alexander Putchkin*. Even the little *Stefan Batory* from Gdynia that folded with the tighter wallets of collapsing communism. And most lamented the FS *Homeric*, the fun-ship interloper amidst a largely Anglo-Saxon fleet.

Trunk-laden on the western voyage, immigrants filled with awe and second thoughts at the endless rocky waste of Labrador and Quebec. Suitcase swollen on the eastern passage, carrying upper bunks of students to wine and lust, and lowers of limping veterans returning to the gore and glory of the beaches of Normandy.

Burned to the waterline. Sold for scrap. Refitted to plod the Caribbean, the Med, the South Atlantic — warm, calm waters far from the quixotic, rollicking North Atlantic. Tied up at wharves, stripped of their cherished belongings, and forgotten by all but the faithful. Never again putting to sea. A nursing-home existence.

And what in their place? An ever-expanding armada of ever-larger cruise ships, bulking up as fast as the bellies queuing at their midnight buffets. Disney Worlds of the water, boasting hot tubs, wave pools, beauty spas, gymnasia, casinos, miniature golf courses, basketball courts, rock-climbing walls, and shopping malls with upscale boutiques, bars, and restaurants. Now one particularly obese lady of the seas, weighing in at 160,000 tons (almost four times the size of the *Titanic*), even has a boxing ring, psychedelic sculpture garden, surfing simulator, and ice rink. Mammoth, ugly beasts flung into the sea to make money, their owners praying they won't sink, but knowing they'll never swim with the grace and purpose of their forebears. Opulent, bloated barges, overstuffed now with widows on too-large inheritances, riding the glass elevators to the dining rooms — eyeing skeptically the grumbling pot bellies surviving on digitalis. Or crammed with Club Med abs and biceps chasing bodies bronzed on tanning beds and toned at Pilates classes. Floating fun fairs for the corpulent and incurious, roaming aimlessly from Miami to Miami like plastic tugs in a bathtub.

After the others had gone, for years, one liner was left alone, regularly braving the open North Atlantic on trans-ocean crossings, carrying its passengers with purpose from A to B. The *Queen Elizabeth 2*. It's true that, like the cruise ships of today, it pampered its clientele with five-star service in six restaurants, five bars, and three lounges, entertained them from one dawn to the next with activities for every taste and age. But crossing the Atlantic on the *QE2* and its predecessors was a very different experience from "cruising," even if today the ship is actually crossing the ocean, calling briefly at ports on the way, enabling its passengers to check off more countries visited, more souvenirs acquired. There was something very different and very special about luxury at sea when the ship itself was not the destination, the primary reason for being there — when your purpose was to move from continent to continent in a stately, elegant fashion, allowing time for cultural transition and to marvel at the power and beauty of the watery space between. But not too much time, too much luxury. That's part of what made it different — just a short week of intimate, glittering contact, knowing that at the end of it in a different port everyone would part forever with separate agendas and untold destinations. That is what made the transatlantic liners so special and, for me at least, the *QE2* the caviar of ships. The last of them. The height of decadence. Before excess.

The best of the cruise ships have caviar and champagne at the captain's cocktail party, no doubt. But only on the *QE2* was it served mid-Atlantic on a rolling sea. Only on the *Queen* would the talk be of the miles steamed that day from New York, of the distance remaining to Bishop's Rock, of the coveted blue ribbon and the last liner to hold it. On no other ship, I am sure, did conversation so readily turn to the history of Cunard and the great vessels of old — the *Lusitania, Mauretania, Aquitania, Queen Mary* — and what would happen to the old queen when the new one ascended the throne.

I miss them all, the flag ships and lesser liners of the Atlantic. On the *Homeric* in '62, we were three honeymoon couples together in the dining room off to graduate school and jobs in Europe. Easy for an Italian crew bred to romance, to flatter. Each evening, when our cabin steward folded back our blankets, he took a négligé from Dot's cupboard and laid it on her bed, propped up on the pillow and cinched at the waist.

When we crossed on the *Batory* in 1979, on our way to England on sabbatical, Lech Walesa was leading the ship-workers' strike in Gdansk, and the atmosphere was electric. The Polish crew were listening to shortwave radios and whispering to us about how bad things were at home. Everything was rumour—where we were in the Atlantic, if the ship had slowed to preserve oil, whether or not the captain was having an affair with a rich heiress on board and planning to defect. Deb revelled in the intrigue; Karen fell in love for the first time; and Tim won a prize at the costume ball.

In '93, on the *Queen* on our way to another sabbatical, we caught the tail end of a hurricane that churned the Atlantic into crests of ten metres or more. At lunchtime a still larger wave toppled tables, chairs, food, and guests onto the floors. We toured the ship deck by deck, inspecting the damage. It looked as if she were back in the Falklands and had actually come under fire. But we marvelled at her stability under such a siege—and at our privilege in seeing the anger of the sea in such safety. In '97, setting off on a European hiking expedition, we crossed when the Atlantic was so flat that, with the ship's efficient stabilizers, I missed the gentle rock that previously each night had carried me into a deep and restful sleep. Everywhere stomachs were at ease, and people ate and drank around the clock on the edge of decadence.

One day, perhaps, we'll cross the Atlantic on the new *Queen Mary 2*, but I don't know. I'm worried when I look at its size and shape. It doesn't have the contours of a liner, and it's over the top in frills like all the giant ships of today. Still, it is Cunard (albeit owned by Carnival Cruises), it's travelling from A to B, and the voyage is brief.

I know there is still nothing quite like being in mid-Atlantic on a star-spangled night when the Milky Way stretches almost to the horizon, like the beam of a search light guiding us toward new experiences and unexpected connections eagerly awaited. Or at midday when a baby's-blanket sky reaches to a sapphire sea in every direction, and I am reclined in a wooden deck chair, recovering from the disasters and reflecting on the delights of a trip that is almost over. It's hard to resist the urge to be there—to imagine

at least that one is on a classic liner again, sipping champagne, the
*QE2*, perhaps, the caviar of ships.

---

**NORTH ATLANTIC CAVIAR**

SERVES 4–6

2 large hard-boiled eggs
1 small jar caviar
¼–½ cup grated
　　Spanish onion
¼–½ cup sour cream
flat-leafed fresh parsley
　　for garnish
8 or more slices dry toast

» Hard-boil the eggs, let cool, and peel. Gently separate the yolks from the whites and grate yolks and whites into two separate piles.

» In the centre of each of four small plates place a small spoonful of the caviar. Surround the caviar with approximately a tablespoonful each of grated egg yolk, egg white, onion, and sour cream at north, south, east, and west. Garnish caviar with a sprig of parsley.

» Cut the crusts off toast and slice into about 1-inch strips. Serve in individual small cups or shallow wine glasses.

» IN THE FINAL SCENE at the airport in *Casablanca*, Bogart is persuading Bergman that she has to get on the plane without him — that her heart may be with Rick, but her duty lies with Victor and the Resistance. In his gruff yet tender voice, Bogie comforts Ingrid, "We'll always have Paris."

Our family spent twenty-two years in Windsor. It isn't Paris, and Highway 2, which takes off east from the airport straight as a runway, isn't the Champs Elysée. But after you pass Tecumseh, the traffic slows as you chug through towns with pedestrian names like Emeryville, Belle River, Stoney Point, and, least melodic of all, Puce. Strung out along the highway, interspersed with the gas stations, warehouses, fruit and vegetable stands, and boats and cars with homemade "For Sale" signs are several of what the French would call "cafés," but we know more appropriately as "greasy spoons." Rectangular boxes with big, glaring signs advertising "Breakfast Served All Day, $4.99." Walls of plywood or fake pine siding. Paintings on black and gold velvet of tropical rivers and forests. Others of purple mountains and azure lakes like the sets of early B movies. All hanging out of kilter, jarred by their own garishness. Tables and chairs with metal legs, the former covered in paper mats with pictures and recipes of popular cocktails, the latter sporting cheap, red vinyl seats splattered in cigarette burns. A big, noisy fan on the wall — near the wooden, swinging door to the kitchen — labouring hard but incapable of diffusing the thick, blue veil hovering over everything.

It was our custom over the years we lived in Windsor to stop at one of these establishments for breakfast whenever we were making an early start for cottage or ski country and didn't want to be bothered having to do a last-minute kitchen cleanup. Those are the times for a full breakfast in highway restaurants. Two fried eggs, bacon and sausage, home fries, wholewheat toast, an extra order to soak up the remaining egg yolk (and to be able to finish with the sweet taste of strawberry jam or marmalade.) Coffee. Lots of coffee with the cups refilled at no extra charge. And a toothpick to go.

That's a meal that lasts all day. Your allotted calories in one quick splurge. No need to waste time stopping again. A comfortable full feeling until you reach the lake or the lodge.

I remember one Christmas holiday I was so strung out on departure that, as we filled up at the neighbourhood gas station, I poured windshield-washing liquid into the aperture marked "transmission fluid." We had to wait while the mechanic hoisted the car into the air, drained and refilled us. Pre-breakfast stomachs grumbled. I was pushed into the back seat of the car, told to shut up and just grade papers. But we did stop for the traditional breakfast along Highway 2 just outside Windsor. Tim needed the sustenance; he was going to do the driving.

Those meals became so associated with travel that after all the kids had left home and Dot and I were feeling restless because it had been a long time since the last trip and the next one was not yet in sight, we'd sometimes drive out along Highway 2 for breakfast anyway. Karen or Deb would call on Saturday night and ask what we'd done that day. "We went to Puce for breakfast." "Nooooo!"

It wasn't just the breakfast food that was appealing. It was also the atmosphere. Two young women, oblivious of craning necks, discussing the bitchy things their supervisor had said the day before, neglected cigarettes smoldering in the aluminum ashtrays beside their coffees. Tables of four or six men in caps with seed-company logos on the peaks, scraps of scrambled egg and toast hardening on their plates. In winter, they would assess the quality of the ice fishing and the prospects of the Wings in the playoffs; in summer the state of the crops and the agony of the Tigers. The salesmen in suits, jackets temporarily removed and ties loosened, alone with their papers and third cups of coffee. The plump, efficient waitress with folds of flesh under her forearms, whisking away the remainder of a morning plate of fries and wiping off our table with a damp blue and white rag. "Need menus, dear? No? I'll be back for your orders in a minute." She seemed to know everyone except us, but it didn't matter; we got the same treatment. Comfortable. Familiar. Canadian.

Those breakfasts in or near Puce always remind me you don't have to have lots of money and go to exotic places to have memorable experiences. You can find them anywhere. We've been fortunate enough to see a lot of the world, but most of that travel has been on tight budgets. Not often have we stayed in fancy hotels and eaten at the finest restaurants. Yet we've spent nights and eaten meals that have been all the more memorable for the modest circumstances in which they occurred — for the surprise of greatness they served up when all we could reasonably have expected was the ordinariness of *prix fixe*. Perhaps most of all there has been the pleasure of living those simple, transient moments together, *en famille*. And when we haven't been able to wander afar, we've sought and found culinary and travel experiences that have delighted us close to home.

One Saturday breakfast along Highway 2, Dot and I were feeling particularly restless and recollections of our last trip no longer assuaged our yearning to be off again. Suddenly, however, a calmness rolled over me, a feeling of contentment, a sense of connection. I reached across the Arborite table for Dot's hand, squeezed it gently, and in my best Bogart voice I rasped, "We'll always have Puce."

## Lunches & Light Meals

Cucumber Sandwiches, Afternoon-Tea Style   262
Goofy Burgers   240
International Scotch Eggs   64
Magic Wings   240
Pan-Bagnat   189
Pissaladière   79
Shwarma Alarma   200
Yesterday's Omelette   245


## Breads, Muffins, Desserts

Barb's Cranberry Scones   156
Dessert Crêpe   222
Indian Pudding   272
Irish Soda Bread   182

*Missing the Bus, Making the Connection* was designed by Dennis Choquette and typeset by Suzanne Burkill, summer 2008. The text face is Monotype Fournier; display type is The Sans. It was printed offset, Smyth-sewn, and bound by Tri-Graphic, Ottawa. The text stock is Domtar Opaque Plainfield, 70 lb., an acid-free, ancient-forest-friendly paper. The cover was designed and executed by Fingerprint Communications, Toronto.